T0227859

Structures and Properties of Clusters: From a few Atoms to Nanoparticles

Lecture Series on Computer and Computational Sciences
Editor-in-Chief and Founder: Theodore E. Simos

Volume 5

Structures and Properties of Clusters: From a few Atoms to Nanoparticles

Editor: George Maroulis

CRC Press
Taylor & Francis Group
Boca Raton London New York

CRC Press is an imprint of the
Taylor & Francis Group, an **informa** business

First published 2006 by Koninklijke Brill NV

Published 2021 by CRC Press
Taylor & Francis Group
6000 Broken Sound Parkway NW, Suite 300
Boca Raton, FL 33487-2742

First issued in hardback 2021

© 2006 by Taylor & Francis Group, LLC
CRC Press is an imprint of Taylor & Francis Group, an Informa business

No claim to original U.S. Government works

ISBN 13: 978-1-138-41298-9 (hbk)
ISBN 13: 978-90-6764-456-3 (pbk)

A C.I.P. record for this book is available from the Library of Congress

COVER DESIGN: ALEXANDER SILBERSTEIN

Brill Academic Publishers
P.O. Box 9000, 2300 PA Leiden
The Netherlands

*Lecture Series on Computer
and Computational Sciences*
Volume 5, 2006, pp. I-IV

Clusters: From a few atoms to nanoparticles

This volume groups together a number of important studies on the structure and properties of clusters. The size of studied systems varies from a few atoms to nanoparticles. In recent years, intense research activity has been observed in many directions in this field. This has resulted in new and novel knowledge with important commercial implications. Clusters have also become a favorite ground for the development and testing of new computational methods, with sound expectations for the creation of highly performant theoretical tools for large scale calculations. Such advances will enable theoreticians not only to follow successfully experimental efforts, but also to make reliable predictions of the evolution of structure and properties with clustering and aggregation.

George Maroulis
Department of Chemistry
University of Patras
GR-26500 Patras, Greece
maroulis@upatras.gr

Dedicated to the memory of Prof. Dr. Jaroslav Koutecký (1922-2005)

Table of Contents

Brill Academic Publishers
P.O. Box 9000, 2300 PA Leiden
The Netherlands

*Lecture Series on Computer
and Computational Sciences*
Volume 5, 2006, pp. 1-8

Positional Isotope Effect for the Water Tetramer

D. J. Anick[1]

Harvard Medical School,
Centre Building 11,
McLean Hospital, 115 Mill St.,
Belmont, Massachusetts 02478, U.S.A.

Abstract: Ab initio studies are carried out for the water tetramer with a single H replaced by D, $(H_2O)_3(HDO)$. The isomer with D in a free position, $H_7D^fO_4$, has ZPE 0.17 kcal/mol higher than the isomer with D in an H-bond, $H_7D^bO_4$. The same ZPE difference is found for $H^bD_7O_4$ vs $H^fD_7O_4$. The difference may be large enough for a preference for H rather than D in a free position to be experimentally measurable. Exploration of the components of ZPE shows that the stretch component alone favors $H_7D^fO_4$, but this is more than compensated by the bend and torsion components.

Keywords: positional isotope effect, water cluster, tetramer, D_2O

1. Introduction

"Isotope effects" are any changes in the physical or chemical properties of a substance due to replacement of constituent atoms by an isotope. H-to-D isotope effects have long been used in studies of the structure of water phases. In some experiments, the properties of the deuteron and proton by themselves are relevant, such as the deuteron's greater coherent scattering length in neutron scattering studies of water and ice [1-3]. In others, H-to-D substitution alters properties of ice by changing the vibrational frequency of the O—H bond [4].

The Born-Oppenheimer approximation at the foundation of *ab initio* calculations posits that all nuclei are so heavy that nuclear masses are irrelevant. Computed electronic orbitals, ground and excited states, potential energy surfaces, and optimum geometries are unaffected by isotopic substitution. Atomic masses can strongly affect molecular vibrations, however, with heavier isotopes resulting in red-shifted vibrational frequencies. Lower frequencies also mean a lower zero point vibrational energy (ZPE). Change in ZPE is the mechanism of the isotope effects considered in this article.

One experiment involving water where the ZPE change due to H-to-D substitution makes a significant difference, is in the behavior of ice-VII under high pressure [5-7]. In H_2O-Ice-VII, tunneling and the appearance of a bimodal position for the proton in the H-bond begin at lower pressures (i.e. at greater O—O distances and at a higher barrier to proton transfer) than for the deuteron in D_2O-Ice-VII. Another experiment demonstrating an isotope effect mediated by ZPE difference concerns diffusion of He through amorphous ice. Kay, Daschbach *et al* [8] found, and used *ab initio* calculations to explain, an "inverse isotope effect" with faster diffusion for He in D_2O than in H_2O.

Since the frequencies associated with specific H's in a water cluster vary with the H's position, and the ZPE is (up to the harmonic approximation) proportional to the sum of all the vibrational frequencies of the cluster, it follows that each symmetry-distinct proton in a water cluster could have its own positional isotope effect. By a "positional isotope effect" (or p.i.e.) we mean a change in ZPE associated with substitution of D for H only at that position.

Only a few studies of p.i.e.'s for water clusters have been published, and they deal with the smallest clusters. Engdahl and Nelander [9] found experimentally that $(H_2O)(HDO)$ species with D in the bonded position were about 60 cm^{-1} (or 172 cal/mol) more stable than arrangements with H in the bonded position. A recent experimental and theoretical study of the Zundel cation $H_5O_2^+$ found that for $H_5O_2^+$ drawn from a 3:1 molar mix of D_2O and H_2O at 80 °K, H was 2.3 times as likely to occupy the bonding position as chance would predict [10]. Sabo *et al* [11] examined rotational constants, torsional

[1] Corresponding author. E-mail: david.anick@rcn.com

modes, and intermolecular stretching modes for H/D-substituted cyclic water trimers, finding good agreement between theory and experiment for the rotational constants and torsional modes.

This article explores the p.i.e. for the cyclic tetramer, H_8O_4. The IR spectrum of this cluster, as well as far-IR tunneling splittings associated with pendent H flipping, has been measured in experimental systems [12-16]. Its optimum geometry is well known to be cyclic, with the oxygen nuclei lying in a nearly planar square with S4 symmetry [17-18]. Four symmetry-equivalent protons are in H-bonds (we call these "bonded" H's or positions) and four symmetry-equivalent protons are free (also called "dangling", "pendent", or "non-H-bonded"). Each O of the tetramer is a donor in one H-bond and an acceptor in one, the "DA" pattern.

Several factors make H_8O_4 a good choice of cluster for examining a positional isotope effect: (1) it is well known and stable at 298 °K; (2) there are just two symmetry-distinct H positions, thereby simplifying the computation and modeling; (3) because it is fairly light (m.w. 72 vs 73 with a single D substitution) size selection by molecular weight should be experimentally feasible; and (4) its DA motif occurs in many water clusters, e.g. it is present in the minimum $(H_2O)_n$ for n = 3,4,5,6,7,9,10, and 11 [17-26], so whatever we learn from H_8O_4 is likely to be transferable to other water clusters.

2. Methods

Except where otherwise stated, the model MP2/aug-cc-pVTZ was used for all reported calculations. This model is widely accepted as being very accurate for water clusters, though scaling is necessary for optimum prediction of frequencies [27-29]. Calculations were done on a Parallel Quantum Solutions (PQS) QuantumCube, using PQS software [30], which computes MP2 Hessians numerically.

All reported results are based on the harmonic approximation. Vibrational frequencies and ZPE computed via MP2 typically require scaling, *i.e.* computed frequencies need to be multiplied by a factor, usually between 0.9 and 1, to bring them into better agreement with experiments [27,31]. For MP2/cc-pVTZ, 0.950±0.072 may be used for frequencies and 0.975 for ZPE [32]. For MP2/aug-cc-pVDZ, 0.959±0.031 for frequencies and 0.979 for ZPE may be used. We decided not to scale in this article, for two reasons. First, scaling would only change answers by a few percent, and by reporting our unscaled data this could easily still be done. Second, comparison of MP2 predictions against actual spectra for water clusters suggest that different scaling factors might be needed for different parts of the spectrum, to achieve optimum agreement. ZPE involves the whole spectrum. Considerations of this nature would be complex and tangential to our purpose.

3. Results and Discussion

We computed spectra for the cyclic tetramers H_8O_4, $H_7D^fO_4$, $H_7D^bO_4$, $H^fD_7O_4$, $H^bD_7O_4$, and D_8O_4. The notation $H_7D^fO_4$ means $(H_2O)_3(HDO)$ with the D in a free position. Likewise $H^bD_7O_4$ consists of $(D_2O)_3(HDO)$ with H in a bonded position (and hence all D's in free positions), and so on. In Table 1 we list the computed total IR stretch intensity for each of four regions: H-bonded O—D stretch (taken as covering 2300 to 2580 cm^{-1}), free O—D stretch (2600 to 2900), bonded O—H stretch (3100 to 3600) and free O—H stretch (3600 – 3900). For the tetramer these ranges will not overlap and we have made them generously wide so that they will include any variations in experimental or computational results. Table 1 also lists the ZPE for each species.

That the ZPE should decrease when D replaces any H was expected. Of interest here, is that the decrease is different for a D^f vs a D^b. Comparison of $H_7D^fO_4$ vs $H_7D^bO_4$ and $H^bD_7O_4$ vs $H^fD_7O_4$ show that the species with D^f sits 174 or 176 cal/mol higher in total energy than the species with D^b. This is in excellent agreement with the Engdahl and Nelander results [9] that the $H_3D^fO_2$ dimers sit about 172 cal/mol higher than the $H_3D^bO_2$ dimer.

We are particularly interested in exploring whether and how an experiment might detect this difference for the tetramer. In an experimental setup like that of Buck *et al* [22], vaporized water emerges from a nozzle carried by an inert gas stream and quickly coalesces into small clusters. The clusters undergo size selection via deflection by a molecular cross beam that imparts a fixed momentum p, which separates them according to p/m. The selected clusters are then probed by IR spectroscopy.

To look for a p.i.e. for H_7DO_4 (resp. HD_7O_4), we would start with a D_2O-H_2O mixture and select for molecular weight 73 (resp. 79). If the distribution of D_2O, HDO and H_2O available from the nozzle and subsequent cluster formation were unbiased, the optimum D_2O:H_2O molar ratio would be 1:7 (resp. 7:1) to maximize the amount of H_7DO_4 (resp. HD_7O_4) formed. However, it is possible that the mixture would need to be made richer in H_2O as there may be some preference for the accretion of D_2O during cluster formation [16,33].

Once molecular weight of 73 (or 79) has been selected, our working hypothesis is that we have a mix of the two species $H_7D^fO_4$ and $H_7D^bO_4$ (or $H^bD_7O_4$ and $H^fD_7O_4$) that interconvert and achieve thermodynamic equilibrium. For $H_7D^fO_4$ and $H_7D^bO_4$, the fractions of $H_7D^fO_4$ and $H_7D^bO_4$ would be $y^f = (1+\exp(-\gamma/RT))^{-1}$ and $y^b = (\exp(\gamma/RT)+1)^{-1}$ respectively, where $\gamma = 174$ cal/mol. Table 2 gives the predicted total (integrated) IR intensity for each of four spectrum regions, at each of three temperatures. Table 3 provides the same data, for the comparison of $H^bD_7O_4$ and $H^fD_7O_4$. Tables 2 and 3 also show what the "unbiased" predictions would be if there were no p.i.e. Of the possible measurements listed in Tables 2 and 3 that could demonstrate a departure from the unbiased figures, the "bonded stretch intensity ratio" (BSIR), i.e. the ratio of the total intensity of bonded O—H stretches to that of bonded O—D stretches, is the most promising. The signals from free stretches will have a smaller signal-to-noise ratio than the bonded stretch signals, and the predicted intensity is less trustworthy for the free stretches. One does not need to know the total quantity of clusters measured, in order to use BSIR. Also, the better BSIR measurement is for the comparison of $H^bD_7O_4$ vs $H^fD_7O_4$ (Table 3), since the error in measuring a ratio of two quantities is least when the log of the ratio is closer to zero.

It is conceivable that $H_7D^fO_4$ and $H_7D^bO_4$ interconvert so easily that distinct minima are not well defined. This would be the case if there is a pathway between them on the PES whose saddle is low enough to permit tunneling from one state to the other. The water tetramer has an extremely complex PES that has been the study of much theoretical and experimental work [34-38]. A much-studied feature of the tetramer is that the free H's can flip between "up" and "down" via tunneling transitions that can be observed via FIR laser spectroscopy [14-16]. However, flips will not change a D^f into a D^b or vice versa. The lowest-energy pathway that converts a D^f to a D^b has a transition state with one bifurcated H-bond. Wales and Walsh [35] labeled this t-state as "udbd" indicating that the H_2O orientations, listed in cyclic order, were free-H-up, free-H-down, bifurcated, and free-H-down. They placed it 3.6 kcal/mol above the global minimum ("udud") configuration. We re-optimized it and found that a better description is udbp, "p" indicating that the last free H is coplanar with the O-O-O-O. By MP2/aug-cc-pVTZ it lies 3.73 kcal/mol above "udud", and after adding in a ZPE contribution to $\Delta G^{\ddagger}$ of -0.74 kcal/mol (computed at MP2/aug-cc-pVDZ level) the barrier becomes 2.99 kcal/mol. It is a transition between a udud and a uddu state. Loerting *et al* [28] found that tunneling plays a role in the concerted 4-proton cyclic transfer for the water tetramer, a pathway with barrier height 10 kcal/mol, so we expect that tunneling will also contribute to a faster interconversion rate via the udbp t-state. However, Brown *et al* [38] considered udbp to be an unlikely explanation for any of the observed tunneling splittings.

Assuming that the D^f and D^b species cannot interconvert by tunneling alone, the interchange rate will decrease with temperature. Below a certain temperature we expect that interconversion will cease for practical purposes, but there may still be a p.i.e. due to positional preference when the tetramer is being formed. In this case the final distribution will depend upon the relative height of the kinetic barriers to adding the HDO in an orientation that makes the D free vs an orientation that makes the H free. Miller *et al* [39-40] succeeded in growing $(H_2O)_n$ clusters by adding one H_2O unit at a time to He droplets at 0.4 °K, while continuously taking IR spectra. If this experiment were repeated using a D_2O:H_2O ratio of approximately 7:1, at some point an HDO would add to $(D_2O)_n$. After accumulating multiple trials for various n it would be clear whether a preference emerged for H^f over H^b, as predicted by the p.i.e.

How can the p.i.e. be explained? One approach is to split ZPE into components. The 9n-6 vibrational frequencies $\{v_i\}$ of an $(H_2O)_n$ cluster correspond to 2n O—H stretch modes (nearly always between 1800 cm^{-1} and 4000 cm^{-1}), n H—O—H bending modes (1300 cm^{-1} to 1800 cm^{-1}), and 6n-6 torsional or librational modes (below 1300 cm^{-1}). These ranges also apply after H-to-D substitution(s) in most cases but for clusters with exceptionally short H-bonds or other anomalies there can be overlap. Since

$$ZPE = \frac{hc}{2} \sum_{i=1}^{9n-6} v_i \qquad (1)$$

(omit the factor 'c' if $\{v_i\}$ are given in Hz rather than cm^{-1}), we can split ZPE into three components,

$$ZPE = ZPE_S + ZPE_B + ZPE_T, \tag{2}$$

where ZPE$_S$ is Eq. (1) summed just over the stretch modes, and likewise for ZPE$_B$ and ZPE$_T$. Writing ZPE_X^0 for the ZPE$_X$ component of H$_8$O$_4$, and ZPE_X^m for the ZPE$_X$ component of H$_7$D^{m}O$_4$, m = b or f,

$$\Delta ZPE_S = ZPE_S^f - ZPE_S^b = -163.2 \text{ cal/mol}; \tag{3}$$

$$\Delta ZPE_B = ZPE_B^f - ZPE_B^b = +146.2 \text{ cal/mol}; \tag{4}$$

$$\Delta ZPE_T = ZPE_T^f - ZPE_T^b = +191.1 \text{ cal/mol}. \tag{5}$$

The total ΔZPE quoted above of +174 cal/mol is the sum of these 3 terms. The corresponding values for ZPE$_X$(H^{b}D$_7$O$_4$)–ZPE$_X$(H^{f}D$_7$O$_4$) are nearly identical: –163.0, +145.8, and +192.7 (total: +175.5).

To understand ΔZPE$_S$, think of it as $(ZPE_S^0 - ZPE_S^b) - (ZPE_S^0 - ZPE_S^f)$. Going from H$_8O_4$ to H$_7$D^{f}O$_4$ converts one free O—H stretch at 3897 cm^{-1} (unscaled MP2 frequencies) to a free O—D stretch at 2824 cm^{-1}, while going from H$_8$O$_4$ to H$_7$D^{b}O$_4$ converts one bonded O—H stretch near 3480 cm^{-1} to a bonded O—D stretch at 2532 cm^{-1}. The difference is (3480–2532)–(3897–2824) = –125 cm^{-1} $\equiv$ –178.7 cal/mol (note: the conversion here includes the factor of ½ in Eq. (1)), in reasonable agreement with Eq. (3). These figures can be further explained if we model the O—H stretch as a spring whose spring constant is unchanged when D replaces H: the reduced mass when it is O—H is (16×1)/(16+1)=16/17 and when it is O—D it is (16×2)/(16+2)=32/18, so the frequency should go down by a factor of $((16/17)/(32/18))^{1/2}$ = 0.7276. Note that the computed frequency ratios obey this rule extremely well: 2824/3897 = 0.7247 and 2532/3480 = 0.7276. Thus ΔZPE$_S$ can be approximated quite closely as (C)×(3897–3475), where the constant C is 0.7276–1.0 = –0.2724.

For ΔZPE$_B$, we find that in the singly-substituted tetramers, the D^f—O—H^b molecule bends at 1511 cm^{-1} while D^b—O—H^f bends at 1410 cm^{-1}. This is the only substantial difference in the bend region, and since 1511–1410 = 101 cm^{-1} $\equiv$ 144.4 cal/mol, we have essentially accounted for ΔZPE$_B$. We know of no simple model that can "explain" the change from the average bend frequency for H$_8$O$_4$, which is 1663 cm^{-1}, to the substituted bend frequencies of 1511 and 1410, in terms of elementary physics.

In order to understand ΔZPE$_T$ we looked at where the 18 torsional modes differed, among H$_8$O$_4$, H$_7$D^{f}O$_4$, and H$_7$D^{b}O$_4$. The highest four torsional modes (modes 15 through 18) for H$_8$O$_4$ feature out-of-plane bends for the four bonding H's. By "out-of-plane" we mean approximately perpendicular to the plane of the H-O-H angle in which the index H occurs. For the highly symmetric H$_8$O$_4$ these four modes are coupled, complicating the picture. The correlation of the top four torsional modes with the out-of-plane bends of the four bonding H's is most clearly seen by examining the normal modes of H$_7$D^{f}O$_4$. Their frequencies for H$_8$O$_4$ range from 757 to 989 cm^{-1} (mean 850). The next four modes (modes 11 through 14) feature out-of-plane bends for the four bonding H's. Again, this is best seen by breaking the symmetry and looking at the normal modes of H$_7$D^{b}O$_4$. In H$_8$O$_4$ the frequency range is 411 to 455 cm^{-1} (mean 440). When a bonded H of H$_8$O$_4$ is replaced by D, a "top four" torsional mode is affected, and its frequency drops to 629 cm^{-1} from (say) 850 cm^{-1}. If instead the D replaces a free H, the "top four" frequencies change little and only a "next tier" mode is affected. It drops from approximately 440 to 366 cm^{-1}. If all other changes are ignored, this analysis gives

$$\Delta ZPE_T \approx (ZPE_T^0 - ZPE_T^b) - (ZPE_T^0 - ZPE_T^f) = (850-629) - (440-366) = 147 \text{ cm}^{-1} \equiv 210.1$$

cal/mol, in reasonable agreement with Eq. (5). For each of the three components, the error in this method of analysis occurs because "other changes" cannot be completely ignored, i.e. frequencies of modes other than those directly featuring the deuteron are also affected a little. Still, this analysis does give the correct sign and ball-park magnitude for each component.

To summarize, the p.i.e. cannot be assigned primarily to any one of the components of ZPE. All three components contribute, at approximately the same magnitude. The direction of the bending and torsional components' contributions is opposite to that of the stretch component.

4. Conclusion

Ab initio calculations demonstrate that a positional isotope effect should exist in the water tetramer, favoring H (resp. D) in the free (resp. bonded) positions. The size of the predicted effect, 174 cal/mol, is similar to that which has previously been observed in the water dimer [9]. We have explored briefly how experimental setups that have been used successfully to examine other small water clusters could be modified to look for the effect. We have made a reasonable start toward understanding the origin, direction, and magnitude of the effect.

An obvious question concerns the validity of extrapolating from the single example of the tetramer to other water clusters, especially those with bonding patterns other than 'DA'. The answer is that the tetramer example does generalize. There are subtle differences among bonding patterns (e.g. 'DAA' vs 'DA') and there is a small cooperativity effect for two D substitutions on the same O, but the principal p.i.e. for all water clusters is a highly consistent preference of around 160 cal/mol favoring H (resp. D) in free (resp. bonded) positions. In a separate article we present a comprehensive statistical study of positional isotope effects in water clusters [41].

Tables

Table 1: List of tetramer species, their ZPE, and computed IR intensity by spectrum region

cluster	# D bonded	# D free	# H bonded	# H free	ZPE (cal/mol)	Predicted Intensity (km/mol)			
						2300-2580	2600-2900	3100-3600	3600-3900
H_8O_4	0	0	4	4	62002	0	0	2854	383
$H_7D^bO_4$	1	0	3	4	59859	374	0	2157	355
$H_7D^fO_4$	0	1	4	3	60033	0	28	2900	287
D_8O_4	4	4	0	0	45458	1449	292	0	0
$H^bD_7O_4$	3	4	1	0	47626	1079	246	769	0
$H^fD_7O_4$	4	3	0	1	47450	1475	219	0	69

Table 2: Predicted mole fractions of $H_7D^bO_4$ and $H_7D^fO_4$ in an equilibrium mixture, predicted IR intensities by spectrum region, and their stretch intensity ratios, at various temperatures

Temp (°K)	fraction $H_7D^bO_4$	fraction $H_7D^fO_4$	Predicted Stretch Intensity (km/mol)				bonded SI ratio	free SI ratio
			2300-2580	2600-2900	3100-3600	3600-3900		
(unbiased)	0.500	0.500	187.0	14.0	2528.5	321.0	13.52	22.93
298	0.573	0.427	214.3	12.0	2474.3	326.0	11.55	27.26
150	0.642	0.358	240.1	10.0	2423.0	330.7	10.09	32.98
100	0.706	0.294	264.0	8.2	2375.5	335.0	9.00	40.69

Table 3: Predicted mole fractions of $H^fD_7DO_4$ and $H^bD_7O_4$ in an equilibrium mixture, predicted IR intensities by spectrum region, and their stretch intensity ratios, at various temperatures

Temp (°K)	fraction $H^fD_7O_4$	fraction $H^bD_7O_4$	Predicted Stretch Intensity (km/mol)				bonded SI ratio	free SI ratio
			2300-2580	2600-2900	3100-3600	3600-3900		
(unbiased)	0.500	0.500	1277.0	232.5	384.5	34.5	0.301	0.148
298	0.574	0.426	1306.2	230.5	327.8	39.6	0.251	0.172
150	0.643	0.357	1333.8	228.6	274.2	44.4	0.206	0.194
100	0.708	0.292	1359.4	226.9	224.5	48.9	0.165	0.215

References

[1] M.-C. Bellissent-Funel, J. Teixeira, L. Bosio, Structure of high-density amorphous water II: Neutron scattering study, J. Chem. Phys. **87** (4), 2231-2235 (1987).

[2] J. Li, Inelastic neutron scattering studies of hydrogen bonding in ices, *J. Chem. Phys.* **105** (16), 6733-6755 (1996).

[3] W.E. Thiessen, A.H. Narten. Neutron diffraction study of light and heavy water mixtures at 25 °C, *J. Chem. Phys.* 77 (5), (1982) 2656-2662.

[4] V. Buch, J.P. Devlin, A new interpretation of the OH-stretch spectrum of ice, *J. Chem. Phys.* **110** (7), 3437-3443 (1999).

[5] E. Katoh, M. Song, Infrared spectroscopic study of H_2O-D_2O mixed ice up to 100 GPa, *Phys. Rev. B* **62** (5), 2976-2979 (2000).

[6] M. Benoit, D. Marx, Michele Parinello, Tunneling and zero-point motion in high-pressure ice, *Nature* **392**, 258-261 (1998).

[7] M. Bernasconi, P. L. Silvestrelli, and M. Parrinello, *Ab Initio* Infrared Absorption Study of the Hydrogen-Bond Symmetrization in Ice, *Phys. Rev. Lett.* **81** (6), 1235-1238 (1998).

[8] J.L. Daschbach, G.K. Schenter, P. Ayotte, R.S. Smith, B.D. Kay, Helium Diffusion through H_2O and D_2O Amorphous Ice: Observation of a Lattice Inverse Isotope Effect, *Phys. Rev. Lett.* **92** (19): 198306 (2004).

[9] A. Engdahl, B. Nelander, On the relative stabilities of H-bonded and D-bonded water dimers, *J. Chem. Phys.* 86 (4), 1819-1823 (1987).

[10] J.P. Devlin, M.W. Severson, F. Mohamed, J. Sadlej, V. Buch, M. Parinello, Experimental and computational study of isotopic effects within the Zundel ion, *Chem. Phys. Lett.* **408**, 439-444 (2005).

[11] D. Sabo, Z. Bačić, S. Graf, S. Leutwyler, Rotational constants of all H/D-substituted water trimers: Coupling of intermolecular torsional and symmetric stretching modes, *J. Chem. Phys.* **110** (12), 5745-5757 (1999).

[12] R.N. Pribble, T.S. Zwier, Probing Hydrogen Bonding in Benzene-(Water)$_n$ Clusters using Resonant Ion-Dip IR Spectroscopy, *Faraday Discuss.* **97**, 229-241 (1994).

[13] F. Huisken, M. Kaloudis, A. Kulcke, Infrared spectroscopy of small size-selected water clusters, *J. Chem. Phys.* **104** (1), 17-25 (1996).

[14] J.D. Cruzan, L.B. Braly, K. Liu, M.G. Brown, J.G. Loeser, R.J. Saykally, Quantifying Hydrogen Bond Cooperativity in Water: VRT Spectroscopy of the Water Tetramer, *Science* **271**, 59-62 (1996).

[15] J.D. Cruzan, M.G. Brown, K. Liu, L.B. Braly, R.J. Saykally, The far-infrared vibration-rotation-tunneling spectrum of the water tetramer-d8, *J. Chem. Phys.* **105** (16), 6634-6644 (1996).

[16] J.D. Cruzan, M.R. Viant, M.G. Brown, R.J. Saykally, Terahertz Laser Vibration-Rotation Tunneling Spectroscopy of the Water Tetramer, *J. Phys. Chem. A* **101**, 9022-9031 (1997).

[17] K. Liu, J. D Cruzan, R.J. Saykally, Water Clusters, *Science* **271**, 929-933 (1996).

[18] S.S. Xantheas, *Ab initio* studies of cyclic water clusters $(H_2O)_n$, $n=1-6$. III. Comparison of density functional with MP2 results *J. Chem. Phys.* **102** (11), 4505-4517 (1995).

[19] R.N. Pribble, T.S. Zwier, Size-Specific Infrared Spectra of Benzene-$(H_2O)_n$ Clusters (n = 1 through 7): Evidence for Noncyclic $(H_2O)_n$ Structures, *Science* **265**, 75-79 (1994).

[20] J. Kim, K.S. Kim, Structures, binding energies, and spectra of isoenergetic water hexamer clusters: Extensive ab initio studies, *J. Chem. Phys.* **109** (14), 5886-5895 (1998).

[21] J. Brudermann, M. Melzer, U. Buck, J.K. Kazimirski, J. Sadlej, V. Buch, The asymmetric cage structure of $(H_2O)_7$ from a combined spectroscopic and computational study, *J. Chem. Phys.* **110** (22) (1999), 10649-10652.

[22] U. Buck, I. Ettischer, M. Melzer, V. Buch, J. Sadlej, Structure and Spectra of Three-Dimensional $(H_2O)_n$ Clusters, n=8,9,10, *Phys. Rev. Lett.* **80** (12) (1998), 2578-2581.

[23] J. Sadlej, V. Buch, J.K. Kazimirski, U. Buck, Theoretical Study and Spectra of Cage Clusters $(H_2O)_n$, n=7-10, *J. Phys. Chem.* A **103**, 4933-4947 (1999).

[24] H.M. Lee, S.B. Suh, J.Y. Lee, P. Tarakeshwar, K.S. Kim, Structures, energies, vibrational spectra, and electronic properties of water monomer to decamer, *J. Chem. Phys.* **112** (22), 9759-9772 (2000).

[25] J. Sadlej, Theoretical study of structure and spectra of cage clusters $(H_2O)_n$, n=11,12, *Chem. Phys. Lett.* **333**, 485-492 (2001).

[26] H.M. Lee, S.B. Suh, K.S. Kim, Structures, energies, and vibrational spectra of water undecamer and dodecamers: An ab initio study, *J. Chem. Phys.* **114** (24), 10749-10756 (2001).

[27] J. Kim, J.Y. Lee, S. Lee, B.J. Mhin, K.S. Kim, Harmonic vibrational frequencies of the water monomer and dimer: Comparison of various levels of *ab initio* theory , *J. Chem. Phys.* **102**, 310-317 (1995); and the references therein.

[28] T. Loerting, K. R. Liedl, B. M. Rode, Predictions of rate constants and estimates for tunneling splittings of concerted proton transfer in small cyclic water clusters, *J. Chem. Phys.* **109** (7), 2672-2679 (1998).

[29] R.A. Christie and K.D. Jordan, Theoretical Investigation of the $H_3O^+(H_2O)_4$ Cluster, *J. Phys. Chem.* A **105**, 7551-7558 (2001).

[30] PQS v. 3.1, Parallel Quantum Solutions, 2013 Green Acres Road, Fayetteville, AR 72703.

[31] A.P. Scott, L. Radom, Harmonic Vibrational Frequencies: An Evaluation of Hartree-Fock,, Møller-Plesset, Quadratic Configuration Interaction, Density Functional Theory, and Semiempirical Scale Factors, *J. Phys. Chem.* **100**, 16502-16513 (1996).

[32] http://srdata.nist.gov/cccbdb/

[33] G.D. Kay, A.W. Castleman, Isotope enrichment during the formation of water clusters in supersonic free jet expansions, *J. Chem. Phys.* **78**, 4297-4302 (1983).

[34] M. Schütz, W. Klopper, H.-P. Lüthi, S. Leutwyler, Low-lying stationary points and torsional interconversions of cyclic $(H_2O)_4$: An *ab initio* study, *J. Chem. Phys.* **103**, 6114-6126 (1995)

[35] D.J. Wales, T.R. Walsh, Theoretical study of the water tetramer, *J. Chem. Phys.* **106**, 7193-7207 (1997).

[36] D. Sabo, Z. Bačić, Four-dimensional model calculation of torsional levels of cyclic water tetramer, *J. Chem. Phys.* **109** (13), 5404-5419 (1998).

[37] S. Graf, S. Leutwyler, An *ab initio* derived torsional potential energy surface for the cyclic water tetramer, *J. Chem. Phys.* **109** (13), 5393-5403 (1998).

[38] M.G. Brown, F.N. Keutsch, L.B. Braly, R.J. Saykally, High symmetry effects on hydrogen bond rearrangement: The 4.1 THz vibrational band of $(D_2O)_4$, *J. Chem. Phys.* **111** (17), 7801-7806 (1999)

[39] C.J. Burnham, S.S. Xantheas, M.A. Miller, B.E. Applegate, R.E. Miller, The formation of cyclic water complexes by sequential ring insertion: Experiment and theory, *J. Chem. Phys.* **117** (3), 1109-1122 (2002).

[40] K. Nauta, R.E. Miller, Formation of Cyclic Water Hexamer in Liquid Helium: The Smallest Piece of Ice, *Science* **287**, 293-295 (2000).

[41] D. J. Anick, Proton and deuteron position preferences in water clusters: an *ab initio* study, *J. Chem. Phys.* **123**, 244309 (2005).

Brill Academic Publishers
P.O. Box 9000, 2300 PA Leiden.
The Netherlands

Lecture Series on Computer
and Computational Sciences
Volume 5, 2006, pp. 9-15

Tight-binding Calcium Clusters from Adaptive Tempering Monte Carlo Simulation

Xiao Dong, Silvina M. Gatica, and Estela Blaisten-Barojas[1]

School of Computational Sciences
George Mason University, MS 5C3, Fairfax, VA 22030, USA

Abstract: The most stable structure of calcium clusters with 14 to 32 atoms is optimized by the Adaptive Tempering Monte Carlo method. The binding energy of the clusters is obtained within the tight-binding approach parameterized in a previous work. The optimization process is started at about 800 K and the tempering brings the structure to the global minimum ending the process at 1 K. It is found that six cluster sizes, 15, 16, 18, 21, 23 and 25 have a global minimum structure not reported in the literature. In this size range, Ca_{15}, Ca_{21} and Ca_{23} are the preferred geometries that can be identified as magic numbers. The tight-binding one-electron levels in the valence band display a large energy gap of 0.5 eV between the last occupied and first unoccupied levels for the magic number clusters. This band gap is 5 to 10 times smaller for other cluster sizes.

Keywords: calcium clusters, multicanonical, tempering, adaptive tempering Monte Carlo

PACS: 36.40.-c, 36.40.Mr, 52.65.Pp, 61.46.+w

1 Introduction

The structure and electronic properties of metallic clusters have long been subject of interest giving rise to several popular approaches such as the jellium model for alkaline metals, in which electron sub-shell closings occur when the number of electrons in the valence band is 2, 8, 18, 20, 34, 40, 58, 68, 90, etc. On the other hand, the alkaline earths metals such as calcium have a different electronic behavior due to the s-p-d character of the conduction band of bulk calcium. Recently an important computational effort led to the discovery of the preferred structures of calcium clusters from Ca_{32} to Ca_{85} within the tight-binding (TB) approach [1]. These clusters do not satisfy the jellium model shell closings. Additionally, small clusters of up to 13 atoms were investigated with the all-electron density-functional approach [2]. Calcium clusters with hundreds of atoms have been studied with empirical classical potentials based on parameterization of bulk properties [3]. This approach, though, is not suitable for smaller clusters since it overestimates the binding energy [2]. However, the structure, energetics and electronic properties of clusters in the range 14-32 have not been reported from quantum mechanical approaches. This is the subject of the present letter. The optimization of the best structure from quantum mechanical methods is a difficult task because clusters present many isomer geometries that are stable. The process of finding the structure with lowest binding energy is more computationally eager than the quantum calculation of the electronic energy of one given geometry. In this letter we propose a simulation method that permits to optimize cluster structures, and that we have linked to a quantum tight-binding approach. The process is the Adaptive Tempering Monte Carlo (ATMC) [4] which is here

---

[1]Corresponding author. E-mail: blaisten@gmu.edu

combined with the TB model from Ref. [1] parametcrized for calcium nanoclusters. The ATMC belongs to a family of algorithms named multicanonical and/or parallel tempering that initiated with the work of Marinari and Parisi [5] and that of Lyubartsev et. al. [6]. This letter is organized as follows. In section 2 we describe the ATMC method. In section 3 we describe the energetics and structural results for Ca_{14} through Ca_{32} and show details on the valence band eigenvalues. In Section 4 we present our conclusions.

2 Adaptive Tempering Monte Carlo linked to Tight-Binding

In the ATMC method [4] the system accesses a multitude of canonical ensembles, each with constant T_iNV, where each T_i characterizes a different canonical ensemble within a predetermined temperature range. Each canonical ensemble is simulated with the usual Metropolis Monte Carlo algorithm, and the various ensembles are connected along the simulation by a super-Markov chain in which the temperature is allowed to hop adaptively according to the following acceptance probability

$$acc = \min\left[1, \exp\left[-(E- < E >_{T_{old}})\left(\frac{1}{k_BT_{new}} - \frac{1}{k_BT_{old}}\right)\right]\right] \tag{1}$$

Here, E is the instantaneous cluster binding energy, k_B is Boltzmann's constant, and $< E >_T$ is the average cluster binding energy at temperature T. T_{new} is obtained form T_{old} by hopping $+\Delta T$ with probability p or $-\Delta T$ with probability q. When Z is the normalizing partition function, the probability p is $\exp[(-(E- < E >)(1/k_BT_{new} - /k_BT_{old})]/Z$ and q = 1 - p. We calculate δE, the standard deviation of the average binding energy $< E >$ at temperature T_{old}, and introduce the parameter a in terms of which the temperature hops by [4]:

$$\Delta T = \frac{T}{1 - \delta E/(ln(a)k_BT)} \tag{2}$$

For the system of calcium clusters, the optimal value of the parameter a is 0.135.

This algorithm enables the system to visit a wide range of temperatures. Every time that the temperature *hops* to a new temperature with probability p, we say that a tempering event took place. Subsequently, the system evolves at the new temperature T_{new} under the new canonical MC in which the step size is also adapted to yield a run in which roughly 50% of configuration changes are accepted. and 50% are rejected. In all simulations, the cluster was started from an arbitrary initial configuration at high temperatures close to the upper limit of the allowed temperature range. For calcium clusters, the upper limit for the temperature is set at $T = 1000$ K. The total binding energy E is calculated with the TB model from Ref. [1]. The TB model and parameters adopted to obtain the binding energy E were previously used by the authors in Ref. [1] where readers are referred for details. The model is based on the Slater-Koster (SK) approach [7] in which s, p and d orbitals span a 9x9 matrix representation of the TB Hamiltonian for each atom in the cluster. The basis set is non-orthogonal and the model has 97 parameters associated to the analytical representation of on-site and hopping integrals. These parameters were fitted to the energy bands and cohesive energy of bulk fcc and bcc calcium [8] and to the *ab initio* energy surfaces of Ca_7 through Ca_{13} [2] and are reported in Ref. [1]. The starting cluster configurations are spherical cuts from a simple cubic lattice. Before the tempering starts, any given cluster is warmed up for 10,000 iterations of a regular canonical ensemble MC at temperature $T = 800$ K. At this point the adaptive tempering starts, and the system adaptively changes temperature until the T_{new} reaches the desired lower limit, which was ~ 1 K in the case of the calcium clusters. A typical example of the temperature evolution as the ATMC progresses is given in Fig. 1 for a cluster with 23 atoms. Fig. 1a shows the evolution of the temperature over approximately 10.000

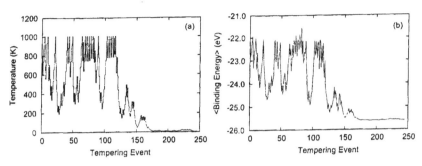

Figure 1: Temperature and average binding energy of Ca_{23} along the ATMC simulation

ATMC iterations. Fig. 1b depicts the corresponding changes in the average binding energy as the tempering process evolves. In this specific example, the temperature changed 247 times.

For some of the clusters studied, the system evolves for a certain number of iterations, reaches a relatively low temperature where it seems to be trapped in a local minimum. Then the ATMC allows the system to overcome barriers and escape from such local minimum leading the system to excursion again to high temperature regions. Finally after more tempering events the system lands in the global minimum. One of such cases is shown in Fig. 2 for a Ca_{14} cluster. As seen in Fig. 2a, at about 100 K the cluster remains quite some time in regions of configuration space with low binding energy (Fig. 2b). However, the cluster is able to hop out of that region and excursion to other regions consistent with high temperatures. After about an extra 10,000 MC iterations the cluster finally finds the global minimum, and the temperature collapses fast to 1 K. For this example, the temperature changed about 1866 times before ending the process.

3 Energetics and Structural Changes

The ATMC method was applied to all calcium cluster sizes containing 13 to 32 atoms. The electronic energy of these clusters was in all cases calculated within the TB model described above. In Fig. 3a we have gathered results of the binding energy E_N per atom. The binding energy is defined as the TB electronic energy of a cluster of N calcium atoms minus N times the TB energy of one calcium atom. In Fig. 3a, the TB results correspond to the empty triangles. For comparison, black triangles in the figure are the TB energies of clusters with geometries borrowed from the Morse potential (parameter $\rho = 3.6$) [9], which have been scaled consistently with the TB energy. It is clear that none of those geometries is preferred over the configurations obtained with the ATMC. Figure 3b shows the second difference of the TB energies obtained by our calculation. Peaks correspond to energetically preferred sizes because a size associated with a peak is more stable that both nearest sizes. It is interesting to note that there is an even-odd alternation where odd sizes are preferred over even sizes. Three of these sizes, 15, 21 and 23 show the most abrupt drop of peak height towards larger sizes. Because of that, these sizes can be called magic numbers. In this TB approach, the core electrons of Ca are frozen, and only the 2 valence electrons are considered. Therefore, the number of electrons corresponding to these magic number clusters is 30, 42 and 46, which are not consistent with shell closings of the jellium model (20, 40, 58, etc).

When analyzing closely the preferred cluster geometries, we find that all of them except for six are relaxed Morse structures in which bond lengths and angles accommodate somehow to adjust for the large surface to volume ratio. These six clusters, Ca_{13}, Ca_{16}, Ca_{18}, Ca_{21}, Ca_{23} and Ca_{25}

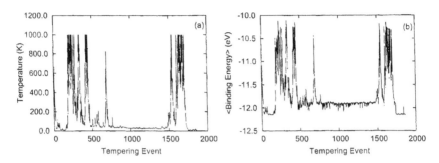

Figure 2: Temperature and average binding energy of Ca_{23} along the ATMC simulation

depicted in Fig. 4, have a preferred structure not previously reported in the literature as the most stable under any model potential (Lennard Jones[10], Morse[11]. Sutton-Chen [12], TB-second-moment many body [13, 14]. Murrell Mottram [15], Dzugutov[16]). The three C_{2v} magic number clusters are among the six new structures. The Ca_{15} cluster is a pentagonal bipyramid with apex vertexes capped by two parallel squares. The Ca_{23} cluster has a structure built on the elongated 19-atom icosahedron capped with one pentagonal pyramid to which two symmetrically opposed sides are decorated by dimers. The Ca_{21} cluster is an incomplete 23-atom cluster in which two atoms are missing, the apex vertex atom and one from the pentagonal pyramid underneath.

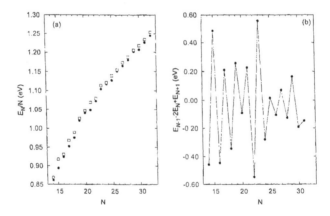

Figure 3: Binding energy and magic numbers of calcium clusters versus size

TB also provides the one-electron quantum levels of the cluster valence band. It is interesting to note that these eigenvalues present a large energy gap between the highest occupied state and lowest unoccupied state of 0.63, 0.47 and 0.48 eV for the magic number clusters Ca_{15}, Ca_{21} and Ca_{23}, respectively. However, the energy gap for all other sizes in the range studied is smaller,

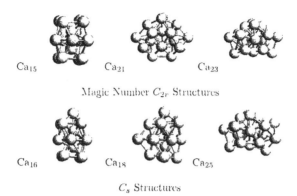

Figure 4: Six new calcium cluster structures. Ca_{15}, Ca_{21} and Ca_{23} are magic numbers

i.e. on the order of 0.05 to 0.1 eV. Fig. 5 illustrates this effect. Eigenvalues are sorted by energy and numbered in increasing order from the bottom of the band. Fig. 5 shows the distribution of TB eigenvalues in a ± 1 eV band around the Fermi energy. Black circles identify occupied states whereas white squares indicate the unoccupied states. Visually one sees that whereas the energy gap for Ca_{15} is large, it is considerably smaller for Ca_{16}. The same effect is shown in Fig. 5 for Ca_{23} and Ca_{21} has a behavior very similar to Ca_{23}. Therefore, electronic effects are fundamental in the determination of the magic numbers in calcium clusters.

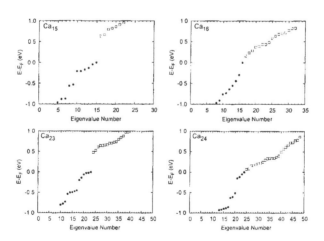

Figure 5: Eigenvalues of Ca_{15}, Ca_{16}, Ca_{23}, Ca_{21}

4 Conclusions

In this letter we have combined the Adaptive Tempering Monte Carlo method to optimize the calculation of the binding energies of calcium clusters within the tight-binding quantum approach. The ATMC is very efficient, optimizes structures in a fraction of the time the simulated annealing method requires, and can easily be coupled to quantum approaches. The cluster sizes studied spanned from Ca_{13} to Ca_{32}. Within this size range, three magic numbers Ca_{15}, Ca_{21} and Ca_{23} were revealed. The structure of these magic number clusters, as well as the structure of three other sizes (16, 18, 25), is new to the literature. It is also observed that a large energy gap of about 0.5 eV exists between the highest occupied TB-eigenstate and the lowest unoccupied TB-eigenstate for the magic number clusters. The corresponding energy gap for all other sizes studied drops to about 0.05-0.1 eV. This correlation is indicative that at these three magic sizes there is an electronic shell closing which is not consistent with that predicted by the jellium model.

Acknowledgment

We acknowledge financial support from the Provost Office of George Mason University for the assistanship allocated to XD.

References

[1] X. Dong, G. M. Wang and E. Blaisten-Barojas, Tight-binding model for calcium nanoclusters: Structural, electronic, and dynamical properties, *Physical Review B* **70** 205409 (2004).

[2] J. W. Mirick, C-H. Chien and E. Blaisten-Barojas, Electronic structure of calcium clusters, *Physical Review A* **63** 023202 (2001).

[3] J. E. Hearn and R.L. Johnson, Modeling calcium and strontium clusters with many-body potentials, *Journal of Chemical Physics* **107** 4674 (1997).

[4] X. Dong and E. Blaisten-Barojas, Adaptive Tempering Monte Carlo Method, *Journal of Computational and Theoretical Nanoscience* **3** 1 (2006).

[5] E. Marinari and G. Parisi, Simulated tempering: a new Monte Carlo scheme, *Europhysics Letters* **19** 451 (1992).

[6] A. P. Lyubartsev, A. A. Martsinovskii, S. V. Shevkunov and P. N. Vorontsov-Velyaminov, New approach to Monte Carlo calculation of the free energy: Method of expanded ensembles. *Journal of Chemical Physics* **96** 1776 (1992).

[7] J. C. Slater and G. F. Koster, Simplified LCAO Method for the Periodic Potential Problem, *Physical Review* **94** 1498 (1954).

[8] G. M. Wang, E. Blaisten-Barojas and D. Papaconstantopoulos, Pressure induced transitions in calcium: a tight-binding approach, *Journal of Physical Chemistry of Solids* **64** 185 (2003).

[9] J. P. K. Doye and D. J. Wales, Structural consequences of the range of the interatomic potential A menagerie of clusters. *Journal of the Chemical Society, Faraday Transactions* **93**. 4233-4244 (1997).

[10] D. J. Wales and J. P. K. Doye, Global Optimization by Basin-Hopping and the Lowest Energy Structures of Lennard-Jones Clusters Containing up to 110 Atoms, *Journal of Physical Chemistry A* **101** 5111-5116 (1997).

[11] J. P. K. Doye, D. J. Wales and R. S. Berry, The effect of the range of the potential on the structures of clusters, *Journal of Chemical Physics* **103** 4234-4249 (1995).

[12] J. P. K. Doye and D. J. Wales, Global minima for transition metal clusters described by SuttonChen potentials, *New Journal of Chemistry* **22** 733-744 (1998).

[13] C. H. Chien, E. Blaisten-Barojas and M. R. Pederson, Many-body potential and structure for rhodium clusters, *Journal of Chemical Physics* **112** 2301 (2000).

[14] G. M. Wang, E. Blaisten-Barojas, A. E. Roitberg and T. P. Martin, Strontium clusters: Many-body potential, energetics, and structural transitions, *Journal of Chemical Physics* **115** 3640 (2001).

[15] J. N. Murrell and R. E. Mottram, Potential energy functions for atomic solids. *Molecular Physics* **69** 571 (1990).

[16] J. P. K. Doye and D. J. Wales, Polytetrahedral Clusters, *Physical Review Letter* **86** 5719-5722 (2001).

Brill Academic Publishers
P.O. Box 9000, 2300 PA Leiden,
The Netherlands

Lecture Series on Computer
and Computational Sciences
Volume 5, 2006, pp. 16-21

Magnetic and spectroscopic properties of deposited transition metal clusters: A case study for Os on Fe(001)

S. Bornemann[1], J. Minár, H. Ebert

Dept. Chemie und Biochemie,
University of Munich,
Butenandtstr. 5-13, D-81377 München, Germany

Abstract: The fully relativistic KKR multiple scattering formalism has been used for a theoretical investigation of small Os clusters deposited on a Fe(001) surface. In order to account for the influence of spin-orbit coupling on the electronic and magnetic properties of such clusters the calculations were done on the basis of the Dirac equation within the framework of spin density functional theory (SDFT). Furthermore, the dichroism in X-ray absorption (XMCD) was investigated for small Os clusters up to a size of three atoms.

Keywords: magnetic clusters, KKR, SDFT, XMCD

PACS: 73.20.-r; 71.15.Rf; 73.22.-f; 87.64.Ni

1   Introduction

During the last few years, magnetic transition metal clusters have come into scientific focus and have been extensively studied by experiment and theory because of their exciting magnetic properties and their possible technical applications to a miniaturized storage of information [1, 2]. Accordingly, great efforts are undertaken to improve the preparation methods for such systems as well as for optimising their magnetic properties such as their magnetic moments and anisotropies [3, 4]. For experimental investigations of the magnetic properties of deposited clusters the technique of magnetic circular dichroism in X-ray absorption (XMCD) has turned out to be a versatile tool as it allows to measure atomic spin and orbital magnetic moments in an element specific way [5, 6]. While the first experiments on clusters were done on rather large systems [5] containing several thousand of atoms, it is now also possible to study very small clusters consisting of only a few atoms or even single isolated atoms [7, 8]. These experimental works on clusters showed clearly that not only the spin but also the spin-orbit induced orbital magnetic moment of small clusters is strongly enhanced compared to the bulk material. However, it is not yet fully understood, how the magnetic properties evolve from single atoms to finite-sized magnetic particles and how the atomic magnetic moments are correlated and dependent on the details of the atomic coordination. Thus, a rather large number of theoretical investigations on deposited clusters have been carried out to find answers to some of the open questions. Most of these investigations were done in a non- or scalar-relativistic way being either based on spin density functional theory or on parameterized tight-binding (TB) model Hamiltonians [9, 10, 11]. Some theoretical work also included the influence of spin-orbit coupling giving in particular access to the magnetic anisotropy and the spin-orbit induced orbital moments [12, 13].

---

[1]Corresponding author. E-mail: sven.bornemann@cup.uni-muenchen.de

In the following we present results of theoretical investigations on very small Os clusters deposited on a Fe(001) surface and we discuss the electronic, magnetic and spectroscopic properties of these systems. Our calculations were done by using the KKR Green's function formalism which is briefly introduced in the following section.

2   Theoretical Framework

The theoretical investigations which are presented below have been performed within the framework of spin density functional theory (SDFT) using the local spin density approximation (LSDA). For the parameterization of the corresponding exchange and correlation potential the results of Vosko et al. have been applied [14]. For a proper account of all relativistic effects the electronic structure calculations were based on the corresponding Dirac equation for spin polarized systems [15]:

$$\left[\frac{1}{i}c\vec{\alpha}\cdot\vec{\nabla} + \frac{1}{2}(\beta - 1)c^2 + V_{eff}(\vec{r})\right]\Psi_i(\vec{r}) = \epsilon_i\Psi_i(\vec{r}) \tag{1}$$

with the effective spin-dependent potential

$$V_{eff}(\vec{r}) = \bar{V}(\vec{r}) + \beta\vec{\sigma}\cdot\vec{B}_{eff}(\vec{r}) . \tag{2}$$

Traditional quantum mechanical methods for the treatment of finite systems as free or deposited clusters are usually based on the Raleigh-Ritz variational principle. The approach used here, however, is based on the spin polarized relativistic multiple scattering or Korringa-Kohn-Rostoker (SPR-KKR) formalism giving direct access to the electronic Green's function $G(\vec{r}_n, \vec{r}_m, E)$ [16]:

$$G(\vec{r}_n, \vec{r}_m, E) = \sum_{\Lambda\Lambda'} Z_\Lambda(\vec{r}_n, E)\tau_{\Lambda\Lambda'}^{nm}(E)Z_{\Lambda'}^\times(\vec{r}_m, E) - \sum_\Lambda Z_\Lambda(\vec{r}_<, E)J_\Lambda^\times(\vec{r}_>, E)\delta_{nm} . \tag{3}$$

Here, $Z_\Lambda(\vec{r}_n, E)$ and $J_\Lambda(\vec{r}_n, E)$ are the regular and irregular solutions, respectively, of the Dirac equation for an isolated potential well and $\tau_{\Lambda\Lambda'}^{nm}(E)$ is the so-called scattering path operator, that describes the electronic propagation from site m to site n accounting for all possible intermediate scattering events in a self consistent way.

To calculate $\tau_{\Lambda\Lambda'}^{nm}(E)$ for a finite free cluster system the so-called real space KKR-matrix, that combines the single-site t-matrices and the KKR-structure constants has to be inverted (see for example [17]). Our implementation of the real space SPR-KKR scheme made use of the atomic sphere approximation (ASA). Dealing with the electronic structure of deposited clusters, on the other hand, we first calculated the Green's function of the undisturbed substrate system with the tight-binding version of the KKR-formalism [18]. The Green's function of the deposited clusters was then obtained self-consistently in a subsequent step by using the following Dyson equation:

$$G(\vec{r}, \vec{r}', E) = G^0(\vec{r}, \vec{r}', E) + \int_\Omega d^3r'' G^0(\vec{r}, \vec{r}'', E)\Delta V(\vec{r}'')G(\vec{r}'', \vec{r}', E) . \tag{4}$$

Here $\Delta V(\vec{r})$ represents the distortion of the potential in the regime of the cluster and its surrounding (Ω), while $G^0(\vec{r}, \vec{r}', E)$ is the reference Green's function representing the undistorted supporting surface.

3   Results and Discussion

In this section the theoretical results for four different small Os clusters deposited on Fe(001) are presented. These are a single Os adatom, an Os dimer and two Os trimers, the first one having an island like shape while the second one is chain like.

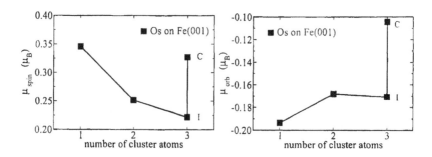

Figure 1: Left: Spin magnetic moments per Os-atom for small Os-clusters on Fe(001). Right: The corresponding orbital moments. For the 3-atom cluster the label C and I indicate chain and island like shape, respectively.

3.1 Electronic and Magnetic Properties

The averaged spin and orbital magnetic moments of all clusters are shown in Fig. 1 as a function of cluster size. One can clearly see the typical cluster behaviour of the surface induced atomic spin magnetic moments. The orbital magnetic moments are roughly of the same order of magnitude as the spin magnetic moments, but are always aligned antiparallel to them. Due to the more pronounced relativistic effects in Os the spin-orbit induced orbital moments are approximately ten times larger for Os when compared to its lighter homologue Ru. Looking at the single adatoms of Os and Ru for instance, we found an orbital moment of -0.194 μ_B in the case of Os and 0.015 μ_B in the case of Ru. For Ru clusters having the same geometry we found, however, that the orbital moments are always aligned parallel to the spin magnetic moments, while in general the spin magnetic moments are roughly three times bigger for Ru when compared to Os. For the two Os trimers one can see the typical dependence of the spin and orbital magnetic moments on the cluster shape reflecting the different hybridisation of the Os atoms for different atomic configurations. Here we found that the chain like trimer has the higher spin magnetic moment but a lower absolute orbital magnetic moment than the island like trimer.

Looking at the density of states (DOS) of the Os adatom in Fig. 2 one can see a rather strong hybridisation of the Os atom with the Fe substrate atoms. The Os atom clearly shows a nonatomic like DOS. This hybridisation leads to an increased bandwidth and thus to an decreased density of states at the Fermi level resulting in a quenching of the spin magnetic moment.

3.2 XAS and XMCD Investigations at the $M_{2,3}$-edge of Os

As a first step of our investigations, as already mentioned above, we performed fully-relativistic self consistent calculations of Os on the Fe(001) surface. The tight-binding (TB) spin polarised relativistic KKR method, that was briefly introduced in section 2, is a very efficient method to calculate electronic properties of the systems investigated here. However, because the TB-version of the KKR-method requires special care when dealing with highly excited electronic states, it was found to be more convenient to use the standard spin polarised relativistic (SPR) version of the KKR method. Thus, the SPR-KKR package [16] has been used to calculate the XAS and XMCD spectra presented here. This means in particular that the SCF potentials of Os clusters on Fe(001) calculated with the TB-KKR scheme were used as an input potential to the real space SPR-KKR method. Because of the low coordination numbers encountered for cluster systems and

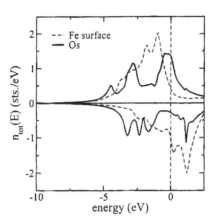

Figure 2: Density of states (DOS) for an Os adatom on Fe(001) (full line) and DOS of Fe surface atom for the unperturbed substrate (dashed line).

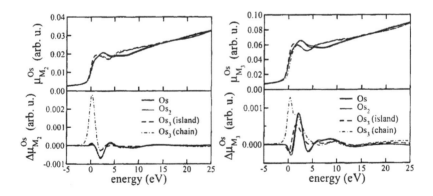

Figure 3: Left: XAS and XMCD spectra for the M_2-edge of Os. Right: The corresponding spectra for the M_3-edge.

the resulting low band width W, correlation effects are expected to be much more important than for comparable bulk systems, as it was demonstrated for example by the work of Nonas et al. [12]. As our method applies the local density approximation (LDA) to the density functional theory (DFT), it might provide an inadequate representation of pronounced correlation effects as they occur for example in some transition metal oxides.

Fig. 3 shows the theoretical results for the XAS and XMCD spectra at the M_2-edge (left panel) and M_3-edge (right panel) of Os and their cluster size dependence. The XAS spectra (upper part of both panels) show a typical line shape as observed for bulk Os with only a minor dependence on the cluster geometry and size. One can see that the XMCD (lower part of both panels) signal decreases with increasing cluster size, however, for the chain like trimer the XMCD signal is much more pronounced due to the lower coordination number when compared the the island like trimer. Thus, the calculated XMCD spectra show clearly the sensitivity of the XMCD signal with respect to the cluster magnetisation and geometry.

Acknowledgment

We acknowledge support by the Deutsche Forschungsgemeinschaft within the Schwerpunktprogramm 1153 *Cluster in Kontakt mit Oberflächen: Elektronenstruktur und Magnetismus.*

References

[1] S. Sun, C. B. Murray, D. Weller, L. Folks and A. Moser, Monodisperse FePt Nanoparticles and Ferromagnetic FePt Nanocrystal Superlattices , *Science* **287** 1989 (2000).

[2] B. Stahl, J. Ellrich, R. Theissmann, M. Ghafari, S. Bhattacharya, H. Hahn, N. S. Gajbhiye, D. Kramer, R. N. Viswanath, J. Weissmüller and H. Gleiter, Electronic properties of 4-nm FePt particles , *Phys. Rev. B* **67** 14422 (2003).

[3] Y. Xu, Z. G. Sun, Y. Qiang and D. J. Sellmyer, Magnetic properties of $L1_0$ FePt and FePt: Ag nanocluster films , *J. Appl. Physics* **93** 8289 (2003).

[4] C. Binns, S. H. Baker, S. Louch, F. Sirotti, H. Cruguel, P. Prieto, S. C. Thornton and J. D. Bellier, Building high-performance magnetic materials out of gas-phase nanoclusters , *Appl. Surf. Sci.* **226** 249 (2004).

[5] K. W. Edmonds, C. Binns, S. H. Baker, S. C. Thornton, C. Norris, J. B. Goedkoop, M. Finazzi and N. B. Brookes, Doubling of the orbital magnetic moment in nanoscale Fe clusters . *Phys. Rev. B* **60**(1) 472 (1999).

[6] P. Ohresser, G. Ghiringhelli. O. Tjernberg, N. B. Brookes and M. Finazzi, Magnetism of nanostructures studied by x-ray magnetic circular dichroism: Fe on Cu(111) , *Phys. Rev. B* **62** 5803 (2000).

[7] P. Gambardella, S. S. Dhesi, S. Gardonio, C. Grazioli, P. Ohresser and C. Carbone. Localized magnetic states of Fe, Co, and Ni impurities on alkali metal films , *Phys. Rev. Letters* **88**(4) 047202 (2002).

[8] P. Gambardella, S. Rusponi, M. Veronese, S. S. Dhesi, C. Grazioli, A. Dallmeyer, I. Cabria, R. Zeller, P. H. Dederichs, K. Kern, C. Carbone and H. Brune, Giant Magnetic Anisotropy of Single Cobalt Atoms and Nanoparticles , *Science* **300** 1130 (2003).

[9] V. S. Stepanyuk, W. Hergert, P. Rennert, K. Wildberger, R. Zeller and P. H. Dederichs, Metamagnetic states of 3d nanostructures on the Cu(001) surface , *J. Magn. Magn. Materials* **165**(1-3) 272 (1997).

[10] V. S. Stepanyuk, W. Hergert, P. Rennert, K. Wildberger, R. Zeller and P. H. Dederichs, Imperfect magnetic nanostructures on a Ag(001) surface , *Phys. Rev. B* **59**(3) 1681 (1999).

[11] J. Izquierdo, D. I. Bazhanov, A. Vega, V. S. Stepanyuk and W. Hergert, Competition between two- and three-dimensional growth of Co clusters deposited on Cu(001): Influence on the magnetic properties , *Phys. Rev. B* **63**(14) 140413 (2001).

[12] B. Nonas, I. Cabria, R. Zeller, P. H. Dederichs, T. Huhne and H. Ebert, Strongly Enhanced Orbital Moments and Anisotropies of Adatoms on the Ag(001) Surface , *Phys. Rev. Letters* **86** 2146 (2001).

[13] B. Lazarovits, L. Szunyogh and P. Weinberger, Fully relativistic calculation of magnetic properties of Fe, Co. and Ni adclusters on Ag(100) , *Phys. Rev. B* **65** 104441 (2002).

[14] S. H. Vosko, L. Wilk and M. Nusair, Accurate spin-dependent electron liquid correlation energies for local spin density calculations: a critical analysis , *Can. J. Phys.* **58** 1200 (1980).

[15] A. H. MacDonald and S. H. Vosko, A relativistic density functional formalism , *J. Phys. C: Solid State Phys.* **12** 2977 (1979).

[16] Fully relativistic band structure calculations for magnetic solids – Formalism and Application,H. Ebert , in: *Electronic Structure and Physical Properties of Solids*, editor: H. Dreyssé, vol. 535 of: *Lecture Notes in Physics,* page 191, Springer, Berlin (2000).

[17] H. Ebert, V. Popescu and D. Ahlers, MXD - model calculations and a fully relativistic theory for magnetic EXAFS , *J. Phys. (Paris)* **7** C2 131 (1997).

[18] R. Zeller, P. H. Dederichs, B. Újfalussy, L. Szunyogh and P. Weinberger, Theory and convergence properties of the screened Korringa-Kohn-Rostoker method , *Phys. Rev. B* **52** 8807 (1995).

Brill Academic Publishers
P.O. Box 9000, 2300 PA Leiden,
The Netherlands

*Lecture Series on Computer
and Computational Sciences*
Volume 5, 2006, pp. 22-29

A Density Functional Study of Structures and Vibrations of Ta$_3$O and Ta$_3$O$^-$

Patrizia Calaminici[1], Roberto Flores–Moreno, Andreas M. Köster

Departamento de Química
CINVESTAV
Av. Instituto Politécnico Nacional 2508
A.P. 14-740, México D.F. 07000 México

Abstract: Density functional calculations of neutral and anionic tantalum trimer monoxide are presented. The calculations were performed employing scalar quasi- relativistic effective core potentials. Different isomers of Ta$_3$O and Ta$_3$O$^-$ were studied in order to determine the ground state structures. For both systems a planar C$_{2v}$ structure with an edge-bound oxygen atom was found as ground state. Equilibrium structure parameters, harmonic frequencies, adiabatic electron affinity and Kohn-Sham orbital diagrams are reported. The calculated values are in good agreement with the available experimental data obtained from negative ion photoelectron spectroscopy. The correlation diagram between the neutral and anionic Ta$_3$O shows that, in agreement with the experimental prediction, the extra electron in the anionic system occupies a nonbonding orbital.

Keywords: Density Functional Theory, Transition Metal Clusters, Effective Core Potential, Photoelectron Spectroscopy, Electron Affinity.

1 Introduction

The gas phase spectroscopic study of transition metal oxides is of experimental and theoretical interest. Experimentally, the properties related to the metal–oxygen bond are crucial for the understanding of chemisorption and the catalytic activities of metal oxides [1, 2, 3, 4, 5]. In particular, tantalum oxides are important in catalysis and the investigation of the tantalum–oxygen chemical bonding is of great interest. Theoretically, molecules containing transition metals are rather challenging due to the open d shells. Simple transition metal oxide molecules provide ideal systems for the investigation of the reliability of theoretical methods [6, 7, 8]. Recently, negative ion photoelectron spectroscopy was applied to the group 5 metal trimer monoxides V$_3$O, Nb$_3$O and Ta$_3$O yielding insight into the bonding of these early transition metal cluster oxides [9]. The experimental data reported in this work provide a benchmark for computational studies of partially ligated early transition metal clusters. Our previous work was devoted to the theoretical study of V$_3$O and Nb$_3$O trimer monoxides and their anions [6, 7, 8]. The vibrationally resolved 488 nm negative ion photoelectron spectrum of Ta$_3$O [9] provides measurements of its electron affinity and vibrational frequencies which can be here summarized as follows. The electron affinity of Ta$_3$O is 1.583 ± 0.010 eV [9]. The metal–oxygen stretching frequency is 710 ± 15 cm^{-1} for the neutral Ta$_3$O. Lower symmetric modes are also active, with frequencies of 225 ± 20 cm^{-1} for the neutral Ta$_3$O and 215 ± 20 cm^{-1} for its anion. The Ta$_3$O spectrum indicates that the extra electron in the anionic system occupies essentially a nonbonding orbital and that the neutral and anionic

---

[1]Corresponding author. E-mail: pcalamin@cinvestav.mx

clusters have planar structures. In this paper we present the results of structural and spectroscopic properties of both neutral and anionic tantalum trimer monoxide obtained from scalar relativistic effective core potential (ECP) Linear Combination Gaussian Type Orbital–Kohn–Sham Density Functional Theory (LCGTO-KS-DFT) calculations. The calculated values of the adiabatic electron affinity and the vibrational frequencies are compared with those recently measured [9]. This work represents the first theoretical investigation on tantalum trimer monoxide and its anion.

2 Computational details

All calculations were performed using the deMon2k program [10]. The exchange-correlation contributions proposed by Vosko, Wilk and Nusair (VWN) [11] was used. The exchange-correlation potential was numerically integrated on an adaptive grid [12]. The grid accuracy was set to 10^{-5} in all calculations. The Coulomb energy was calculated by the variational fitting procedure proposed by Dunlap, Connolly and Sabin [13, 14]. Scalar quasi-relativistic ECPs [16, 17] were used. For the ECP integrals a half-numeric integrator was recently implemented in deMon2k. Details of this implementation will be discussed elsewhere [15]. A valence space of 6 and 13 electrons for the oxygen and tantalum atoms was employed, respectively. The reliability of these ECPs was tested with calculations on the ground state of the TaO molecule. For the fitting of the density the auxiliary function set A2* were automatic generated. In the Appendix section a description about the automatic generation of the auxiliary functions is presented. In order to localize different minima on the potential energy surface (PES) of the neutral and anionic tantalum trimer, the structures of both clusters have been optimized considering as starting points different initial geometries and multiplicities. To avoid spin contamination the calculations were performed with the restricted open shell Kohn–Sham (ROKS) method. A quasi-Newton method [19] with analytic energy gradients was used for the structure optimization. The convergence was based on the gradient and displacement vectors with a threshold of 10^{-4} and 10^{-3} a.u., respectively. A vibrational analysis was performed in order to discriminate between minima and transition states. The second derivatives were calculated by numerical differentiation (two-point finite difference) of the analytic energy gradients using a displacement of 0.002 a.u. from the optimized geometry for all 3N coordinates. The harmonic frequencies were obtained by diagonalizing the mass-weighted Cartesian force constant matrix.

3 Results and Discussion

In order to test the reliability of the used quasi-relativistic ECPs for the oxygen and tantalum atoms test calculations have been performed on the ground state of the TaO molecule. The emission spectrum of TaO has been observed at high resolution using a Fourier transform spectrometer providing for the first time the experimental bond length and vibrational frequency of this molecule in gas phase [20]. The ground state of TaO has bond length r_e of 1.6873430(29) Å with a vibrational frequency ω_e of 1028.9060(15) [20]. For the $^2\Delta$ ground state of the TaO molecule we calculate a bond length of 1.725 Å and a harmonic frequency of 1005 cm $^{-1}$. These results made us optimist that the used ECPs are appropriate for the determination of the ground state of tantalum trimer monoxide and its anion. Figure 1 summarizes the results of the obtained ground state structures of Ta₃O (top) and Ta₃O⁻ (bottom). The calculated bond distances are reported in Å. Both Ta₃O and Ta₃O⁻ ground state have planar C_{2v} structure with the oxygen atom bridging two tantalum atoms. This result is in perfect agreement with the experimental hypothesis that the neutral and anionic Ta₃O clusters have planar structures with doubly bridging oxygen atoms. Moreover, we also note that the equilibrium geometries of both ground state structures are very similar (Fig. 1). The ground state structure of the neutral Ta₃O could be assigned from our calculation to a $^2B_2$ state. We assign a $^1A_1$ state as the ground state structure of the anionic system. Both neutral and cationic ground state structures are followed by planar structures in the quartet ($^4A_1$) and triplet ($^3A_1$) potential energy surface, respectively. Similar results were found for the ground state structure of the neutral and anionic V_3O and Nb_3O clusters [6, 7, 8]. The quartet state lies 0.81 eV above the neutral ground state while the energy difference between the singlet and the triplet anionic states is 0.31 eV. Higher multiplicities have been also studied. However, the found minima in the sextet and quintet PES are lying much higher in energy with respect to the assigned ground states. In Figure 2 the schematic molecular orbital correlation diagram from the anionic $^1A_1$ ground state to the neutral $^2B_2$ ground state is shown. Both neutral and anionic ground state structure are lying in the page plane and the oxygen atom is at the left side of each structure. This figure shows that, in agreement with the experimental prediction, the extra electron in the anion of Ta_3O occupies a a_1 orbital which is nonbonding between the cluster fragment and the oxygen atom. In order to further characterize the calculated ground state structures of Ta_3O and Ta_3O^- the harmonic vibrational frequencies have been calculated. The results are collected in Table I. The lowest frequency for both systems is a stretching mode in the molecular plane. This indicates that the corresponding excited states may be planar as was found in our study. Two total symmetric a_1 modes in the neutral Ta_3O appear at 215 and 726 cm^{-1} (Table I). These are the two active modes in the negative ion photoelectron spectrum. Their frequencies agree well with the experimental observed ones of 225 ± 20 cm^{-1} and 710 ± 15 cm^{-1} in the neutral Ta_3O. Also the total symmetric a_1 mode of 212 cm^{-1} calculated for the Ta_3O^- cluster is in good agreement with the experimentally assigned mode of 215 ± 20 cm^{-1}. The calculated adiabatic electron affinity is equal to 1.59 eV. This value is in very good agreement with the experimental reported value of 1.583 ± 0.010 eV from negative ion photoelectron spectroscopy [9]. We can compare the calculated adiabatic electron affinity value with the adiabatic electron affinity we have previously calculated for the V_3O (1.30 eV) and the Nb_3O (1.39 eV) systems. We notice that the calculated adiabatic electron affinity increases going down in the triad from V_3O to Nb_3O and Ta_3O, in agreement with the experimental observation [9].

4 Conclusions

In this article we have presented DFT calculations of neutral and anionic tantalum trimer monoxides. The calculations have been performed at the local level of theory employing quasi-relativistic effective core potentials for the tantalum and oxygen atoms. Both neutral and anionic system have a planar C_{2v} ground state structure and low multiplicity. Both grounds states are followed by excited states which have planar C_{2v} structure, too. Ground state structures, as well as the structures of the excited states, have been characterized by spectroscopic term symbols. The calculated harmonic vibrational frequencies and adiabatic electron affinity were compared with the experimental values recently obtained from negative ion photoelectron spectroscopy. The agreement between calculated and experimental values is good. The molecular orbital correlation diagram between the two ground state structures shows that the extra electron in the anionic system occupies a nonbonding orbital. This work represents the first theoretical study on tantalum trimer monoxide and its anion and provides additional insight for the understanding of the ground and low-lying states of the group 5 M_3O^- and M_3O clusters.

5 Appendix: Automatic Generation of Auxiliary Functions

With the auxiliary function definition GEN-An and GEN-An^*, $n = 2$, 3 and 4, automatically generated auxiliary function sets are selected in deMon2k. The GEN-An sets consist of s, p and d Hermite Gaussian functions. The GEN-An^* sets possess also f and g Hermite Gaussians. Because the auxiliary functions are used to fit the electronic density they are grouped in s, spd and $spdfg$ sets. The exponents are shared within each of these sets [21]. Therefore, the auxiliary function notation (3,2,2) describes 3 s sets with together 3 functions, 2 spd sets with together 20 functions and 2 $spdfg$ sets with together 42 functions. The range of exponents of all auxiliary functions is determined by the smallest, ζ_{min}, and largest, ζ_{max}, primitive Gaussian exponent of the chosen basis set. Therefore, the GEN-An and GEN-An* automatically generated auxiliary function sets are different for different basis sets. The number of exponents N (auxiliary function sets) is given by:

$$N = \text{Int}\left(\frac{\ln(\zeta_{max}/\zeta_{min})}{\ln(6-n)} + 0.5 \right) \tag{1}$$

Here n is 2, 3 or 4 according to the chosen GEN-An or GEN-An* set. The exponents are generated (almost; as it is explained below) even tempered and splitted into s, spd and, if a GEN-An* set is requested, $spdfg$ sets, The tightest (largest) exponents are assigned to the s sets, followed by the spd and. if exist, $spdfg$ sets. The basic exponent from which the generation starts is defined as:

$$\zeta_o = 2\zeta_{min} (6-n)^{(N-1)} \tag{2}$$

When ECPs are used the equation (2) changes to:

$$\zeta_o = 2\zeta_{min} (6-n)^{N} \tag{3}$$

This gives to the auxiliary set more penetration to the core than that obtained from the valence basis set using the (2).

Furthermore, the set allowed are only spd and $spdfg$ for polarized auxiliary sets. This is in accordance to the fact that the core density (s-type) in not present at all.

From this ζ_o exponent the two tightest s set exponents, ζ_1 and ζ_2 are generated according to the formulas:

$$\zeta_1 = \left(1 + \frac{n}{12-2n} \right) \zeta_o \tag{4}$$

$$\zeta_2 = \frac{\zeta_o}{6-n} \tag{5}$$

The other s set exponents are generated according to the even tempered progression:

$$\zeta_{i+1} = \frac{\zeta_i}{6-n} \tag{6}$$

The ζ_o exponent of the following spd sets is also generated according to the progression (6). Based on this ζ_o exponent the exponents of the first two spd sets are calculated with the formulas (4) and (5). The following spd set exponents are then calculated again according to the even tempered progression (6). In the same way the $spdfg$ set exponents are calculated. In the case of 3d elements an extra diffuse s auxiliary function set is added.

Table 1: Vibrational frequencies [cm^{-1}] of the Ta_3O and $Ta3O^-$ ground state structures. The assignment of each normal mode and its symmetry is also given.

Cluster	Mode	Symmetry	ν [cm^{-1}]
Ta_3O	ν	b_2	199
	ν	a_1	215
	π	b_1	262
	ν	a_1	270
	ν	b_2	606
	ν	a_1	726
Ta_3O^-	ν	b_2	172
	ν	a_1	212
	π	b_1	254
	ν	a_1	269
	ν	b_2	519
	ν	a_1	673

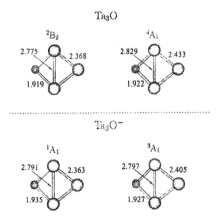

Figure 1: Ground state and first excited state structures of Ta_3O (top) and Ta_3O^- (bottom) clusters. Bond lengths are in Å.

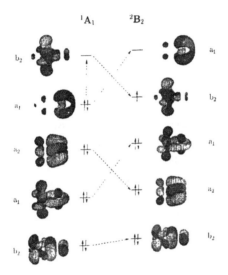

Figure 2: Schematic molecular orbital correlation diagram from the anionic (^{1}A$_1$) ground state to the neutral (^{2}B$_2$) ground state. Both neutral and anionic ground state structure are lying in the page plane and the oxygen atom is at the left side of each structure.

Acknowledgments

This work was financially supported by the CONACYT projects 36037-E and 40379-F. R.F.-M. gratefully acknowledge CONACYT for the Ph.D. fellowship n. 163442.

References

[1] R. Fournier and I Pápai, Recent Advances in Density Functional Methods, edited by D.P. Chong, World Scientific, Singapore, Part I, 219.285(1995)

[2] P.B. Armentrout and B.L. Kickek. Organometallic Ion Chemistry, edited by B.S. Freiser, Kluwer Academic, Dordrecht, 1-45(1996)

[3] M. Calatayud. A. Markovits, C. Minot, Electron-count control on adsorption upon reducible and irreducible clean metal–surfaces, *Catalysis Today* **89** 269-278(2004)

[4] C. Kolczewski. K. Hermann. Ab initio DFT studies of oxygen K edge NEXAFS spectra for the $V_2O_3(0001)$ surface, *Theoretical Chemistry Accounts* **114** 60-67(2005)

[5] K.M. Neyman. F. Illas, Theoretical aspects of heterogeneous catalysis: Applications of density functional methods, *Catalysis Today* **105** 2-16(2005)

[6] P. Calaminici and A.M. Köster, Structures and Vibrations of V_3O and V_3O^-: A Density Functional Study, *International Journal of Quantum Chemistry* **91** 317-320(2003).

[7] P. Calaminici. A.M. Köster and D.R. Salahub, Negative Ion Photoelectron Spectra Simulation of V_3O from a Density Functional Study, *Journal of Chemical Physics* **118** 4913-4919(2003).

[8] P. Calaminici, R. Flores–Moreno and A.M. Köster, Structure and Vibrations of Nb_3O and Nb_3O^-: A Density Functional Study, *Journal of Chemical Physics* **121** 3558-3562(2004).

[9] S.M.E. Green, S. Alex, N.L. Fleischer, E.L. Millam, T.P. Marcy, and D.G. Leopold, Negative ion photoelectron spectroscopy of the group 5 metal trimer monoxides V_3O, Nb_3O and Ta_3O, *Journal of Chemical Physics* **114** 2653-2668(2001).

[10] A.M. Köster, P. Calaminici, R. Flores-Moreno, G. Geudtner, A. Goursot, T. Heine, F. Janetzko, S. Patchkovskii, J.U. Reveles, A. Vela and D.R. Salahub, deMon2k, The deMon developers (2004)

[11] S.H. Vosko, L. Wilk and M. Nusair, Accurate spin–dependent electron liquid correlation energies for local spin density calculations: a critical analysis. *Canadian Journal of Physics* **58** 1200-1211(1980).

[12] A.M. Köster, R. Flores–Moreno and J.U. Reveles, Efficient and reliable numerical integration of exchange–correlation energies and potentials, *Journal of Chemical Physics* **121** 681-690(2004).

[13] B.I. Dunlap, J.W.D. Connolly and J.R. Sabin, On first-row diatomic molecules and local density models, *Journal of Chemical Physics* **71** 4993-4999(1979).

[14] W. Mintmire and B.I. Dunlap, Fitting the Coulomb potential variationally in linear-combination-of-atomic-orbitals density-functional calculations, *Physical Review A* **25** 88-95(1982).

[15] R. Flores-Moreno, A. Vela and A.M. Köster, Numerical evaluation of pseudopotential integrals, to be submitted

[16] A. Bergner, M. Dolg, W. Küchle, H. Stoll and H. Preuß, *Ab initio* energy-adjusted pseudopotentials for elements of groups 13-17, *Molecular Physics* **80** 1431-1441(1993).

[17] D. Andrae, U. Häußermann, M. Dolg, H. Stoll and H. Preuß, Energy-adjusted *ab initio* pseudopotentials for the second and third row transition elements, *Theorica Chimica Acta* **77** 123-141(1990).

[18] A.M. Köster, P. Calaminici, Z. Gómez and U. Reveles, Density Functional Theory Calculations of Transition Metal Clusters, R.G. Parr Festschrift, Vol. II, (Editor: K. Seni, University of Hyderabad, India), World Scientific Publishing Co. Inc., New Jersey, 1439-1475(2002).

[19] J.U. Reveles and A.M. Köster, Geometry Optimization in Density Functional Methods, *Journal of Computational Chemistry* **25** 1109-1116(2004).

[20] S.M. Ram and P.F. Bernath, Fourier Transform Emission Spectroscopy of TaO. *Journal of Molecular Spectroscopy* **191** 125-136(1998).

[21] J. Andzelm, N. Russo and D.R. Salahub, Ground and excited states of group IVA diatomics from local-spin-density calculations: Model potentials for Si, Ge, and Sn, *Journal of Chemical Physics* **87**, 6562-6572(1987).

Brill Academic Publishers
P.O. Box 9000, 2300 PA Leiden,
The Netherlands

Lecture Series on Computer
and Computational Sciences
Volume 5, 2006, pp. 30-40

A Density Functional Study of Structure and Stability of Ni$_8$, Ni$_8{}^+$ and Ni$_8{}^-$ Cluster

Patrizia Calaminici[1a], **Marcela R. Beltrán**[b]

[a]Departamento de Química
CINVESTAV
Av. Instituto Politécnico Nacional 2508
A.P. 14-740, México D.F. 07000 México

[b]Universidad Nacional Autonoma Mexico,
Instituto Investigacion de Materiales,
Mexico City, D.F. 01000 México

Abstract: Density functional calculations of neutral, cationic and anionic nickel octamer are presented. The structure optimization and frequency analysis were performed on the local density approximation (LDA) level with the exchange correlation functional by Vosko, Wilk and Nusair (VWN). Improved calculations for the stability were based on the generalized gradient approximation (GGA) where the exchange correlation functional of Perdew and Wang (PW) was used. For neutral, cationic and anionic cluster several isomers and different spin multiplicities were investigated in order to find the lowest structures. Structural parameters, relative energies, binding energies, harmonic frequencies, adiabatic ionization potential and electron affinity will be presented. The calculated values are compared with available experimental data.

Keywords: Density Functional Theory, Transition Metal Clusters, Nickel Clusters, Structures, Relative Energy.

This manuscript is dedicated to the memory of Professor Jaroslav Koutecky for his very important achievements and unforgettable contribution in the study of transition metal clusters.

---

[1]Corresponding author. E-mail: pcalamin@cinvestav.mx

1   Introduction

The study of transition metal (TM) clusters has become an increasingly interesting topic in the past three decades from both experimental and theoretical point of views due to their particular physical, chemical, electronic and magnetic properties related to their peculiar geometrical structures, and to their role on the development of these properties toward the bulk (see for example Refs. [1, 2, 3, 4, 5, 6] and references therein). In this sense the knowledge of their properties furnishes information how the transition from atom or molecule to the solid state may occur. The determination of structural properties and the growth pattern of the clusters therefore offer a first step toward the understanding of the development of a solid. If we classify solids by their bonding properties we can distinguish three categories with strong bonding usually referred to be as ionic, semiconducting or metallic solids. Among the $3d$ TM clusters, Ni systems have received most of attention both experimentally and theoretically [7, 8, 9, 10, 11, 12, 13, 14, 15, 16, 17, 18, 19, 20, 21]. In particular the localized behavior of the unfilled $3d$ electrons in nickel clusters results in a big complexity which has animated many groups to study how this effects dominates in most of the properties of these systems. From the theoretical point of view, nickel clusters have constituted one of the most studied sets of clusters since they are excellent systems for exploring new theoretical approaches and several manuscripts have been already published. Even if to review the full literature about this topic is not a purpose of the present work, in order to get an idea of the different theoretical approaches applied in the study nickel clusters, we would like to address the reader to the following papers and their therein references [10, 11, 12, 13, 14, 15, 16, 17, 18, 19, 20, 21]. Despite many articles have published on the different isomers of neutral small nickel clusters less attention has been paid to the study of structure and properties of cationic and anionic systems. In this letter a particular effort was done in order to answer some of the questions related to the structure and electronic properties of cationic and anionic nickel octamer. In the following sections we present the structures of several isomers of Ni_8, $Ni_8{}^+$ and $Ni_8{}^-$ cluster obtained from all-electron Linear Combination Gaussian Type Orbital–Kohn–Sham Density Functional Theory (LCGTO-KS-DFT) calculations. Different topologies and spin multiplicity were considered in order to scan as much as possible each potential energy surface (PES) and find the lowest energetic structures. The stability of the structures is tested by a frequency analysis. Structural parameters, harmonic frequencies, binding energy, ionization potential and electron affinity are reported. The calculated values are compared with available data from the literature. We believe this is the most extensive theoretical investigation performed on the ground and low-lying states of the neutral Ni_8, cationic Ni_8^+ and anionic Ni_8^- cluster.

2   Computational details

All calculations were performed using the density functional theory (DFT) deMon2k program [22]. The exchange-correlation potential was numerically integrated on an adaptive grid [23]. The grid accuracy was set to 10^{-5} in all calculations. The Coulomb energy was calculated by the variational fitting procedure proposed by Dunlap, Connolly and Sabin [24, 25]. The structure optimizations were performed in the local density approximation (LDA) with the exchange-correlation functional of Vosko, Wilk and Nusair (VWN) [26]. DFT optimized double zeta plus valence polarization (DZVP) all-electron basis sets were employed [27]. The VWN same functional was used for the frequency analysis in order to be able to distinguish between stable structures and transition state structures. Since such calculations are insufficient for energetic considerations, single point energies were finally calculated using the same basis and auxiliary function set with the exchange-correlation functional proposed by Perdew and Wang (PW86) [28, 29]. This approach has already been proven reliable for other small TM clusters [4]. For the fitting of the density the auxiliary function set A2 were automatic generated. The way how the automatic generation of the auxiliary functions is performed will be presented somewhere else [30] . In order to localize different minima on the potential energy surface (PES) of the neutral, cationic and anionic nickel octamer, the structures of the three clusters have been optimized considering as starting points different initial geometries and multiplicities. To avoid spin contamination the calculations were performed with the restricted open shell Kohn–Sham (ROKS) method. A quasi-Newton method [31] with analytic energy gradients was used for the structure optimization. The convergence was based on the gradient and displacement vectors with a threshold of 10^{-4} and 10^{-3} a.u., respectively. For the vibrational analysis the second derivatives were calculated by numerical differentiation (two-point finite difference) of the analytic energy gradients using a displacement of 0.002 a.u. from the optimized geometry for all 3N coordinates. The harmonic frequencies were obtained by diagonalizing the mass-weighted Cartesian force constant matrix.

3 Results and Discussion

The optimized structure parameters, the relative energies and the spin multiplicity of the minima structures we found for the neutral nickel octamer are presented in Figure 1. The corresponding results obtained for the minima structures of the ions are presented in Figure 2 and 3, respectively. All optimized bond distances are given in Å.

In Figs. 1, 2 and 3 the relative energy values obtained with the VWN functional are given in round brackets, whereas the values obtained with the PW86 functional are given in square brackets.

For Ni_8, $Ni_8{}^+$ and $Ni_8{}^-$ we investigated several initial structures as the bisdisphenoid, capped pentagonal bypiramid, cube, bi-capped tripyramidal prism, bi-capped octahedron, a square antiprism and a D_{2d} star structure. In all cases, the energy was minimized by optimization of the structural parameters and several spin multiplicities were considered. Some of the starting initial geometries during the optimization collapsed in some of other structures. For example, in our study we did not found any minima with cubic structure although the cubic topology was considered as initial guess in different multiplicities.

For the neutral Ni_8 cluster the multiplicities 11, 9, 7, 5 and 3 were studied for all possible isomers. For the charged systems the multiplicity 10, 8, 6 and 4 were investigated.

For the neutral nickel octamer eight minima were found (Fig. 1). For Ni_8, the D_2 bisdisphenoid structure in multiplicity 9 (structure a) was found as ground state. This structure has a twofold HOMO state full filled. This result is in agreement with both experimental data [32] and another theoretical study [19]. This isomer is followed by a C_{2v} bi-capped prism (structure b)) with the same multiplicity at only 0.09 eV (Fig. 1). The next two found minima, a C_{2v} bi-capped prism (structure c)) and a D_{2d} bisdisphenoid (structure d)) structure, are in the sextet PES, at 0.19 and 0.27 eV above the ground state structure. Follows at higher energy a T_d bi-capped tripyramidal structure in multiplicity 9 (structure e)) and three isomers in multiplicity 5 (structures f), g) and h) in Fig. 1). The minima structures in multiplicity 11 are not reported since these structures were found much higher in energy as respect the ones reported in Fig. 1.

In the case of the cation $Ni_8{}^+$, eleven minima structures were found (Fig. 2). Similar to the neutral nickel octamer, for the cationic nickel octamer we found as ground state structure the D_2 bisdisphenoid structure in higher multiplicity. The Ni-Ni bond distance of the two atoms which cap the square pyramid is about 0.06 Å shorter as respect the one on the neutral ground state structure. The cationic ground state is followed by five other isomers within an energy range of only 0.19 eV. A D_2 bisdisphenoid structure on the octuplet PES (structure b)), a C_{2v} bi-capped prism in multiplicity 10 and the same isomer in multiplicity 8 (structures c) and d), respectively), a D_2 bisdisphenoid structure on the sextet PES (structure e)) and a T_d bi-capped tripyramidal structure in multiplicity 8 (structure f)). Other five isomers follow well separated in energy with respect the ground state structure (Fig. 2).

Nine minima structures were found for the anionic nickel octamer (Fig. 3). Different from the neutral and anionic case, the ground state structure of Ni_8^- is found as a T_d bi-capped tripyramidal structure on the octuplet PES structure a)). It is followed at only 0.07 eV by a D_2 bisdisphenoid (structure b)) in the same multiplicity. Also this case, GGA corrections are crucial for the correct determination of the ground state structure. In fact, the LDA level of theory predicts the change of order of structure a) and b) (see Fig. 3). As Fig. 3 shows, all remaining seven minima found for the anionic nickel octamer are well separated in energy with respect the ground state structure. As we can see from Fig. 2, the order of the minima a) and b) is exchanged when the local approximation is used. Therefore, the GGA corrections are very important for the correct prediction of the global minimum and for the relative stability of isomers.

In order to characterize the calculated ground state structure of nickel octamer and its ions and to give clues for further desirable experimental investigations, the harmonic vibrational frequencies have been calculated. The calculated harmonic frequencies for all minima are listed in Table 1. All the presented structures have no imaginary frequency and therefore they are real minima on the PES (Table 1).

In Table 2 the calculated binding energy, adiabatic ionization potential and adiabatic electron affinity are listed. The binding energy per atom calculated with the VWN functional is 4.1 eV, whereas the PW86 functional gives a value of 3.38 eV (Table 2).

With the LDA level of theory the calculated adiabatic ionization potential and the adiabatic electron affinity are 6.78 eV end 2.29 eV, respectively. The GGA corrections give 6.72 and 2.37 eV, respectively. The experimental adiabatic ionization potential [33] is 6.13 eV, which is about 0.6 eV lower than our LDA and GGA values. We also calculated the adiabatic ionization potential considering the structures b) reported in Figs. 1 and 2. The obtained value with the PW86 gradient corrected functional is 6.48 eV, much closer to the experimental value. This result gives evidence that due to the very small energy difference between ground state and low-lying states the last ones could not be excluded in the calculation of properties like adiabatic ionization potential in small nickel clusters.

The calculated adiabatic electron affinity for is in good agreement with the experimental value of 1.97 ± 0.05 eV [34].

4 Conclusions

In this work we have reported the LCGTO-DFT local and GGA first principle all-electron calculations for the structural and spectroscopic properties of neutral, cationic and anionic nickel octamer. Several topological structures in different PES were investigated for the neutral cluster as well as for the ionic systems. All found minima were characterized by vibrational analysis in order to guide future experiments, which we hope will be forthcoming. The inclusion of gradient corrections is very important because of the very small energy separation between different low-lying isomers. Binding energies, adiabatic ionization potential and adiabatic electron affinity have been reported. Due to the very small energy difference between ground state and low-lying states different isomers might be considered for the comparison of the calculated energy properties with the available experimental values. Experimental investigations which provide vibrational resolved photo-electron spectra for small nickel clusters are highly desirable in order to be able to give a final answer concerning the ground state structure of these systems.

Acknowledgments

Financial support from the Conacyt projects 36037-E and 40393-F and computational support from the DGSCA-UNAM is gratefully acknowledged.

Patrizia Calaminici and Marcela Beltrán

Table 1: Vibrational frequencies [cm^{-1}] of the neutral Ni$_8$, cationic Ni$_8^+$ and anionic Ni$_8^-$ cluster. The calculations were performed with the VWN/DZVP/GEN-A2 method. The cluster structures are given in Figure 1, 2 and 3.

Ni$_8$	Frequencies	Ni$_8^+$	Frequencies	Ni$_8^-$	Frequencies
a)	87, 118, 132, 141, 156, 169, 171, 177, 188, 193, 252, 252, 253, 262, 285, 288, 312, 320	a)	84, 115, 131, 133, 144, 171, 173, 176, 186, 191, 237, 245, 250, 259, 278, 313, 316, 319	a)	90, 95, 104, 118, 158, 162, 167, 171, 191, 195, 222, 229, 241, 257, 261, 304, 318, 337
b)	81, 94, 98, 120, 138, 163, 165, 178, 195, 199, 227, 235, 238, 257, 267, 311, 319, 338	b)	81, 106, 117, 125, 133, 149, 172, 176, 189, 195, 229, 245, 251, 260, 280, 317, 319, 329	b)	98, 109, 118, 127, 133, 155, 167, 170, 182, 187, 231, 244, 257, 258, 278, 307, 314, 320
c)	78, 93, 115, 119, 151, 163, 170, 171, 185, 206, 220, 221, 249, 266, 269, 305, 330, 344	c)	97, 99, 111, 122, 136, 147, 164, 175, 183, 188, 231, 256, 259, 269, 278, 302, 320, 327	c)	46, 64, 81, 119, 142, 151, 160, 167, 186, 207, 217, 235, 244, 246, 265, 297, 320, 344
d)	103, 105, 112, 113, 135, 146, 170, 172, 184, 185, 225, 245, 248, 272, 279, 313, 318, 327	d)	62, 85, 91, 115, 138, 159, 161, 178, 191, 204, 222, 222, 243, 248, 267, 306, 326, 337	d)	43, 59, 99, 117, 123, 144, 147, 181, 184, 200, 210, 237, 239, 245, 270, 307, 326, 344
e)	60, 65, 107, 132, 135, 151, 159, 185, 196, 210, 216, 235, 249, 262, 284, 308, 328, 347	e)	115, 119, 123, 128, 166, 174, 180, 191, 195, 213, 233, 247, 250, 267, 270, 311, 320, 341	e)	134, 194, 214, 220, 223, 231, 234, 249, 257, 261, 274, 294, 295, 311, 325, 344, 362, 366
f)	37, 61, 74, 100, 113, 118, 136, 161, 176, 195, 207, 221, 227, 273, 284, 323, 326, 340	f)	61, 66, 104, 126, 130, 153, 161, 184, 190, 193, 218, 220, 242, 250, 278, 316, 325, 347	f)	114, 117, 125, 125, 162, 165, 165, 181, 184, 193, 245, 245, 261, 266, 281, 281, 316, 323
g)	42, 93, 119, 135, 149, 152, 159, 172, 199, 218, 223, 242, 258, 290, 297, 339, 359, 373	g)	54, 71, 104, 132, 138, 157, 166, 177, 183, 204, 209, 225, 241, 253, 281, 311, 322, 343	g)	125, 131, 144, 156, 158, 170, 171, 190, 208, 222, 245, 247, 259, 266, 284, 299, 310, 345
h)	69, 72, 103, 118, 153, 162, 188, 204, 210, 228, 239, 264, 279, 291, 300, 313, 330, 337	h)	96, 104, 122, 129, 133, 149, 175, 182, 183, 192, 224, 250, 258, 278, 278, 312, 319, 325	h)	76, 86, 109, 116, 126, 130, 159, 161, 162, 196, 216, 240, 248, 267, 269, 292, 310, 313
		i)	20, 75, 91, 109, 118, 168, 179, 202, 208, 209, 221, 253, 261, 275, 287, 306, 317, 342	i)	103, 112, 119, 116, 126, 130, 159, 161, 162, 196, 216, 240, 248, 267, 269, 292, 310, 313
		l)	83, 90, 95, 102, 131, 134, 147, 169, 184, 206, 221, 234, 242, 257, 266, 311, 320, 333		
		m)	108, 131, 139, 142, 152, 157, 162, 175, 219, 224, 240, 251, 256, 265, 285, 311, 320, 359		

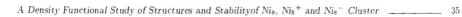

Table 2: Binding energy (eV), ionization potential (eV) and electron affinity (eV) for Ni_8. The calculations were performed with the VWN/DZVP/GEN-A2 and the PW86/DZVP/GEN-A2 methods. The PW86/DZVP/GEN-A2 values are in parenthesis.

BE	BE per atom	Adiabatic IP	Adiabatic EA
32.8 (27.06)	4.1 (3.38)	6.78 (6.72)	2.29 (2.37)

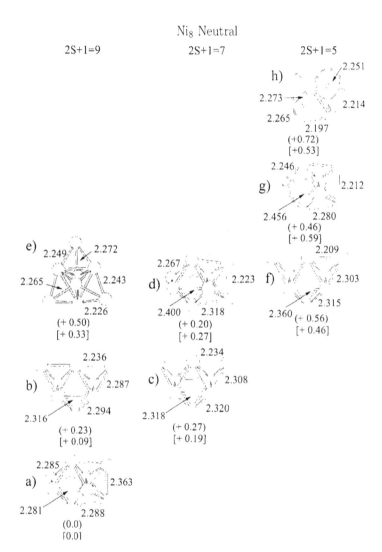

Ni₈ Neutral

2S+1=9   2S+1=7   2S+1=5

Figure 1: Ground state and excited state structures of Ni₈ cluster. The calculations were performed with the VWN/DZVP/GEN-A2 method. The relative energy is given in eV. VWN values are in round brackets and PW86 values are in square brackets. Bond lengths are given in Å.

Ni₈ Cation

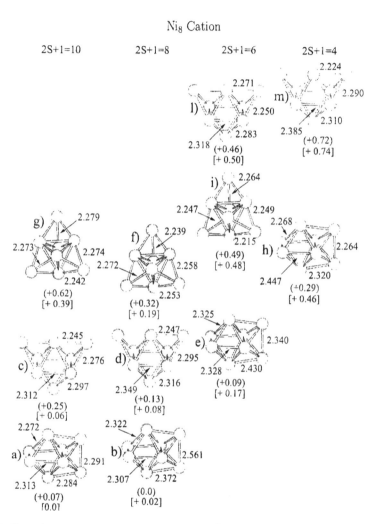

Figure 2: Ground state and excited state structures of Ni_8^+ cluster. The calculations were performed with the VWN/DZVP/GEN-A2 method. The relative energy is given in eV. VWN values are in round brackets and PW86 values are in square brackets. Bond lengths are given in Å.

Ni₈ Anion

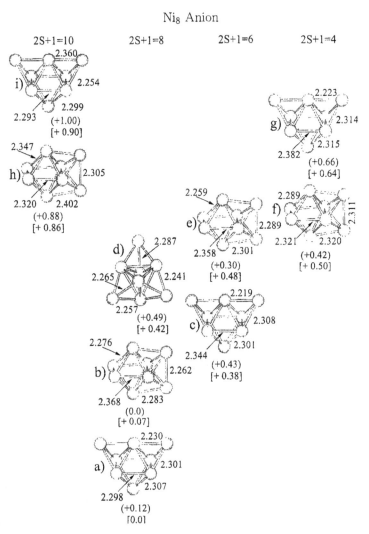

Figure 3: Ground state and excited state structures of Ni₈⁻ cluster. The calculations were performed with the VWN/DZVP/GEN-A2 method. The relative energy is given in eV. VWN values are in round brackets and PW86 values are in square brackets. Bond lengths are given in Å.

References

[1] M.D. Morse, Clusters of Tansition Metal Atoms, *Chemical Reviews,* **86** 1049-1109(1986).

[2] J.A. Alonso, Electronic and Atomic Structure, and Magnetism of Transition Metal Clusters, *Chemical Reviews* **100** 637-677(2000).

[3] V. Bonacic-Koutecky, L. Cespiva, P. Fantucci, J. Koutecky, Effective core potential-configuration interaction study of electronic structure and geometry of small neutral and cationic Ag_n clusters: Predictions and interpretation of measured properties, *Journal of Chemical Physics* **98** 7981-7994(1993)

[4] K. Jug, B. Zimmermann, P. Calaminici, A. M. Köster, Structure and Stability of Small Copper Clusters Cu_n ($n \leq 10$), *Journal of Chemical Physics* **116**, 4497–(2002)

[5] P. Calaminici, A.M. Köster, N. Russo, P.N. Roy, T. Carrington Jr., D.R. Salahub, V_3: Structure and Vibrations from Density Functional Theory, Franck-Condon Factors and the PFI-ZEKE Spectrum, *Journal of Chemical Physics* **114**, 4036-4044(2001)

[6] J. Jellinek and I.L. Garzon, Structural and Dynamic Properties of Transition-Metal Clusters, *Zeitschrift für Physik. D, Atoms, molecules and clusters* **20** 239-242(1991).

[7] E.K. Parks, K.P. Kerns and S.J. Riley, The structure of Ni_{46}, Ni_{47}, and Ni_{48}, *Journal of Chemical Physics* **114** 2228-2236(2001).

[8] M.B. Knickelbein, Nickel clusters: The influence of adsorbates on magnetic moments, *Journal of Chemical Physics* **116** 9703-9711(2002).

[9] F. Liu, R. Liyanage and P.B. Armentrout, Guided ion beam studies of the reaction of $Ni_n{}^{(+)}$ (n = 2-16) with D2: Nickel cluster-deuteride bond energies *Journal of Chemical Physics* **117** 132-141(2002).

[10] F.A. Reuse and S.N. Khanna, Photoabsorption spectrum of small Ni_n (n=2-6, 13) clusters, *The European Physical Journal D - Atomic, Molecular and Optical Physics* **6** 77-81(1999).

[11] T.L. Wetzel and DePristo, Structures and energetics of $Ni_{24}Ni_{55}$ clusters, *Journal of Chemical Physics* **105** 572-580(1996).

[12] F. Ruette and C. Gonzalez, The importance of global minimization and adequate theoretical tools for luster optimization: the Ni_8 cluster case, *Chemical Physics Letters* **359** 428-433(2002).

[13] S.N. Khanna and P. Jena, Magnetic moment and photo-detachment spectroscopy of Ni_5 clusters, *Chemical Physics Letters* **336** 467-472(2001).

[14] S.N. Khanna, M.R. Beltran and P. Jena, Relationship between photoelectron spectroscopy and the magnetic moment of Ni_7 cluster, *Physical Review B* **64** 235419-235422(2001).

[15] G.M. Pastor, R. Hirsch and B. Muhlschlegel, Magnetism and structure of small clusters: An exact treatment of electron correlations, *Physical Review B* **53** 10382-10396(1996).

[16] M. Castro, C. Jamorski and D.R. Salahub, Structure, bonding, and magnetism of small Fe_n, Co_n, and Ni_n clusters, $n \leq 5$, *Chemical Physics Letters* **271** 133-142(1997).

[17] G.A. Cisneros, M. Castro and D.R. Salahub, DFT study of the structural and electronic properties of small Ni_n (n=2-4) clusters, *International Journal of Quantum Chemistry* **75** 847-861(1999).

[18] G.L. Estiu and M.C. Zerner, Structural, electronic, and magnetic properties of small Ni clusters *Journal of Physical Chemistry* **100** 16874-16880(1996).

[19] N. Desmarais, C. Jamorski, F.A. Reuse and S.N. Khanna, Atomic arrangements in Ni_7 and Ni_8 clusters, *Chemical Physics Letters* **294** 480-486 (1998).

[20] Z. Xie, Q.-M. Ma, Y. Liu, Y.-C. Li, First-principle study of the stability and Jahn-Teller distortion of nickel clusters, *Physics Letters A* **342** 459-467(2005).

[21] M.C. Michelini, R. Pis Diez, A.H. Jubert, Density Functional Study of Small Ni_n Clusters, with n=2-6, 8, using the Generalized Gradient Approximation, *International Journal of Quantum Chemistry* **85** 22-33(2001).

[22] A.M. Köster, P. Calaminici, R. Flores-Moreno, G. Geudtner, A. Goursot, T. Heine, F. Janetzko, S. Patchkovskii, J.U. Reveles, A. Vela and D.R. Salahub, deMon2k, The deMon developers (2004)

[23] A.M. Köster, R. Flores–Moreno and J.U. Reveles, Efficient and reliable numerical integration of exchange-correlation energies and potentials, *Journal of Chemical Physics* **121** 681-690(2004).

[24] B.I. Dunlap, J.W.D. Connolly and J.R. Sabin, On first-row diatomic molecules and local density models, *Journal of Chemical Physics* **71** 4993–4999(1979).

[25] W. Mintmire and B.I. Dunlap, Fitting the Coulomb potential variationally in linear-combination-of-atomic-orbitals density-functional calculations, *Physical Review A* **25** 88-95(1982).

[26] S.H. Vosko, L. Wilk and M. Nusair, Accurate spin–dependent electron liquid correlation energies for local spin density calculations: a critical analysis, *Canadian Journal of Physics* **58** 1200-1211(1980).

[27] N. Godbout, D.R. Salahub, J. Andzelm and E. Wimmer, Optimization of Gaussian-Type Basis-Sets for Local Spin-Density Functional Calculations .1. Boron Through Neon, Optimization Technique and Validation *Canadian Journal of Physics* **70** 560-571(1992)

[28] J.P. Perdew and Y. Wang, Accurate and simple density functional for the electronic exchange energy: Generalized gradient approximation, *Physical Review B* **33**, 8800-8802(1986); Erratum: *Physical Review B* **40** 3399(1989).

[29] J.P. Perdew, Density-functional approximation for the correlation energy of the inhomogeneous electron gas, *Physical Review B* **33**, 8822-8824(1986); Erratum: *Physical Review B* **34** 7406(1986).

[30] P. Calaminici, R. Flores Moreno, A.M. Köster, A Density Functional Study of Structures and Vibrations of Ta_3O and Ta_3O^-, *Computing Letters*, submitted

[31] J.U. Reveles and A.M. Köster, Geometry Optimization in Density Functional Methods, *Journal of Computational Chemistry* **25** 1109-1116(2004).

[32] H. Basch, M.D. Newton, J.W. Moskovitz, The electronic structure of small nickel atom clusters, *Journal of Chemical Physics* **73** 4492-4510(1980).

[33] M.B. Knickelbein, S. Yang, S.J. Riley, Near-threshold photoionization of nickel clusters: Ionization potentials for Ni_3 to Ni_{90}, *Journal of Chemical Physics* **93** 94-104(1990).

[34] S.-R. Liu, H.-J. Zhai and L.-S. Wang, Evolution of the electronic properties of small Ni_n^- (n=1-100) clusters by photoelectron spectroscopy, *Journal of Chemical Physics* **117** 9758-9765(2002).

Brill Academic Publishers
P.O. Box 9000, 2300 PA Leiden,
The Netherlands

Lecture Series on Computer
and Computational Sciences
Volume 5, 2006, pp. 42-49

Close-packing transitions in clusters of Lennard-Jones spheres

F. Calvo[†,1], M. Benali[*], V. Gerbaud[*], and M. Hemati[*]

(†) Laboratoire de Physique Quantique, IRSAMC, Université Paul Sabatier, 118 Route de Narbonne, F31062 Toulouse Cedex, France
(*) Laboratoire de Génie Chimique, UMR 5503, BP 1301, 5 rue Paulin Talabot 31106 Toulouse Cedex, France

Abstract: The structures of clusters of spherical and homogeneous particles are investigated using a combination of global optimization methods. The pairwise potential between particles is integrated exactly from elementary Lennard-Jones interactions, and the use of reduced units allows us to get insight into the effects of the particle diameter. As the diameter increases, the potential becomes very sharp, and the cluster structure generally changes from icosahedral (small radius) to close-packed cubic (large radius), possibly through intermediate decahedral shapes. The results are interpreted in terms of the effective range of the potential.

1 Introduction

Atomic and molecular clusters display very rich structural properties [1, 2, 3]. Due to their large surface/volume ratio, these finite systems often show symmetry elements that are not observed in bulk matter. For instance, fivefold and icosahedral geometries, while being forbidden in periodic systems, are ubiquitous in clusters ranging from rare-gas [4] to simple metals [5]. Clusters of molecules also display such pentagonal elements, even though the appearance of the bulk crystalline features usually occurs at smaller sizes with respect to atomic systems. In general, the icosahedral structure remains the most stable at small sizes, and more compact shapes become favored above some crossover size. The transition takes place near 1500 atoms for argon [4], near 200 molecules for N_2 [6], and only 30 for CO_2 [7]. The preference of larger molecules toward close-packed structures has been confirmed in the $(C_{60})_n$ system [8].

The interaction between larger structures is usually harder to consider because of the internal degrees of freedom. Several studies have emphasized the possible rearrangements during the soft collision between clusters [9, 10]. Thanks to their outer ligand layer, colloidal particles are less sensitive to such isomerizations. However, unless the liquid suspension is removed they do not form superstructures. The interaction between colloidal particles, even with only a few hundred atoms, cannot be calculated exactly at the level of atomic details. Instead, coarse-grained approximations such as those introduced by Hamaker [11] provide the main features governing this interaction. In the present paper, we investigate clusters of spherical particles assumed to be homogeneously filled with Lennard-Jones (LJ) centers. By varying the radius of the particles from small to large values, we explore the transition from the atomic scale to the mesoscale, and its consequences on the shape of the nano-assemblies.

---

[1]Corresponding author. E-mail: florent.calvo@irsamc.ups-tlse.fr

Finding the stable structures of a many-particle system, even bound by simple forces, can be very difficult because of the huge number of minima on the potential energy surface (PES) [12]. Powerful numerical algorithms have been dedicated to solve this task, especially the basin-hopping, or Monte Carlo+minimization algorithm of Wales and Doye [13]. Such an approach is useful in the case where the cluster contains relatively few particles (below about 100), but is not practical for large sizes, for which we will use extrapolations to the cohesion energies for the magic number series. The article is organized as follows. In the next section, we describe the interaction between particles and discuss them in terms of an effective range. Section 3 presents our results on the structure as a function of both the number of particles and the particles' radius. We finally summarize and conclude in Sec. 4.

2 Methods

We consider spherical particles (1) and (2) with common radius R and constant volumic density ρ. The interaction between two elements of volume $\rho d^3 r_1$ and $\rho d^3 r_2$ distant by $r' = |\mathbf{r}_1 - \mathbf{r}_2|$ is assumed to be a Lennard-Jones form

$$d^6 V = 4\varepsilon \left[\left(\frac{\sigma}{r'} \right)^{12} - \left(\frac{\sigma}{r'} \right)^6 \right] \rho^2 d^3 r_1 d^3 r_2. \tag{1}$$

$$
\begin{aligned}
V^{(n)}(d) =\ & -\frac{4\pi^2}{(n-2)(n-3)(n-4)(n-5)} \left[\frac{1}{n-6} \left(\frac{2}{d^{n-6}} - \frac{1}{(d+2R)^{n-6}} - \frac{1}{(d-2R)^{n-6}} \right) \right. \\
& -\frac{1}{d(n-7)} \left(\frac{2}{d^{n-7}} - \frac{1}{(d+2R)^{n-7}} - \frac{1}{(d-2R)^{n-7}} \right) \\
& \left. +\frac{R^2}{d} \left(\frac{2}{d^{n-5}} + \frac{1}{(d+2R)^{n-5}} + \frac{1}{(d-2R)^{n-5}} \right) \right]
\end{aligned}
\tag{2}
$$

for $n > 6$, and

$$V^{(6)}(d) = -\frac{\pi^2}{2} \left[\ln \frac{(d+2R)(d-2R)}{d^2} + \frac{R^2}{d} \left(\frac{2}{d} + \frac{1}{d+2R} + \frac{1}{d-2R} \right) \right] \tag{3}$$

for $n = 6$ [11]. The resulting interaction between two identical spheres is proportional to ρ^2 and ε. Furthermore, if we assume that the LJ parameter σ fixes the scale of all distances, setting it to 1 leads to

$$V(d) = 4\varepsilon\rho^2 \left[V^{(12)}(d) - V^{(6)}(d) \right]. \tag{4}$$

Due to the presence of many terms in the potential, there is no explicit expression for the equilibrium distance d_0 or the binding energy V_0 as a function of R. In practice, for a given radius, we minimize $V(d)$ numerically to find d_0 and V_0 at constant ρ and ε. The potential is then scaled by V_0, which amounts to choosing a reduced energy unit. Doing so enables us to compare configuration energies for different diameters.

The effective potential between two Lennard-Jones spheres shows complex but interesting variations with the distance d. At large $d \gg 2R$, the spheres are seen as pointlike and the usual 12–6 LJ interaction is recovered. At low values of $d \sim 2R + \delta$, $\delta \ll 2R$, $V(d)$ behaves as $1/\delta^7$. Typical scaled pair potentials are represented in Fig. 1 for $R = 0.1$, 0.5, 1, and 5. As R increases, the equilibrium distance d_0 gets closer to $2R$, and the potential looks much stiffer. At large R, d_0 tends to $2R$ and $V_0 \rightarrow -\infty$, the interaction becomes that of infinitely attractive hard spheres. One can associate an inverse range μ to the potential by fitting it to a Morse function, $V_{\text{Morse}}(d) = e^{\mu(d-d_0)}[e^{\mu(d-d_0)} - 2]$. The variations of μ versus the spheres radius are also represented in the inset of Fig. 1. For $R \rightarrow 0$,

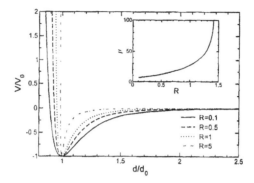

Figure 1: Scaled pair potentials between two Lennard-Jones spheres of radius R, as a function of the reduced distance with respect to the equilibrium value. The curves corresponding to $R = 0.1$, 0.5, 1, and 5 are plotted. Inset: approximate inverse range μ of the potential versus the sphere radius.

μ tends to 6, the value of the Lennard-Jones atomic potential. The range decreases monotonically with increasing R, first slowly up to $R \sim 1$, then more abruptly. The effective range is quite small ($\mu > 15$) at $R = 1$. For comparison, the Girifalco potential [14] mimicking the interaction between two buckyballs has μ close to 14 [15].

The strong variations exhibited by the effective range of the potential should have important consequences on the properties of clusters of LJ spheres. From previous work by Doye, Wales and their coworkers [16, 17, 18, 19], significant differences in cluster structure are expected between the small and large radius regimes, or between the atomic scale and the meso scale.

3 Close-packing transitions

We have attempted to locate the most stable conformations of clusters of spherical particles interacting via the pair potential described in the previous section. Global optimization of cluster structure being computationally heavy, this problem has been addressed using the powerful basin-hopping algorithm of Wales and Doye [13]. Briefly, this method samples the set of isomers by performing large amplitude random displacement moves followed by a local minimization (quench). We have studied the size range $8 \leq N \leq 60$, and 5×10^4 quenches were performed for each set of size and radius. We have also borrowed the putative global minima of LJ and Morse clusters given in the Cambridge Cluster Database [20] as extra starting points for our optimizations.

We have represented in Fig. 2 some typical examples of the most stable structures found at sizes 13, 24, 29, 34 and 37 and for different values of R. These structures illustrate the three main families of clusters that were found during the global optimization process.

The smallest spheres form clusters similar to atomic LJ clusters, generally with an icosahedral shape and elements of fivefold symmetry. These structures are highly coordinated, but also highly strained: most pair interactions deviate from the equilibrium distance [17]. Below $R = 1$ many global minima adopt a more compact decahedral shape, less coordinated and less strained than icosahedra. Above $R = 1$ more and more close-packed cubic structures appear. These are the fewest coordinated, but are practically free of strain.

The general phenomenology of structural transitions in clusters of LJ spheres follows that of Morse clusters [16, 17, 18], suggesting that geometry is primarily driven by the effective range of

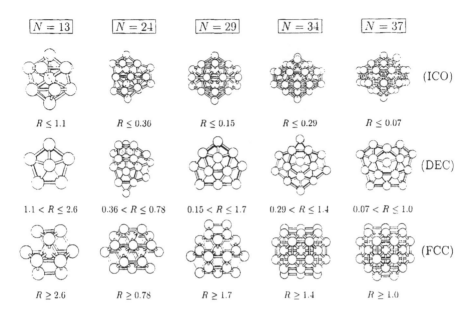

Figure 2: Typical global minima found for $N = 13, 24, 29, 34$, and 37. All these sizes change from an icosahedral structure at low radius to a close-packed cubic structure at large radius, with an intermediate decahedral shape at medium radius.

the interaction. This may not have been obvious at first sight, because the attractive interaction behaves as $1/(d - 2R)$ at low d, then as $1/(d - 2R)^6$ at large distances. However, the hard-core repulsion becomes nearly a contact interaction, and the potential well gets closer to the particles' diameter. Therefore, the similarity of the potential with a Morse form comes from the repulsive part, rather than from the attractive part.

The observation that cluster structure changes from icosahedral to decahedral, then to cubic seems to hold in most cases. Yet this rule has notable exceptions for sizes, which are naturally most stable in decahedral or cubic conformations in LJ atomic clusters (at $N = 75$ or 38, respectively), or when icosahedral structures are marginally stable. Fig. 3 shows the various ranges of stability of the three families of structures as a function of R, for sizes below 60 particles. Despite strong size effects, some trends are obvious on this figure. Most sizes exhibiting a two-step structural transition through an intermediate decahedral shape are indeed located near the first decahedral magic number at $N = 18$, or the secondary magic number for the same series, $N = 38$. In cases near $N = 18$, the decahedral structure remains exceptionally stable even at very high values of R.

At $N = 38$ the global minimum is already close-packed at $R \to 0$, and remains so for larger particles. Only few sizes show a stable decahedral structures above this size, but we expect such geometries to be present again close to the next magic number at $N = 75$. The critical radius where icosahedral structures are no longer the lowest in energy roughly decreases with size, and reaches about 0.7 for $N = 60$. Interestingly, the effective range is about 14 for this radius, at which clusters of C_{60} show complex structural variations [8].

It is often convenient to monitor the relative stability of clusters using the second energy

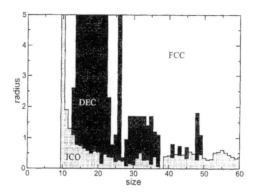

Figure 3: Relative ranges of stability of the icosahedral (ICO), decahedral (DEC) and cubic (FCC) global minima, as a function of particle radius R and number of particles $10 \le n \le 60$.

difference, $D_2 E(n) = E(n+1) + E(n-1) - 2E(n)$, where $E(n)$ is the cohesion energy of cluster at size n. The variations of $D_2 E$ with n are represented in Fig. 4 for the radii $R = 0.1$, 0.5, 1, and 5. Each curve $D_2 E(n)$ displays peaks at the most stable sizes, but these magic numbers change with R. At low radius, they are consistent with the primary and secondary number series characteristic of Mackay ($N = 13, 46, 49, 55$) and anti-Mackay ($N = 19, 23, 26$) icosahedra. At large R, the prominent peaks at $N = 12, 38, 50$ and 59 indicate the completion of volume or surface layers in the cubic geometry. The magic numbers are harder to interpret in terms of geometry for intermediate radius, because of the strong competition between structural types.

To a large extent, the energy differences displayed in Fig. 4 are also similar to the results obtained by Doye, Wales and Berry [17]. However, one should not conclude that the stable structures of clusters of LJ spheres are identical to that of Morse clusters with the same effective range. While this is true for the vast majority of cases, several global minima found in the present study at large radius were not reported in Morse clusters, to the best of our knowledge. For instance, the close-packed structure obtained for $N = 34$ is slightly lower in energy than those reported in the Cambridge Cluster Database [20]. The interaction between large spheres has a very short range, hence the number of different minima on the PES is expected to be huge for clusters [21]. Because this interaction is not rigorously of the Morse form, there may well be small differences in the ordering between the isomers, especially at nonmagic sizes.

Finally, we have studied the large sizes regime, by restricting ourselves to the complete shell magic numbers of the icosahedral, decahedral, and cubic families. Such a coarse-grained approximation has been often used in the past to estimate crossover sizes for the appearance of bulk features in atomic clusters [3]. It has also recently been extended to include temperature [23], pressure [24] and quantum delocalization [22] effects. In the present work, a series of magic number structures are optimized at fixed R, and their energies are fitted as an expansion in $n^{-1/3}$:

$$E(n, R)/n = \alpha(R) + \beta(R)n^{-1/3} + \gamma(R)n^{-2/3} + \delta(R)n^{-1}. \tag{5}$$

The four terms in the above expansion can be seen as representing the contributions of volume, surface, edge, and vertex atoms, respectively. From the values of $(\alpha, \beta, \gamma, \delta)$ for two different structural families the relative stabilities and the possible crossover sizes can be determined. Here we have optimized clusters containing up to about 10^4 particles. In general, and in agreement with the results known on atomic LJ clusters [22], the icosahedral structure are most stable at small

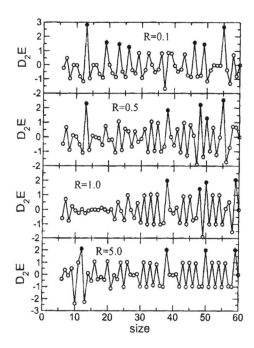

Figure 4: Second energy differences D_2E as a function of size, for different particle radii (from top to bottom) $R = 0.1, 0.5, 1, 5$. The energies are scaled with respect to the binding energy V_0 of the dimer at equilibrium, and particularly stable sizes (magic numbers) are emphasized as solid dots.

sizes, cubic structures are optimal at larges sizes, decahedral shapes being of intermediate stability.

The variations of the crossover sizes with increasing radius are represented in Fig. 5 as a (radius, size) phase diagram. At $R = 0.1$, the ICO→DEC→FCC transitions occur at large sizes, namely $n^*(\text{ICO→DEC}) \simeq 1400$ and $n^*(\text{DEC→FCC}) \simeq 10000$. These values are rather close to the crossover sizes in LJ atomic clusters [22]. Icosahedral shapes become rapidly less stable at intermediate or large R: already at $R = 0.4$, the two-layer Mackay icosahedron ($n = 55$) is no longer the most stable, in rough agreement with the more detailed picture of Fig. 3. Eventually, above $R = 1$, only the cubic structures are significantly lower in energy than the two other families.

The above results are consistent with our previous findings on smaller clusters, and tell us that clusters of LJ spheres behave mostly as hard spheres as soon as $R \gtrsim 1$. The close-packing scheme adopted by these particles significantly enriches the energy landscape of the clusters [19]. From a numerical point of view, it should also simplify the optimization procedure, because only geometries based on the cubic ordering could be sampled. In this respect, lattice-based searches should be used preferentially.

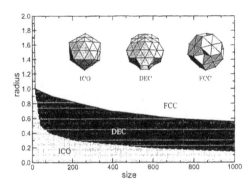

Figure 5: Relative stabilities of the icosahedral (ICO), decahedral (DEC) and close-packed cubic (FCC) structures of large clusters of LJ spherical particles as a function of size, for increasing particle radius.

4 Summary and conclusions

The stable structures of clusters of spherical particles bound by elementary Lennard-Jones forces have been investigated in the small and large sizes regimes. Assuming that the particles were homogeneously filled, the exact pair interaction was calculated as a function of the radius R and the distance d between the centers of mass. The pair potential was scaled and reduced units were used to allow for a comparison upon changing R.

As the radius is increased, we generally find that clusters become more and more compact, exhibiting first icosahedral, then decahedral. and finally close-packed cubic shapes. Finite-size effects remain rather strong in the size range $n \leq 60$, as the onset of the close-packed character appears at different radius depending on n. The possible occurence of magic numbers corresponding to the different packing schemes is another complicating factor. Larger clusters were seen to favor also cubic structures as soon as the radius exceeds the LJ atomic distance σ.

Most of the present results could be interpreted from the effective range of the pair interaction. which decreases very sharply with increasing R, as well as from the numerous data on Morse clusters. These similarities suggest that the thermodynamical [25, 26] and dynamical [27] properties of the present aggregates and their bulk forms will also show intriguing properties.

At least two extensions of the present work are anticipated. Heterogeneous clusters offer a much more challenging test for global optimization, for which designated algorithms have recently been developed [28]. Clusters of particles with two or more kinds of diameters should show a far richer structural diagram than homogeneous systems, even possibly different from the typical geometries reported here. Another extension would be to account for temperature effects. However, the divergence of the binding energy with increasing radius will require giving up the power law repulsive part. A softer exponential function should provide a more realistic description of the short-range Pauli repulsion between the particles.

Beyond finite systems, one could also think of looking at bulk fluids. Slow dynamics is expected for binary systems in which the packing fraction is varied. Conventional Monte Carlo simulations usually fail for these systems, but the convergence can be greatly enhanced using cluster algorithms, originally introduced for hard-sphere mixtures [29] and extended to continuous fluids [30].

References

[1] R. L. Johnston *Atomic and Molecular Clusters* (Taylor & Francis, London, 2002).

[2] B. Hartke, Angew. Chem. **41**, 1468 (2002).

[3] F. Baletto and R. Ferrando, Rev. Mod. Phys. **77**, 371 (2005).

[4] B. Raoult, J. Farges, M.-F. de Feraudy, and G. Torchet, Philos. Mag. B **60**, 881 (1989).

[5] T. P. Martin, T. Bergmann, H. Göhlich, and T. Lange, Chem. Phys. Lett. **172**, 209 (1990).

[6] F. Calvo, G. Torchet, and M.-F. de Feraudy, J. Chem. Phys. **111**, 4650 (1999).

[7] J.-B. Maillet, A. Boutin, and A. H. Fuchs, J. Chem. Phys. **111**, 2095 (1999).

[8] J. P. K. Doye, D. J. Wales, W. Branz, and F. Calvo, Phys. Rev. B **64**, 235409 (2001).

[9] F. Calvo and F. Spiegelman, Phys. Rev. B **54**, 10949 (1996).

[10] D. Y. Sun and X. G. Gong, Phys. Rev. B **54**, 17051 (1996).

[11] H. C. Hamaker, Physica **10**, 1058 (1937).

[12] F. H. Stillinger, Phys. Rev. E **59**, 48 (1999).

[13] D. J. Wales and J. P. K. Doye, J. Phys. Chem. A **101**, 5111 (1997).

[14] L. A. Girifalco, J. Phys. Chem. **96**, 858 (1992).

[15] D. J. Wales and J. Uppenbrick, Phys. Rev. B **50**, 12342 (1994).

[16] P. A. Braier, R. S. Berry, and D. J. Wales, J. Chem. Phys. **93**, 8745 (1990).

[17] J. P. K. Doye, D. J. Wales, and R. S. Berry, J. Chem. Phys. **103**, 4234 (1995).

[18] J. P. K. Doye and D. J. Wales, J. Chem. Soc., Faraday Trans. **93**, 4233 (1997).

[19] M. A. Miller and D. J. Wales, J. Chem. Phys. **111**, 6610 (1999).

[20] The Cambridge Cluster Database, http://www-wales.ch.cam.ac.uk:/CCD.html

[21] D. J. Wales, *Energy Landscapes*, Cambridge University, Cambridge, 2003.

[22] J. P. K. Doye and F. Calvo, J. Chem. Phys. **116**, 8307 (2002).

[23] J. P. K. Doye and F. Calvo, Phys. Rev. Lett. **86**, 3570 (2001).

[24] F. Calvo and J. P. K. Doye, Phys. Rev. B **69**, 125414 (2004).

[25] C. Rey, J. García-Rodeja, L. J. Gallego, and M. J. Grimson, Phys. Rev. E **57**, 4420 (1998).

[26] M. Moseler and J. Nordiek, Phys. Rev. B **60**, 11734 (1999).

[27] J. P. K. Doye and D. J. Wales, J. Phys. B **29**, 4859 (1996).

[28] F. Calvo and E. Yurtsever, Phys. Rev. B **70**, 045423 (2004).

[29] C. Dress and W. Krauth, J. Phys. A **28**, L597 (1995).

[30] J. Liu and E. Luijten, Phys. Rev. Lett. **92**, 035504 (2004).

Brill Academic Publishers
P.O. Box 9000, 2300 PA Leiden
The Netherlands

*Lecture Series on Computer
and Computational Sciences*
Volume 5, 2006, pp. 50-54

Dynamic Breaking and Restoring of Finite Water Chains inside Carbon Nanotubes

Yi Liu and Styliani Consta[1]

Department of Chemistry,
The University of Western Ontario,
London, Ontario, Canada N6A 5B7

Abstract: Car-Parrinello molecular dynamics simulations combined with an electrostatic point charge model reveal that quasi one-dimensional (1D) water chains break down and restore dynamically inside the carbon nanotube (6, 6). The models of finite water chains include a pair of hydronium and hydroxyl ions separated by several water molecules. Fluctuations of the hydrogen-bonded path interrupt the continuous proton transport along the 1D water chains considerably. Driven by electrostatics, protons can move either toward or away from the breaking point of the water chains depending on the dipole orientation of the end water. As a result, both the hydronium and the hydroxyl ions are repelled by the breaking point of the water chains.

Keywords: water chain; water cluster; carbon nanotubes; proton transport.

PACS: 61.46.+w, 71.15.Pd, 61.20.Ja

1.   Introduction

Water adsorbed in a carbon nanotube (CNT) usually forms several coaxial tubular structures near the CNT wall and a bulk-like liquid core depending on the radius of the CNT [1-6]. For small CNTs, e.g., an armchair type CNT (6, 6) with a radius of 4.1 Å, the narrow hollow core only allows the formation of a quasi one-dimensional (1D) water chain. Recently this water chain structure and its effect on proton transport have been studied by both experiments [6] and simulations [1-5] because not only it is important in many potential applications, but also it can serve as a prototype model for the behavior of water chains in biological ion channels [7]. In view of applications in nanotechnology, the CNT-based electronic devices should function well in supersaturated moisture. Therefore, it is of great importance to understand the structure of water clusters confined inside CNTs and its effect on proton transport. It has been reported that the rotation of water molecules [8] and the hydrogen-bonding defects [4] limit the mobility of protons in water chains. In this letter, we point out that another important process, chain breaking, also affects the dynamics of proton transport along water chains significantly.

2.   Computational method

Car-Parrinello molecular dynamics (CPMD) permits one to study dynamic processes where the breaking of chemical bond is involved as in proton transport. In CPMD method, electronic degrees of freedom are described based on density functional theory (DFT), while ionic degrees of freedom are treated classically [9]. In this study, Troullier-Martins ionic pseudopotentials and PBE exchange-correlation approximation [10] are used. The wave functions are expanded with a kinetic energy cutoff of 70 Ry. We chose the fictitious electronic mass of 1100.0 a.u. and replaced hydrogen atoms with deuterium atoms. These choices allow us to use a large time step of 0.17 fs. Even though recent studies [11] suggest that a smaller electronic mass should be used, we expect that the value used here will not change the conclusion obtained in this study. Quantum effects of proton, though not included in this work, should not change the qualitative picture discussed here.

3.   Results and discussion

3.1 Finite neutral water chains inside the CNT

To understand the structure of water clusters inside the CNT, we first studied the water dimer, which is the second most abundant cluster except monomer in the gas phase. A water dimer was inserted into a 120-atom CNT (6, 6) (radius 4.11 Å) whose optimized configuration was taken from our previous study [12]. The simulation box has a size of $(12.4 \times 20 \times 20)$ Å^3. CPMD simulations in the constant number of moles (N), volume (V) and temperature (T) ensemble were performed at T = 300 K using the Nosé-Hoover thermostat [13]. Transient time of 1 ps was followed by simulation of 2 ps for sampling of data. The oxygen-hydrogen radial distribution functions (RDF) of the water dimer with and without the CNT were calculated and the results are shown in Fig. 1. As seen in Fig. 1 (a), the first peak that corresponds to the covalent O-H bonds becomes lower and broader for the confined water dimer. This indicates that the covalent O-H bonds are weakened inside the CNT. For the free water dimer, there is a bimodal distribution corresponding to the non-H-bonded covalent O-H bonds at 0.985 Å, and the H-bonded covalent O-H bond at 1.005 Å, respectively. However, they merge into a single peak at 0.985 Å for the confined water dimer. This implies that the confined water dimer has a tendency to break down to separated monomers and all the O-H bonds become indistinguishable inside the CNT. This is also confirmed by the change of the second peak corresponding to the H-bond [Fig. 1 (b)]. Inside the CNT, the second peak centered at 1.95 Å collapses slightly and extends to higher distances, which indicate the stretching of the H-bond. From MD trajectories we observe that one water molecule sometimes was pinned on the CNT wall due to the interaction between H and C atoms and this may facilitate the stretching of the H-bond of the water dimer. The RDF of the confined water dimer found in this study is different from that of the infinite water chain. Mann et. al. [5] showed that there is a bimodal peak in RDF for the infinite water chain inside the CNT (6, 6). This means that there are two distinct covalent O-H bonds in a well-ordered infinite water chain under periodic boundary conditions. However, our results for the dimer suggest that finite water chains inside the CNT may not be always connected and rigid.

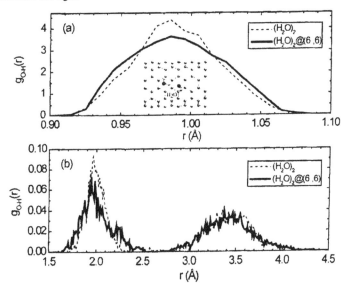

Fig. 1 Oxygen-hydrogen radial distribution functions, $g_{OH}(r)$, for the free and the confined water dimer inside the CNT (6, 6). The bin width of 0.01 Å is used. The $(H_2O)_2$ model used in the CPMD simulations is shown in the inset of Fig. 1 (a).

In order to examine if there is enough space for the fluctuations of the water dimer, we calculated the radial density profile for the water dimer inside the CNT. We observe that the water dimer stands at least 1.8 Å away from the CNT wall, and can move quite freely within a coaxial cylindrical region of radius equal to 2.1 Å. This region is large enough to allow the water dimer to orientate almost perpendicularly to the CNT axis.

Simulations of a $(H_2O)_5$ chain inside the CNT show that the longer water chain is very flexible and breaks down and restores constantly due to thermal motion. The CNT plays a dual role in affecting the behavior of the finite water chain. On one hand it facilitates the break down of the H-bonds. On the other hand it prevents the chain from permanent breaking and helps to restore the chain. This scenario differs from that in bulk liquid water [14]. In bulk water, the H-bonded paths can also break down, but they rearrange themselves and form new connected H-bonded networks. The dynamic breaking and restoring of finite water chains may have significant effects on various transport processes such as proton transport. Next we will study the effect of the fluctuations in the structure on the proton transport along water chains.

3.2 Proton transport along water chains inside the CNT

We first constructed an electrostatic lattice model of a finite $(H_2O)_{151}$ chain (length 40 nm), in which a pair of separated $H_3O^{+\delta}$ and $OH^{-\delta}$ was embedded (inset of Fig. 2). The $O^{-2\delta}$ and $H^{+\delta}$ are assigned effective point charges with $\delta \approx 0.47e$, respectively, which are taken from the empirical SPC water potential model [15]. Even though the chosen partial charges are arbitrary, the following discussion does not depend on the choices of point charges and the geometrical details of the models. The electrostatic potential was calculated along a line 4.0 Å below the water chain to avoid singularity (Fig. 2). The two outside peaks centered at ± 230 Å correspond to the two end waters of the chain. The positive peak (up) corresponds to the left end ion, $H^{+\delta}$, while the negative peak (down) corresponds to the right end ion, $O^{-2\delta}$. The two inside peaks at ± 80 Å correspond to $H_3O^{+\delta}$ (positive) and $OH^{-\delta}$ (negative), respectively. Protons would have a trend to transfer from $H_3O^{+\delta}$ to $OH^{-\delta}$ driven by such an electrostatic potential. A vacancy was introduced by removing the central water molecule in order to mimic the breaking of the water chain. This vacancy produces a pair of potential barrier and trap in the center of the chain as represented by the dotted line. The left peak (up) corresponds to the end $H^{-\delta}$ and would repel the proton coming from its left side. On the other hand, the right peak (down) corresponds to the end $O^{-2\delta}$ and would attract the proton coming from its right side. As a result, both the hydronium and the hydroxyl ions would be repelled by the breaking point. If the breaking occurs between the two counterions, it would prevent or hinder the ion recombination. However, if the breaking occurs outside the two counter ions, it would accelerate the ion combination. These predictions based on the electrostatic model need to be demonstrated using a more realistic model.

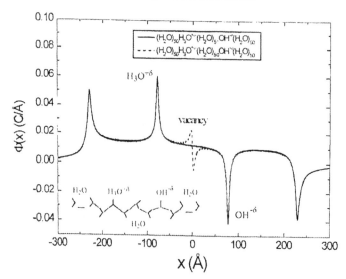

Fig. 2 Electrostatic potential, $\Phi(x)$, for a continuous $(H_2O)_{151}H_3O^{-\delta}OH^{-\delta}$ chain (solid line) and a broken $(H_2O)_{150}H_3O^{+\delta}OH^{-\delta}$ chain with a vacancy (dotted line). The arrangement of H_2O molecules is schematically shown in the inset.

To verify the picture obtained from the electrostatic point charge model, we further studied the effect of the structure fluctuations on the proton transport using CPMD methods. Constant energy CPMD simulations were carried out after the system was equilibrated at T= 300 K. The CNT (6, 6) was modeled using a finite segment with 216 C atoms terminated with H atoms. A finite $(H_2O)_9$ chain was placed into the tube interior including H_3O^- and OH^- separated by 5 H_2O molecules (15.8 Å) [Fig. 3 (a)]. A large supercell with a size of $(33 \times 15 \times 15)$ Å^3 was chosen to minimize the electrostatic interaction between ions in periodic images. In spite of the low dimensionality of the quasi 1D system, the mechanism of ion combination is complex and involves several processes, e.g., proton translocation and bonding defect translocation [8]. These processes have already been studied for biological channels [8] and CNTs [4,5]. We observed that the H-bonded protons move along the H-bonded path in a collective manner, resulting in the exchange of a covalent O-H bond and a H-bond (Grotthuss mechanism [16]). Though the final proton translocation always proceeds from H_3O^+ to H_2O or from H_2O to OH^-, the protons often cross the free energy barrier several times before completing the jump. These observations are supported by the previous studies [4,5,8]. To our knowledge this study is the first report of the effect of the chain breaking in proton transport. To this aim, the H-bond length and the difference between the covalent O-H bond and H-bond length during CPMD trajectories were calculated [Fig. 3 (b)]. Here, the criterion for chain breaking (forming) is that the H-bond length, r_{O1H1}, is greater (less) than 2.5 Å. The chain breaking and reforming were observed and the interval between them was about 100 fs, comparable with the time needed to complete one proton jump between two H_2O molecules. It shows that the OH^- induced proton transport is interrupted due to the chain breaking. The protons move towards and OH^- moves away from the breaking point until the OH^- reaches the center of the chain segment to maximize its solvation. As predicted from the electrostatic point charge model, the H_3O^+ or OH^- indeed diffuses away from the breaking point. In general, the direction of the proton transport is determined by the dipole orientation of the end H_2O molecules located at the breaking point. When the broken chain is restored, the protons continue to move along the initial direction which is determined by the interplay between the ion attraction and the ion solvation. It is also found that the proton transport switches its direction about 40 fs later than the starting of the chain breaking due to the inertia of the moving proton.

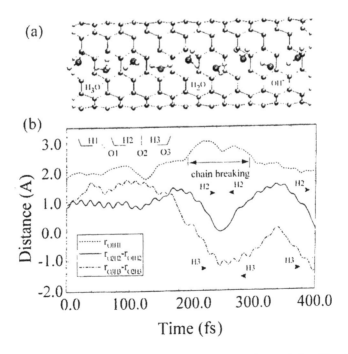

Fig. 3 (a) $(H_2O)_9$ chain model used in the CPMD simulations. (b) Time evolution of bond length difference, $r_{O2H2}-r_{O1H2}$ and $r_{O3H3}-r_{O2H3}$ as well as the H-bond length, r_{O1H1}, in the CPMD simulations using the $(H_2O)_9$ chain model.

4.   Conclusion

The dynamic fluctuations of finite quasi 1D water chains were observed inside the CNT (6, 6) and its effect on proton transport was studied by using CPMD simulations and an electrostatic point charge model. The fluctuations of the H-bonded path affect the dynamics of proton transport along water chains significantly. The proton transfer is driven by electrostatics and protons can move either toward or away from the breaking point of the water chain depending on the dipole orientation of the end water molecule. As a result, the chain breaking always repels the hydronium and the hydroxyl ions from the breaking point. Thus chain breaking may either hinder or accelerate the ion combination depending on whether the breaking occurs between the counterions or not. The physical fragmentation of water chains is an important effect that should be considered in understanding the dynamics of proton transfer or other transport processes occurring in quasi 1-D water chains.

Acknowledgements

We thank the SHARCNET at UWO and the Premier's Research Excellence Award (Canada) for funding.

References

[1] G. Hummer, J. C. Rasalah and J. P. Noworyta, Nature **414**, 188 (2001).

[2] K. Koga, G. T. Gao, H. Tanaka and X. C. Zeng, Nature **412**, 802 (2001).

[3] J. Martí and M. C. Gordillo, Phys. Rev. E **64**, 21504 (2001).

[4] C. Dellago, M. M. Naor and G. Hummer, Phys. Rev. Lett. **90**, 105902 (2003).

[5] D. J. Mann and M. D. Halls, Phys. Rev. Lett. **90**, 195503 (2003).

[6] Y. Maniwa et al., J. Phys. Soc. of Japan **71**, 2863 (2002).

[7] M. Wikström, Curr. Opin. Struct. Biol. **8**, 480 (1998).

[8] R. Pomés and B. Roux, Biophys. J. **75**, 33 (1998); **82**, 2304 (2002).

[9] R. Car and M. Parrinello, Phys. Rev. Lett. **55**, 2471 (1985); J. Hutter et al., CPMD Program, version 3.7.1, Copyright IBM Corp 1990-2001, Copyright MPI für Festkörperforschung, Stuttgart, Germany 1997-2001.

[10] N. Troullier and J. L. Martins, Phys. Rev. B **43**, 1993 (1991); J. P. Perdew, K. Burke and M. Ernzerhof, Phys. Rev. Lett. **77**, 3865 (1996).

[11] P. Tangney and S. Scandolo, J. Chem. Phys. **116**, 14 (2002); J. C. Grossman, E. Schwegler, E. W. Draeger, F. Gygi, and G. Galli, J. Chem. Phys. **120**, 300 (2004); I. W. Kuo, C. J. Mundy, M. J. McGrath, J. I. Siepmann, J. V. Vondele, M. Sprik, J. Hutter, B. Chen, M. L. Klein, F. Mohamed, M. Krack, and M. Parrinello, J. Phys. Chem. B **108**, 12990 (2004).

[12] Y. Liu, R. O. Jones, X. Zhao, and Y. Ando, Phys. Rev. B **68**, 125413 (2003).

[13] S. Nosé, J. Chem. Phys. **81**, 511 (1984); W. G. Hoover, Phys. Rev. A **31**, 1695 (1985).

[14] P. L. Geissler, C. Dellago, D. Chandler, J. Hutter, and M. Parrinello, Science **291**, 2121 (2001).

[15] H. J. C. Berendsen, J. P. M. Postma, W. F. van Gunsteren, and J. Hermans, in _Intermolecular Forces_, edited by B. Pullman (Reidel, Higham, Mass., 1981).

[16] N. Agmon, Isr. J. Chem. **39**, 493 (1999).

Brill Academic Publishers
P.O. Box 9000, 2300 PA Leiden
The Netherlands

Lecture Series on Computer
and Computational Sciences
Volume 5, 2006, pp. 55-60

Frequency dependence of chiral carbon nanotubes electronic hyperpolarizability determined with sum over states method

L. De Dominicis[1]

Department of Advanced Technologies
ENEA Frascati
Via E. Fermi 45 - 00044 Frascati (Rome), Italy

Abstract: This study reports the results of direct implantation of symmetry into calculations of carbon nanotubes (CNTs) second order nonlinear optical properties. In particular, it is described a code based on sum over states (SOS) method and suitable to evaluate quantitatively the frequency dependence of CTNs first hyperpolarizability. The main advantage of performing SOS calculations with symmetrized eigenfunctions relies on the direct identification of the essential channels giving a contribution to first hyperpolarizability. As an explicative example the results of calculation for the (4,1) chiral topology are reported and the transitions responsible for resonant enhancement are identified.

Keywords: Carbon nanotubes; line groups; hyperpolarizability

PACS: 31.15. Hz, 42.65.An, 42.65.Ky

1. Introduction

Carbon nanotubes (CNTs) are synthetic structures whose discovery dates back to 1991 [1]. From a topological point of view CNTs are obtained by rolling up a graphite sheet into a cylinder with nanometer size diameter and length up to some μm. This topological transformation maps the symmetry group of graphite into a new class G of symmetry operations leaving the CNT structure invariant. In particular, for most of the wrapping axis directions, CNTs have a chiral topology characterized by invariance under screw axes symmetry transformations. The peculiar CNT topology determines most of the properties of the CNT π electronic energy eigenstates and ultimately their optical response. On one hand, the quantum confinement, due to the large aspect ratio, results in a parameterization of the eigenstates in terms a band index m and of a large number of closely allowed wavevectors k. On the other side, the property of the complete set of eigenstates of transforming like a basis for the irreducible representation of the chiral symmetry group G establishes, in view of the Wigner-Eckart theorem [2], well defined optical selection rules involving k and m.

Wavefunctions symmetry properties have been demonstrated to play a crucial role in chiral carbon nanotubes (CNTs) linear optical response. The most striking demonstration of the deep influence of symmetry direct implantation into CNTs linear optical properties calculations is reported in the works of Bozović and Damnjanović [3-5]. The first attempts of introducing symmetry into CNTs second order nonlinear optical (NLO) study were focused on the determination of the transformation properties of the CNT first hyperpolarizability tensor β_{ijk} for both chiral and achiral topologies. By following an approach based on the point group isogonal to the whole non-symmorphic line group G it was established that hyperpolarizability vanishes in achiral topologies while only the β_{yyz} components are non vanishing in chiral topologies [6].

In this work it is explored the possibility of performing quantitative evaluation of the frequency dependence of $|\beta_{yz}|$ for chiral CNTs in the region ranging from 1 to 3.5 eV. Calculations have been performed with sum over states (SOS) method taking into account the transformation properties of the electronic eigenfunctions as dictated by the whole space symmetry group G. In the SOS method the optical properties are related to the energy eigenvalues and dipole matrix elements of the global many electron eigenstates. Usually only a set of states are essential for calculation and the transitions between these essential states form channels which provide a physical insight of the underlying nonlinear optical processes.

---

[1] Corresponding author. E-mail: dedominicis@frascati.enea.it

If x, y, z define the axes of a reference frame intrinsic to the CNT and with z along the cylinder axis the chiral component of the CNT first hyperpolarizability in the SOS picture is given by [7]

$$\beta_{xyz}(2\omega;\omega,\omega)=e^3\sum_{lmn}\left[\frac{\langle l|x|m\rangle\langle n|y|m\rangle\langle n|z|l\rangle}{(\omega_{nl}-2\omega-i\gamma_{nl})(\omega_{ml}-\omega-i\gamma_{ml})}+\ldots\ldots\right] \tag{1}$$

where summation runs over the π electrons energy eigenstates, ω_{nl} is the difference between the states energy, γ_{nl} is the sum of the inverse of states lifetime and dots are permutations of the reported term. The CNTs electronic eigenstates $|l\rangle$ are labelled as $|k,m,\Pi\rangle$, where the quantum number Π gathers the wavefunction parity under the symmetry transformations of the group G. The selection rules for the dipole matrix elements $\langle l|\vec{r}|n\rangle=\langle k_l,m_l,\Pi_l|\vec{r}|k_n,m_n,\Pi_n\rangle$ result, in view of Eq.(1), in well defined state to state contributions to first hyperpolarizability. Once that the different contributions to first hyperpolarizability have been identified, quantitative calculations are made possible by constructing symmetry adapted eigenfunctions $|k,m,\Pi\rangle$ with modified projector technique in tight binding approximation [5]. In section II the transformation properties of π electrons, as dictated by the irreducible representations of G, are described and the states contribution to first hyperpolarizability identified. Section III is devoted to the description of the main ideas underlying the code developed to evaluate quantitatively the frequency dependence of $|\beta_{xyz}|$ and the results of explicit calculation for the (4,1) chiral topology are reported.

2. CNT symmetry properties and states contribution to electronic hyperpolarizability

Chiral CNT topology is completely defined by a couple of positive integers (n_1, n_2) with $n_1 \neq n_2$. In terms of (n_1, n_2) it is possible to define the following basic parameters for chiral CNT symmetry description

$$q = 2(n_1^2+n_2^2+n_1n_2)/NR \qquad r=\frac{q}{N}Fr\left[\frac{N}{qR}\left(3-2\frac{n_1-n_2}{n_1}\right)+\frac{n}{n_1}\left(\frac{n_1-n_2}{N}\right)^{\varphi\left(|\gamma_N|-1\right)}\right] \qquad a=\sqrt{\frac{3q}{2RN}}a_0 \tag{2}$$

where N is the greatest common divisor of n_1 and n_2, with $R=3$ or $R=1$ whether $(n_1 - n_2)/3N$ is an integer or not, $Fr[x]$ is the fractional part of x, $\varphi(n)$ the Euler function and $a_0=2.461$Å. The helicity parameter r is an index of chirality with $r=1$ for achiral CNTs. The parameter q gives the number of carbon atoms inside the CNT unit cell, which is the portion of cylinder which under proper translations reproduces the whole CNT structure and whose length is given by a. The elements of the CNT line symmetry group G are screw axes $(C_q^r|Na/q)^t$, consisting of a rotation of $2\pi rt/q$ around the tube axis followed by a translation of Nta/q along the tube axis direction, with t integer. Other elements are rotations C_N^s of $2\pi s/N$ around tube axis ($s=0,1,\ldots N-1$) and rotations (U,U') of π around a direction perpendicular to the tube axis. The electronic eigenstates of a π electron moving in such a topological space transform like the basis of the irreducible representation of G with the symmetry properties listed in tab.1 [5]

Tab.1 Transformation properties of the chiral CNT electronic eigenfunctions. The band index m is an integer in the (-q/2,q/2] domain, while $k \in [0, \pi/a)$

Parameterization	State symmetry		
$k=0$	$_0E_m$	$_0A_0^\perp$	$_0A_{q/2}^\perp$
$k\in(0,\pi/a)$	$_kE_m$		

The dimension of a representation gives the degeneracy of the energy level $\varepsilon_m(k)$. The A states are one-dimensional while the E states span a two dimensional representation. For chiral CNTs, the A states have the superscript $+$ or $-$ according to the parity of the eigenfunction under the U symmetry operation. With the formalism, the position operator is decomposed into the irreducible component $_0E_1 + _0A_0^-$ thus resulting in the following allowed optical transitions in dipole approximation [2]

$$\left\langle _0A_0^\pm \middle| z \middle| _0A_0^\mp \right\rangle \left\langle _0A_{q,2}^\pm \middle| z \middle| _0A_{q,2}^\mp \right\rangle \left\langle _iE_m \middle| z \middle| _iE_m^* \right\rangle \tag{3}$$
$$\left\langle _0A_0^\pm \middle| x,y \middle| _0E_1 \right\rangle \left\langle _iE_m \middle| x,y \middle| _iE_{m+1}^* \right\rangle \left\langle _0A_{q,2} \middle| x,y \middle| _0E_{q,2-1} \right\rangle$$

Where the asterisk indicates an electron in conduction band and we have $\Delta k=0$ for all transitions, while $\Delta m=0$ and $\Delta m=1$ for z and x,y transitions respectively. The selection rules in Eq.(3) allow to identify the state to state transitions contributing to β_{xz} in Eq.(1). In fact, the necessary condition for a non-vanishing contribution is the existence of three electronic eigenstates satisfying, in view of the selection rules in Eq.(3), the condition

$$\left\langle k,m,\Pi \middle| x \middle| k,m\pm 1,\Pi' \right\rangle \left\langle k,m,\Pi' \middle| y \middle| k,m\pm 1,\Pi'' \right\rangle \left\langle k,m,\Pi'' \middle| z \middle| k,m,\Pi \right\rangle \neq 0 \tag{4}$$

The contributions $\beta_{xz}^{(0)}$ from $k=0$ and $\beta_{xz}^{(k,m)}$ for k inside the ID for a given m, as determined from the allowed transitions, are shown in fig.1 and fig.2.

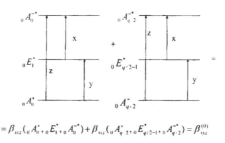

$$= \beta_{xyz}(_0A_0^+, _0E_1^*, _0A_0^{-*}) + \beta_{xyz}(_0A_{q,2}^-, _0E_{q,2-1}^*, _0A_{q,2}^{-*}) = \beta_{xyz}^{(0)}$$

Figure 1. Diagrams of states contribution to hyperpolarizability for $k=0$

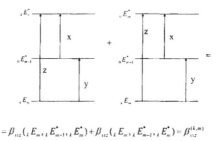

$$= \beta_{xyz}(_iE_m, _iE_{m+1}^*, _iE_m^*) + \beta_{xyz}(_iE_m, _iE_{m-1}^*, _iE_m^*) = \beta_{xyz}^{(k,m)}$$

Figure 2. Diagrams of state contributions to hyperpolarizability for k inside the ID

The hyperpolarizability of a chiral CNT is obtained by integrating $\beta_{xyz}^{(k,m)}$, after summation over band index m, for k inside the irreducible domain (ID) $(0,\pi/a)$ and adding the $k=0$ contribution $\beta_{xyz}^{(0)}$.

$$\beta_{xyz}(2\omega;\omega,\omega) = \beta_{xyz}^{(0)} + \lim_{\varepsilon \to 0} \sum_{m=-q/2+1}^{q/2} \left(\int_{0+\varepsilon}^{(\pi+a)-k} \beta_{xyz}(_k E_m,_k E_{m+1}^*,_k E_m^*)dk + \int_{0+\varepsilon}^{(\pi+a)-k} \beta_{xyz}(_k E_m,_k E_{m-1}^*,_k E_m^*)dk \right) \qquad (5)$$

3. Calculation of hyperpolarizability in a symmetry adapted basis

The quantitative determination of the magnitude of the β_{xyz} tensor component is based on the explicit knowledge of the spatial dependence of the $|k,m,\Pi\rangle$ electronic wavefunctions. These functions, transforming like a basis of the irreducible representation of the symmetry group G, can be obtained with the modified projector technique method in tight binding approximation [5]. The so obtained symmetrized wavefunctions preserve the transformation properties as dictated by the irreducible representation of the symmetry group G. In the following, in order to simplify notation and calculations, the attention is restricted to CNTs with $N=1$ and hence $s=0$. Despite the extension of calculations to CNTs with $N\neq1$ is straightforward, it must be noted that almost the CNTs chiral topologies are characterized by $N=1$. For such a class of CNTs the position vector $\vec{R}_{tu}$ of a carbon atom is obtained with the transformation $\vec{R}_{tu} = \left(C_q^t | a/q \right)^t U^u \vec{R}_{00}$ with $u=0,1$ and where $\vec{R}_{00}$ is the position vector of the atom chosen as origin, given in cylindrical coordinates by [2]

$$\vec{R}_{00} = \left(\rho_0,\phi_0,z_0 \right) = \left(D/2, \ 2\pi \frac{n_1+n_2}{qR}, \ \frac{n_1-n_2}{\sqrt{6qR}} a_0 \right) \qquad D = \frac{1}{\pi}\sqrt{Rq/2a_0} \qquad (6)$$

If $|tu\rangle$ indicates an orbital centred on the atoms at $\vec{R}_{tu}$, we have $|tu\rangle = \left(C_q^t | a/q \right)^t U^u |00\rangle$, where $|00\rangle$ is the orbital centred on the atom at the origin. Armed with this formalism, it is possible to write down (tab.2) the symmetry adapted electronic eigenfunctions in tight binding approximation, also called generalized Bloch eigenfunctions, as calculated by Damnjanovic [5] with the modified projector technique method.

Tab.2 Irreducible representation and generalized Bloch functions for the electronic states of a chiral carbon nanotubes. G_C is the dimension of the symmetry group and

$$\psi_m^k(t) = \frac{ka+2\pi\,m\,r}{q}t\,, \quad h_m^k = Arg(h_m^1(k))\,, \quad h_m^1(k) = \sum_t H_{t1}e^{i\psi_m^k(t)}\,, \quad H_{t1} = \langle 00|H|t1\rangle$$

Eigenfunction symmetry	Generalized Bloch functions
$_0A_m^\Pi$	$\|0m\Pi\rangle = \frac{1}{\sqrt{G_C}}\sum_t e^{-i\psi_m^0(t)}\left(\|t0\rangle + \Pi\|t1\rangle\right)$
$_kE_m$	$\|km\rangle = \frac{1}{\sqrt{G_C}}\sum_t e^{-i\psi_m^k(t)}\left(\|t0\rangle \pm e^{ih_m^k}\|t1\rangle\right)$
$_kE_m^*$	$\|km\rangle = \frac{1}{\sqrt{G_C}}\sum_t e^{-i\psi_m^k(t)}\left(\|t1\rangle \pm e^{ih_m^k}\|t0\rangle\right)$

The introduction of the generalized Bloch states allows to obtain an explicit form for the matrix elements in Eq.(3) and then ultimately of $\beta_{xyz}^{(0)}$ and $\beta_{xyz}^{(k,m)}$. An explicit form of $|\beta_{xyz}(2\omega;\omega,\omega)|$ refereed to the CNT unit cell is then obtained once that the summation is truncated at $t=q$, only nearest neighbours integrals are taking into account and the various contribution are summated and integrated over the variable m and k respectively. Nevertheless the quantitative calculation of $|\beta_{xyz}(2\omega;\omega,\omega)|$ requires the exact knowledge of CNT energy band structures $\varepsilon_m(k)$. For states with symmetry E_m the energy dispersion relations have been assumed given by [8]

$$\varepsilon_m(k) = \pm |V| \sqrt{\sum_{i=1}^{3}(1+\cos\psi_i)} \qquad (7)$$

where the coupling constant $|V|$ is set to 2.5eV, the sign + and − are for conduction and valence band respectively and

$$\psi_1 = -ka\frac{n_2}{q} + 2\pi m\frac{2n_1+n_2}{qR} \qquad \psi_2 = ka\frac{n_1}{q} + 2\pi m\frac{n_1+2n_2}{qR} \qquad \psi_3 = \psi_2 - \psi_1 \qquad (8)$$

In this case a further simplification occurs, because summation and integration variables are separable allowing to obtain the various contributions to $|\beta_{nz}(2\omega;\omega,\omega)|$ in a closed form.

The problem of numerical estimation of $|\beta_{nz}(2\omega;\omega,\omega)|$ is now reduced to the choice of an atomic wavefunction $|tu\rangle$. At first approximation a localized state $|tu\rangle$ is assumed as a p orbital pointing along the normal of the CNT surface and centred on the atom at position $\vec{R}_{tu}$

$$\langle \vec{r}|tu\rangle = \phi_{tu}^p(\vec{r}) = \vec{c}_{tu} \cdot (\vec{r} - \vec{R}_{tu}) \exp\left[-\frac{Z|\vec{r}-\vec{R}_{tu}|}{2a_B}\right] \qquad (9)$$

where $\vec{c}_{tu}$ is a versor normal to CNT surface at atomic position, $Z=3.65$ is the effective nuclear charge as calculated following the Slate method and a_B the Bohr radius. The results of numerical estimation of $|\beta_{nz}(2\omega;\omega,\omega)|$ for the (4,1) chiral topology and referred to the unit cell are shown in fig.3a, while fig3b reports the symmetry assignation of the energy bands for the investigated CNT.

Calculations have been performed under the Matchad 7.0 environment installed on a AFS (Andrew File System) cell of the computational centre server of ENEA Frascati and equipped with four processors. The computational time for the investigated topology was nearly 36 hr. In the calculations the states lifetime has been assumed $\gamma=0.1$ eV on the basis of measurements of electron-electron scattering dynamic [9]. Two well distinct resonances are predicted at $\omega_1=2.18$ eV and $\omega_2=2.52$ eV where the first hyperpolarizability per unit cell, for the investigated topology, reaches a value of the order of 10^{-28} e.s.u.. The analysis of energy band structure allowed to identify the relevant transitions responsible for the resonance enhancement at ω_1 and ω_2 and results are listed in tab.3

Resonance (eV)	States Contribution
$\omega_1=2.18$	$_{0,12}E_3 \rightarrow _{0,12}E_3^*$
	$_{0,36}E_{-3} \rightarrow _{0,36}E_{-3}^*$
	$_{0,36}E_{-2} \rightarrow _{0,36}E_{-2}^*$
	$_{0,41}E_{-3} \rightarrow _{0,41}E_{-4}^*$
	$_{0,7}E_{-6} \rightarrow _{0,7}E_{-6}^*$
$\omega_2=2.52$	$_{0,31}E_3 \rightarrow _{0,31}E_3^*$
	$_{0,25}E_{-3} \rightarrow _{0,25}E_{-3}^*$
	$_{0,25}E_{-2} \rightarrow _{0,25}E_{-2}^*$
	$_{0,19}E_{-3} \rightarrow _{0,19}E_{-4}^*$
	$_{0,63}E_{-3} \rightarrow _{0,63}E_{-4}^*$
	$_{0,53}E_{-6} \rightarrow _{0,53}E_{-6}^*$

Tab.3 States contribution to resonant enanchement of $|\beta_{nz}(2\omega;\omega,\omega)|$ for (4,1) topology. An asterisk indicates a state in the conduction band. The parameter k is given in unit of π/a.

Fig.3 Frequency dependence of $|\beta_{nz}(2\omega;\omega,\omega)|$ per unit cell for (4,1) CNT topology (a). In (b) are shown the energy dispersion relations for the valence band of (4,1) CNT. The numbers indicate the parameter m in the E_m symmetry assignation. The conduction bands are obtained with a mirror reflection along the E=0 line.

The number of essential transitions listed in tab.3 and contributing to the resonant enhancement of $|\beta_{zz}(2\omega;\omega,\omega)|$ also account for the larger magnitude at ω_2 with respect to ω_1.

In the limit of the approximations used, the hyperpolarizability scales with the third power of the number of atoms involved in calculations, so it is possible to estimate in nearly 10^{-30} e.s.u. the single carbon atom contribution to CNT first hyperpolarizability

4. Conclusions

The frequency dependence of the first electronic hyperpolarizabilty for the (4,1) CNT topology has been calculated adopting the sum over states method with symmetrized eigenfunctions. On resonant excitation in the visible region of the electromagnetic spectrum, around 2.1 and 2.5 eV, the model estimates, for $|\beta_{zz}(2\omega;\omega,\omega)|$, a value of nearly 10^{-28} e.s.u per unit cell. This is a value of the same order of hyperpolarizability in most efficient second order nonlinear optical materials [10]. The extensive nature of hyperpolarizability, together with the possibility of grown CNTs with length up to some μm, opens up the possibility of engineering carbon based structure with giant first hyperpolarizability. Nevertheless, the main limitation to this task comes from the fail of dipole approximation as CNTs length grows and from the occurrence of symmetry breaking mechanisms, like plastic local deformation of the hexagonal carbon atoms distribution along CNT structure.

Acknowledgments

The author is indebted with R. Fantoni and S. Botti for helpful discussions at several stages of the work. P. D'Angelo is gratefully acknowledged for support at AFS cell server.

References

[1] S. Iijima, Nature, 354, 56 (1991)

[2] M. Damnjanović, I. Milošević, T. Vuković and T. Marinković, J. Phys. A, 37, 4059 (2004)

[3] M. Damnjanović, I. Milošević, T. Vuković and R. Sdredanović, Phys. Rev. B., 60, 2728 (1999)

[4] I. Božović, N. Božović and M. Damnjanović, Phys. Rev. B. 62, 6971 (2000)

[5] M. Damnjanović, T. Vuković and I. Milosević, Phys. Rev. B, 65, 45418 (2002)

[6] L. De Dominicis, R. Fantoni, S. Botti and L. Asylian, Las. Phys. Lett, 1, 598 (2004)

[7] R.W. Boyd, Nonlinear Optics (Academic Press, New York, 1992) p.139

[8] M. Damnjanović, T. Vuković and I. Milosević, J. Phys. A., 33, 6561 (2000)

[9] T. Hertel, G. Moos, Chem. Phys. Lett., 320,359 (2000)

[10] P. Innocenzi, G. Brusatin, A. Abbotto, L. Beverina, G.A. Pagani, M. Casalboni, F. Sarcinelli, and R. Pizzoferrato, Journal of Sol-Gel Science and Technology, 26, 967 (2003)

Brill Academic Publishers
P.O. Box 9000, 2300 PA Leiden,
The Netherlands

Lecture Series on Computer
and Computational Sciences
Volume 5, 2006, pp. 61-66

Structural stability of $C_m Ti_n$ microclusters and nanoparticles: Molecular–dynamics simulations

O.B. Malcıoğlu and Ş. Erkoç[1]

Department of Physics,
Middle East Technical University,
06531 Ankara, Turkey

Abstract: The minimum energy structures of $C_m Ti_n$ microclusters and nanoparticles have been investigated theoretically by performing molecular dynamics (MD) simulations. Selected crystalline and completely random initial geometries are considered. The potential energy function (PEF) used in the calculations includes two - and three–body atomic interactions for C-Ti binary systems. Molecular–dynamics simulations have been performed at 1 K and 300 K. It has been found that initial geometry has a very strong influence on relaxed geometry.

Keywords: Titan-carbide clusters, binary compounds, empirical potential, molecular dynamics

PACS: PACS Numbers: 74.70.Ad , 34.20.Cf , 36.40.-c , 83.10.Mj

1 Introduction

Material behavior at nanometer scale often leads to some very interesting results. Striped from the usual approximations available at larger dimensions, one needs different methods to theoretically explain and predict observations. Titanium and Titanium composites are widely used in industry. However, Titanium by itself is very prone to oxidation. Treatment with Carbon leads to structures that are resilient to oxidation in atmospheric conditions. Titanium Carbide is a very hard material and may be utilized as a coating film in industry. A number of experimental data suggest that this material has some extraordinary behavior. If industrial applications are to be realized, geometrical properties of the material and results of different compositions need to be studied extensively. It is observed that size ratios of Titanium and Carbon in the treatment lead to different diffusion directions [1]. This indicates different cluster formation mechanisms and most probably clusters with different properties. It is also observed that some "magic" combinations of Titanium and Carbon lead to very strong clusters that can be theoretically explained by cage geometries [2]. There is a reported structural difference in astronomical data [3] than the bulk data, and cage geometries may be an explanation.

Titanium atoms interconnected with hexagonal configuration of Carbon are predicted to have Hydrogen affinity [4]. Furthermore , it is reported that this affinity can be reversed by heating. Thus C-Ti clusters may be a promising candidate for Hydrogen storage.

---

[1]Corresponding author, Şakir Erkoç, E-mail: erkoc@erkoc.physics.metu.edu.tr

In this work, effect of initial geometry on the relaxed structure of C-Ti clusters is investigated. Although a vast number of specimens were put into simulation, only a selected few are presented.

First group of specimens have random initial geometries. This initial condition correspond to vapor deposition or similar techniques. An ensemble of 1000 specimens were relaxed for each material composition in this technique. Geometry of the specimen with lowest energy is considered for discussion.

Second group of initial geometries consist of different face centered crystalline structures. In general, Fd3m (diamond-like) and Fm3m (NaCl-like) symmetries are investigated. This initial condition correspond to diffusion-replacement reactions.

2   Method of Calculations

In order to obtain the minimum energy structures of CTi binary clusters, we conducted molecular dynamics (MD) simulations based on an empirical PEF parametrized for CTi binary system [5]. In this work, the many–body expansion form of the interaction potential energy function has been truncated after the second term so that only the two– and three–body interactions were included.

$$\Phi = \sum_{i<j} U_{ij} + \sum_{i<j<k} W_{ijk} \tag{1}$$

The Lennard–Jones (LJ) [6] potential has been taken for the two–body part, and the Axilrod–Teller (AT) triple–dipole potential [7] for the three–body part, their explicit forms respectively are

$$U_{ij} = \epsilon_0 \left[\left(\frac{r_0}{r_{ij}} \right)^{12} - 2 \left(\frac{r_0}{r_{ij}} \right)^{6} \right] \quad , \quad W_{ijk} = \frac{Z \left(1 + 3 \cos \theta_i \cos \theta_j \cos \theta_k \right)}{\left(r_{ij} \, r_{ik} \, r_{jk} \right)^3} , \tag{2}$$

where $r_{ij} = |\mathbf{r}_i - \mathbf{r}_j|$ is the inter-atomic distance between the atoms i and j; r_0 is the equilibrium distance of the pair potential, where the pair energy assumes its minimum value, ϵ_0; θ_i, θ_j, and θ_k are the angles of the triangle formed by the three atoms i, j, k; and Z is the three–body (intensity) parameter. This combination of PEF, LJ + AT, has proved its usefulness and was successfully used for different cluster systems, for instance for AlTiNi clusters [8], as well as for surface and bulk properties of some semiconductors and metals [9]. The parameter set used for the CTi binary system is presented in Table 1 for the PEF expressed in Eqs. 1 and 2.

Table 1: Empirical potential energy function parameters used for the CTi binary system [5].

Two–body parameters			Three–body parameters	
Dimer	ϵ_o (eV)	r_o (Å)	Trimer	Z (eV Å^9)
C–C	6.21	1.480	C–C–C	292.1
Ti–Ti	2.00	2.300	Ti–Ti–Ti	1764.0
C Ti	5.17	1.638	C C Ti	60.0
			C–Ti–Ti	160.0

This parameter set for CTi binary system was determined to investigate the structural properties of Ti adsorbed single–wall carbon nanotubes [5].

In this work the equations of motion for the CTi system have been solved by employing a MD technique based on the Nordsieck–Gear algorithm [10, 11], through seventh–order predictor-corrector method [12]. The simulations were performed in such a way that each system under study was considered as an isolated system; equivalently saying, no periodic boundary condition (PBC) has been used. By taking the MD temperature as 1 K and 300 K, we considered both a low–temperature and a room–temperature study. For the calculation of each system 50000 time steps (each time–step was 2.6×10^{-16} s) were enough to reach thermal equilibrium. Temperature rescaling was maintained during the whole simulation. Thermal equilibrium was controlled by checking the time–averaged energy after each 100 steps. The statistical averages are also checked in every 500 steps. The structures of the systems discussed in this work are snapshots of the final MD step.

3 Results and Discussions

In clusters, particularly in metal nanoparticles spherical symmetry is dominant in relaxed geometries. Interestingly, in all material combinations studied, a spherically symmetric minimum energy specimen was not encountered. As an example, results from C25Ti75 ensemble is presented in Figure 1. Energy spectrum shows that size of the ensemble is sufficient. It must be noted that geometry presented is not the most probable configuration. In fact, a spherical geometry should have a lower energy if one investigates the PEF used, but it seems that the dominant planar configuration of Carbon and Titanium is a rather high potential barrier. Since the relaxation procedure was carried out at 1 K, this potential barrier seems to hold the system in rather a distorted situation. It may be speculated that in the presence of a matrix surface, with right environmental conditions, this material may have extraordinary coating properties.

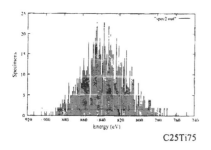

C25Ti75

Lowest Energy Geometry

Figure 1: Energy spectrum and minimum energy geometry of an ensemble of C25Ti75, with random initial geometries at 1 K. Spectrum represents the distribution of energies of possible isomers of C25Ti75 in an ensemble of 1000 random initial geometry specimens.

A similar ab-initio study [2] suggest that C14Ti13 has a significantly stable cubic structure. As explained later this cubic configuration is extraordinarily stable as long as the particular symmetry is satisfied. But, can this effect be observed using a different initial crystalline geometry? Above mentioned potential barrier is the main concern at this point. The minimum energy geometry of C14Ti13 using a different inital structure is presented in Figure 2. The above mentioned trend is still present, and the resultant geometry lacks any symmetry at all. Result of a similar calculation with only slightly changing the material composition is also presented in this figure. This change results in a very loosely bonded Carbon atom which will most probably be lost in heat treatment. Since the above mentioned barrier is quite abundant and persistent, it may be speculated that cubic symmetry may only be obtained using external catalytic influences in synthesis methods that are represented by random initial geometry.

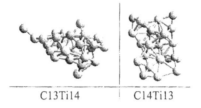

C13Ti14 | C14Ti13

Figure 2: Minimum energy geometries after relaxation of C13Ti14 and C14Ti13 at 1 K. The initial starting structure of these models were FCC (with Fm3m symmetry).

In the same paper, [2], it has been reported that C12Ti8 has some extraordinary structural properties that can be explained by a cage structure. Using random initial geometries, one ends up with the non-symmetrical geometries mentioned above. Interestingly, using specific crystalline initial geometry, one obtains a cage-like structure after relaxation. In Figure 3, relaxation results of two different (crystalline) initial geometries having same symmetry (Fd3m) in their unit cells is shown. Cubic geometry ended up with an amorphous-like result, whereas geometry with truncated edges (thus having different planes exposed to outside) ended up as an empty shell. This empty shell can be viewed as a distorted cage-like structure. Annealing would possibly remove the irregularities, since they seem to be loosely bonded.

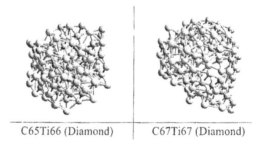

C65Ti66 (Diamond) | C67Ti67 (Diamond)

Figure 3: Relaxed structures of CTi clusters with Fd3m starting symmetry at 1 K. Left figure is relaxed geometry of C65Ti66 with cubic initial geometry. The relaxed structure is amorphous like. Right figure is the relaxed geometry of C67Ti67 which has truncated edges in its initial geometry. The relaxed structure is again amorphous like, but its central region is hollow resembling a cage like geometry.

An empirical study on CTi clusters suggest that cubic blends with Fm3m symmetry in their unit cells (NaCl-like) are extraordinarily stable. This feature is clearly observed in Figure 4. It seems that irrespective of the size, this symmetry leads to extraordinarily persistent geometrical configuration, even after exposure to heat. However, when the same primitive cells are arranged in a rectangular prism, the stability is lost. In Figure 5, this configuration is shown. Even at 1 K, the structure becomes highly disoriented.

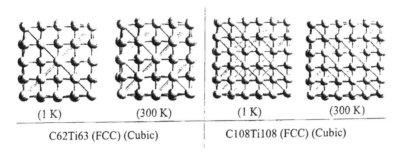

| (1 K) | (300 K) | (1 K) | (300 K) |

C62Ti63 (FCC) (Cubic) | C108Ti108 (FCC) (Cubic)

Figure 4: Relaxation results of cubic CTi initial geometries with Fm3m symmetry.

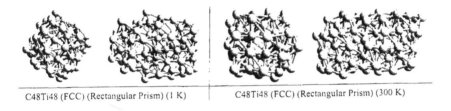

C48Ti48 (FCC) (Rectangular Prism) (1 K) | C48Ti48 (FCC) (Rectangular Prism) (300 K)

Figure 5: Relaxation result of a CTi cluster having rectangular prism configuration of unit cells with Fm3m symmetry.

As a conclusion, it may be stated that different initial geometries lead to drastic changes in the relaxed structure. Since different initial geometries correspond to different mechanisms in experimentation, method of fabrication should play an important role in the resultant structure. Spontaneous re-organization of CTi into empty shells in nanometer dimensions is possible, which is an interesting result by itself. In randomly created initial geometries, there is a large occurrence of planar configurations of Carbon and Titanium atoms, which may lead to a good coating material. Clusters having a cubic configuration of Fm3m primitive cells have an extraordinary geometrical stability, which is lost when cubic configuration changes.

References

[1] A. Ikegami, Y. Kimura, H. Suzuki. T. Sato, T. Tanigaki, O. Kido, M. Kurumada, Y. Saito, C. Kaito, Surf. Sci. 540 (2003) 395.

[2] M.-M. Rohmer, M. Benard. C. Bo, J.-M. Poblet, J. Am. Chem. Soc. 117 (1995) 508.

[3] G. Von Helden, A.G.G.M. Tielens, D. Von Heijinsbergen, M.A. Duncan, S. Hony, L.B.F.M. Waters, G. Meijer, Science 288 (2000) 313.

[4] S. Ciraci, S. Dag, T. Yildirim, O. Gulseren, R.T. Senger, J. Phys.: Condens. Matter 16 (2004) 901.

[5] H. Oymak and Ş. Erkoç, Chem. Phys. 300 (2004) 277.

[6] J.E. Lennard-Jones, Proc. Phys. Soc., London, A 43 (1931) 461.

[7] B.M. Axilrod, E. Teller, J. Chem. Phys. 11 (1943) 299.

[8] Ş Erkoç, H. Oymak, J. Phys. Chem. B 107 (2003) 12118.

[9] Ş. Erkoç, Ann. Rev. Comp. Phys. 9 (2001) 1–103.

[10] A. Nordsieck, Math. Compute. 16 (1962) 22.

[11] C.W. Gear, Numerical Initial Value Problems in Ordinary Differential Equations, NJ: Prentice–Hall, Englewood Cliffs, 1971.

[12] D.J. Evans, G.P. Morriss, Comp. Phys. Rep. 1 (1984) 297.

Brill Academic Publishers
P.O. Box 9000, 2300 PA Leiden,
The Netherlands

Lecture Series on Computer
and Computational Sciences
Volume 5, 2006, pp. 67-76

Density Functional Study of Beryllium Clusters

Yan Sun[1], René Fournier[2]

Department of Chemistry, York University
4700 Keele Street, Toronto, Ontario, M3J 1P3   Canada

Abstract: Beryllium clusters Be_n (n=2-20) were studied by Kohn-Sham theory with the local spin density approximation. We used a Tabu Search algorithm for structure optimization. The lowest energy structures fall into three distinct categories: compact structures typical of pairwise potentials for n=3-7; cage structures where all atoms have nearly equal coordinations for n=8-14; compact fragments of the hcp crystal at n=15-20. The electronic structure gradually evolves from van der Waals interactions (n =2,3) to metallic ($n \geq 13$). All clusters have singlet ground-states except $n = 6$ and $n = 9$ which are triplets. We also found low-lying excited triplet states at n=8 and 19 and a low-lying quintet state at n=7. In agreement with the jellium model, we find that clusters with n=4, 10, 17, and 20 atoms are especially stable and that the structures for n =4, 10, and 20 are quasi-spherical.

Keywords: Clusters, Structure, Global Optimization, Density Functional Theory

PACS: 36.40.-c, 34.20.Cf, 68.35.Bs, 68.47.De

1   Introduction

Group II elements have an s^2 closed-shell ground state atomic configuration and it is well known that the diatomic molecules and small clusters of these elements are bound by van der Waals type interactions. On the other hand, the bulk solids of these elements are metallic because the s and p bands overlap. This makes the size evolution of the electronic structure and other properties in clusters of group II elements particularly interesting. Beryllium is the lightest element in group II and the easiest to model theoretically. There have been several theoretical works on beryllium clusters[1, 2, 3, 4], but experiments have been limited to Be_2[5]. Wang and co-workers[1] used a genetic algorithm (GA) combined with an empirical potential to generate candidate structures for Be_n(n=3-21), and then did Kohn-Sham-Density Functional Theory (KS-DFT) calculations with a BLYP functional. Srinivas and Jellinek[2] investigated the geometrical and electronic properties of Be_n(n =2-9) by DFT with the BPW91 exchange-correlation functional and a 631/31 basis set. Beyer and co-workers[3] performed DFT calculations with the B3LYP exchange-correlation functional and a 6-311++G(3df) basis set on Be_n(n =2-8). Kawai and co-workers[4] did the most comprehensive set of calculations. They studied Be_n(n =2-20) by the Car-Parinello Simulated Annealing (CP SA) method to search for the global minima which was followed by local optimization. All their calculations were done in the local density approximation (LDA) with a plane wave basis and pseudopotentials. Here, we reinvestigate the n=2-20 series. There are three essential differences between our work and that of Kawai *et al.*. First, we did the global search for the

---

[1] Department of Physics, York University
[2] Corresponding author. E-mail: renef@yorku.ca

energy minimum by "Tabu Search in Descriptor Space" (TSDS)[6] directly on the KS-DFT energy surface. Second, we use a localized basis set of Gaussian functions instead of plane waves and we do not use any pseudopotential. Third, we considered higher spin states in cases where the HOMO-LUMO gap was very small. Srinivas and Jellinek also considered different spin states in their study of Be_n (n=2-9) with the BLYP functional. The low energy structures that we find are mostly similar to those of Kawai *et al.*, but there are some differences (including triplet state global minima for Be_6 and Be_9). We also give a different analysis of the geometric structure.

2 Computational details

2.1 Calculation of total energy

We used KS-DFT and the program deMon-KS3p2[7]. For the exchange-correlation energy, we used the local spin density (LSD) functional of Vosko, Wilk and Nusair[8] (VWN). We chose the VWN functional because it predicts structures of small niobium[11], lithium[9], and silver[10] clusters that are in good agreement with experiment and the highest levels of theory, and also gives rather good ionization energies (IEs) for clusters of these metals[11, 9, 10]. Newer functionals such as BP86 and B3LYP give better accuracy than VWN for the binding energies of organic molecules, but they do not give a clear improvement for the properties of metals and geometric structures of clusters and solids. The higher computing cost for these functionals does not make them advantageous for metal clusters, especially when the main goal is to study geometric structure and qualitative aspects of electronic structure.

2.2 Global minimum search

Structure optimization of clusters is difficult because of the huge number of possible isomers. For example, there are at least 1506 distinct local minima for a 13-atom Lennard-Jones (LJ) clusters[12]. For this reason, cluster structure global optimizations are often done with empirical potentials, sometimes followed by local optimizations with more accurate methods such as DFT. Another optimization strategy is to do Car-Parinello (CP) simulated annealing. However, the required number of simulation steps is in the tens of thousands or more, so although the cost of DFT energy evaluation is relatively small in the CP method, these calculations are still costly. We take a different approach and carry the global optimization directly on the KS-DFT energy surface. This means that we can afford only a few thousand DFT energy evaluations per optimization at most. Since the computer cost for one KS-DFT energy evaluation is much larger than any operation in a global optimization, we devised a relatively complex hybrid algorithm (TSDS) for optimization[6]. The main features of TSDS are that: (a) we associate global descriptors to every geometric structure; (b) we estimate the DFT energy of newly created structures by interpolation using the descriptors and DFT energies of previous clusters; (c) we generate and screen many structures at each step of the optimization but retain only one of them for a (costly) DFT calculation; (d) we do a random but biased search that preferentially visits regions of descriptor space where: (*i*) the search has rarely been in the past, and (*ii*) the average energy, estimated by interpolation, is low. The two opposing criteria in (d) are inherent to any global optimization problem. In TSDS, control parameters vary their relative importance so that the emphasis is on criterion (*i*) (exploration) at the beginning of the optimization and on criterion (*ii*) (exploitation) near the end. In our TSDS optimization runs we typically took 300 to 2500 steps to find our lowest energy minima, compared to roughly 50,000 steps for a typical CP-SA run.

Here are examples of descriptors that we use. First, we define the coordination c_i of atom i as the effective number of atoms located within the first coordination shell:

$$c_i = \sum_{j \neq i} f(r_{ij}) \tag{1}$$

$$
\begin{aligned}
f(r) &= 1 & \text{if} & \quad < R_{nn} \\
&= 0 & \text{if} & \quad r > 1.4R_{nn} \\
&= \frac{1.4R_{nn} - r}{0.4R_{nn}} & \text{if} & \quad R_{nn} \leq r \leq 1.4R_{nn}
\end{aligned}
\tag{2}
$$

where R_{nn} is the experimental bulk nearest neighbour distance. This definition gives a coordination of 12 for the fcc and hcp crystal structure and 11.7 for bcc. This definition of c_i is what we used for analyzing results; the definition used in TSDS had a slightly different function $f(r)$. We get many descriptors from these atomic coordination numbers:

$$mean(c) = (1/n) \sum_{i=1}^{n} c_i \tag{3}$$

$$rmsd(c) = (\sum_{i=1}^{n} [(c_i - mean(c))^2 / n])^{1/2} \tag{4}$$

$$c_- = Min\{c_i\} \tag{5}$$

$$c_+ = Max\{c_i\} \tag{6}$$

Two descriptors, the asphericity ζ and shape η, are derived from the three moments of inertia $I_a \geq I_b \geq I_c$:

$$\zeta = \frac{(I_a - I_b)^2 + (I_b - I_c)^2 + (I_c - I_a)^2}{I_a^2 + I_b^2 + I_c^2} \tag{7}$$

$$\eta = (2I_b - I_a - I_c)/I_a \tag{8}$$

We used these descriptors for TSDS optimization. In addition, we used another descriptor after TSDS for analyzing the structures. We define an effective number of interior atoms m as follows. We calculate the asphericity ζ_j around an atom j by using Eq. 7 and the moments of inertia of the neighbours of atom j. Then, we assign a number m_j to atom j which expresses whether it is an interior atom ($m_j=1$), a surface atom ($m_j=0$), or something intermediate. We get an effective number of interior atoms by adding all the m_j's.

$$m_j = exp(-(\zeta_j/\zeta_0)^2) \tag{9}$$

$$m = \sum_i m_j \tag{10}$$

We take $\zeta_0 = 0.05/(ln(2))^{1/2} = 0.0601$ which implies that an atom with $\zeta_i = 0.05$ is effectively a half-interior atom ($m_i = 0.5$). The value of ζ_j is typically greater than 0.2 for surface atoms and smaller than 0.02 for interior atoms, so, with $\zeta_0 = 0.0601$, we have a sharp distinction between interior and surface atoms in most cases.

2.3   Local Optimization

Following TSDS, clusters are sorted according to a score that depends on two things: their energy, and their similarity (on the basis of descriptors) to clusters of lower energy. We do local optimization by using VWN and a 6-311G** basis set on the fifteen best structures. In addition, we also performed local optimization on various fragments of the bulk hcp lattice because this type of structure was found to be stable in Ref. [4].

3   Results

It is convenient to divide the cluster sizes in three groups. Clusters in the first group (n=3–7, Fig. 1) adopt structures characteristic of the Lennard-Jones potential ("argon") and of most classical potentials including different variants of the embedded atom model. In the range n=8–14, beryllium adopts cage-like structures (Fig. 2): there are no interior atoms and little variations among atomic coordinations. The range n =15–20 is characterized by compact fragments of the hcp crystal (Fig. 3).

3.1 Be_2 to Be_7

Our lowest energy structures generally agree with the results of BLYP[1], BPW91/631/31[2] and B3LYP/6-311++G (3df)[3]. In the range n =2–5, van der Waals interactions are important and the lowest energy isomers have high symmetry structures similar to rare gas clusters. However, sp hybridization and metallic bonding develop gradually and this shows up in the decrease in mean interatomic distances (from 2.40 Å for Be_2 to 1.92 Å in Be_7), in the relatively large atomization energies of Be_6 (10.75 eV) and Be_7 (13.57 eV), and in the lower symmetry of Be_6 (D_{2h}) and Be_7 (C_1). On the singlet surface of Be_6 we find a C_{2v} structure which agrees with what was found by BLYP[1], BPW91/631/31[2] and B3LYP/6-311++G(3df)[3]. We find that the ground-state triplet is the lowest in energy: it has D_{2h} symmetry and is less distorted (relative to an octahedron) than the C_{2v} singlet. The BLYP[1] and B3LYP[3] calculations gave the C_{2v} singlet as the ground state whereas the BPW91[2] study found the O_h symmetry quintet to be the most stable. In our calculations, this quintet is higher than the triplet but by only 0.03 eV. Be_7 is a strongly distorted pentagonal bipyramid (PBP) with a singlet ground state and C_1 symmetry, in agreement with previous theoretical work[1, 3]. However, the capped octahedron is the global minimum in Ref. [2], but is 0.1 eV higher in our calculations. We find the quintet D_{5h} PBP only 0.04 eV higher.

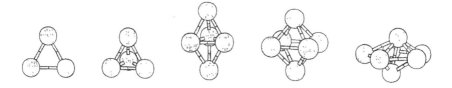

Fig. 1. Lowest energy isomers of Be_n, n=3–7.

3.2 Be_8 to Be_{14}

Metallic bonding fully develops at $n \geq 8$ and clusters start to show bulk-like behavior. We found the minimum energy structure of Be_8 to be a distorted dodecahedron, in agreement with other DFT studies[2, 3, 4]. It is similar to Ag_8[10], and different from the rare gas structure. It is 1.48 eV lower than a D_{6h} fragment of the hcp lattice. The minimum of Be_9 is a tricapped trigonal prism (TTP) with triplet ground state and C_s symmetry, in agreement with Ref. [2]. It is a slightly distorted version of the D_{3h} TTP. It lies 0.96 eV below the hcp fragment and 0.30 eV below the lowest energy singlet which has C_{2v} symmetry and was reported as the global minimum in previous work using LDA[4] theory. The HOMO-LUMO gap in the TTP triplet Be_9 is essentially zero, suggesting the possibility of a quintet ground state. However, we found the quintet to be 1.1 eV higher in energy. The lowest energy isomer of Be_{10} is a D_{4d} bicapped square antiprism and can be viewed as a hcp crystal fragment. A similar structure with an additional central atom was the global minimum found for Li_{11}[9]. The lowest Be_{11} structure has C_{2v} symmetry. Its energy is 0.3 eV lower than a C_{2v} hcp fragment. The minimum energy structures of Be_{10} and Be_{11} both are prolate cage structures where all atoms have a coordination of 4 or 5. The energy minima of Be_{13} and Be_{14} are also prolate cages, ie, they have no interior atoms, all their atoms have similar coordinations (4, 5, or 6), and the shape parameter $\eta \geq 0.20$. Be_{12} is different: its lowest energy isomer is not cage-like, as indicated by Fig. 2 and the relatively large $mean(c)$ and $rmsd(c)$ (Table I). It has C_1 symmetry and is 0.51 eV lower than a C_{2v} hcp fragment. However, we found two low-lying isomers of Be_{12} that both have cage-like structures. The first one is only 0.03 eV higher than the global minimum. It has C_{2v} symmetry and these descriptors: $mean(c) = 5.0, rmsd(c) = 0.6, \zeta = 0.04, \eta = 0.17$. The other, at +0.08 eV relative to the global minimum, is a distorted icosahedron missing a central atom. Its descriptors are: $mean(c) = 5.0, rmsd(c) = 0.0, \zeta = 0.003, \eta = 0.07$. The fact that this isomer is much more stable than the icosahedron with a missing *surface* atom illustrates the general tendency of Be clusters to minimize $rmsd(c)$ rather than maximize $mean(c)$. The minimum reported in a BLYP study[1], an icosahedron with a missing surface atom, is one of the isomers discovered during TSDS optimization, but it is 1.21 eV higher than the global minimum on the LSD potential surface. The lowest energy isomer of Be_{13} is the same C_{2v} hcp fragment that was found by Wang and coworkers[1]. The global minimum of Be_{14} is also an hcp fragment. It has D_{4d} symmetry and agrees with results of Ref. [4].

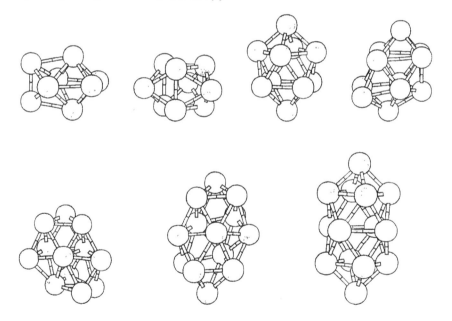

Fig. 2. Lowest energy isomers of Be_n, n=8–14.

3.3 Be$_{15}$ to Be$_{20}$

Our global minima structures for $n = 15$–20 agree with those found by BLYP[1] and LDA[4] with the exception of $n = 16$. These structures can all be obtained by taking fragments of the hcp lattice. The first beryllium cluster with an interior atom is Be$_{15}$. It has a C$_s$ structure consistent with a hcp fragment. The global minimum of Be$_{16}$ is a C$_{2v}$ hcp fragment. The TSDS missed this structure and found instead an isomer that is 0.22 eV higher in energy. The energy minimum reported in Ref. [4] is even higher in energy (0.27 eV above the global minimum). The global minimum of Be$_{17}$ is a hcp fragment, but a very peculiar one. It has a high symmetry (D$_{4d}$) strongly oblate ($\eta = -0.26$) structure. Be$_{18}$ has a slightly oblate ($\eta = -0.08$) C$_{2v}$ structure. and Be$_{19}$ is a less oblate ($\eta = -0.04$) C$_s$ structure. Be$_{19}$ has a triplet excited state 0.16 eV higher than the singlet ground state. Be$_{19}$ is another case where TSDS missed the global minimum and found instead a structure that is 0.20 eV higher in energy. Finally, the lowest energy isomer of Be$_{20}$ found by TSDS is the same C$_{2v}$ hcp fragment found in previous work.

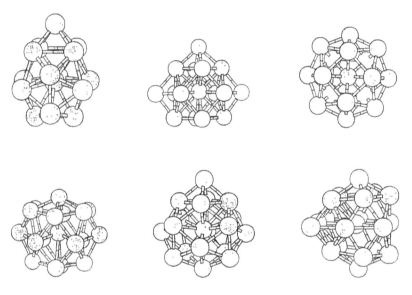

Fig. 3. Lowest energy isomers of Be$_n$, n=15-20.

3.4 Structural trends.

The most significant descriptors are listed for each global minimum structure in Table I. The mean coordination ($mean(c)$) increases gradually. as is typical of most atomic clusters, except for a clear jump from $n=14$ to $n=15$ which corresponds to the first cluster having an interior atom. The fluctuation in coordinations ($rmsd(c)$) is quite small for $n < 15$. much smaller than the energy minima structures of the Lennard-Jones potential and DFT structures we obtained for Ag and Li clusters[9, 10]. This descriptor also increases sharply at $n=15$. The asphericity is small ($\zeta < 0.05$) every time the number of electrons matches a shell-closing number of the jellium model,

Table 1: Energy, atomization energy (AE), and descriptors (Eq. 3, 4, 7, 8) of the lowest energy clusters. The ground state energy of the Be atom is -14.4458 a.u. The value of η is underlined where it agrees with the ellipsoidal jellium model[15].

N	Total Energy (a.u.)	AE (eV)	$mean(c)$	$rmsd(c)$	ζ	η
2	-28.9118	0.55				
3	-43.4283	2.47	2.0	0.0	0.33	$\underline{-0.50}$
4	-58.0125	6.24	3.0	0.0	0.00	$\underline{0.00}$
5	-72.5473	8.66	3.6	0.5	0.21	$\underline{0.49}$
6	-87.0722	10.81	4.3	0.0	0.01	-0.10
7	-101.6194	13.57	4.5	0.9	0.16	$\underline{-0.32}$
8	-116.1892	16.95	4.7	0.7	0.13	$\underline{0.29}$
9	-130.7755	20.77	4.8	0.6	0.03	$\underline{-0.14}$
10	-145.3720	24.87	4.8	0.4	0.04	$\underline{0.22}$
11	-159.9258	27.81	5.0	0.6	0.06	$\underline{0.21}$
12	-174.4712	30.52	5.4	1.3	0.08	$\underline{0.22}$
13	-189.0418	33.92	5.3	0.9	0.19	$\underline{0.35}$
14	-203.6122	37.31	5.2	0.6	0.22	$\underline{0.50}$
15	-218.1735	40.45	6.2	1.7	0.09	$\underline{0.20}$
16	-232.7554	44.15	6.4	1.8	0.09	-0.13
17	-247.3612	48.51	6.3	1.7	0.06	$\underline{-0.26}$
18	-261.9220	51.64	6.4	1.8	0.04	-0.08
19	-276.5030	55.31	6.5	1.9	0.01	-0.11
20	-291.0916	59.20	6.5	2.0	0.00	$\underline{-0.01}$

$N=n_e/2=4$, 10, and 20, but also for $N=n_c/2=6, 9, 18, 19$. The ellipsoidal jellium model predicts that metal clusters should adopt oblate ($\eta < 0$), prolate ($\eta > 0$), or spherical ($\zeta = \eta = 0$) shapes depending on the number of electrons[15]: in 14 out of 18 cases (those with underlined values of η in Table I) our global minima are in line with these qualitative predictions.

Table II compares the number of interior atoms (m, Eq. 10) of Be_n to Li_n and Ar_n. Clusters of beryllium have less of a tendency to form structures with interior atoms than Ar_n. while clusters of lithium have a higher tendency to do so. We attribute this difference to the fact that a Li atom has a much more diffuse electron density than a Be atom, so it can more easily accomodate a range of atomic coordinations and interatomic distances.

The long-range part of the electron density in atoms must be important for their ability to accomodate different interatomic distances. On the other hand, the case with which atoms acquire electric charge should relate to their ability to accomodate different coordinations. The former depends on the IE of the atom[16] and the latter depends on its absolute hardness (AH) defined as AH=(IE-EA)/2, where EA is the electron affinity[17]. So, we think that some aspects of the geometric structure of clusters can be rationalized by considering atomic properties. Specifically, we predict that elements with a large IE (*unlike* Li) tend to adopt structures where nearest-neighbour distances are all nearly equal, and that elements that have a large AH and bind strongly (like Be_n, Zn_n. and Cd_n, but excluding their very small van der Waals clusters) tend to adopt structures with a small $rmsd(c)$. The formation of cage cluster structures in elements with a large AH like C and Be ($8 \leq n \leq 14$) could be rationalized as extreme examples of that tendency since $rmsd(c)$ is zero, or nearly zero, for cages.

Table 2: Number of interior atoms (Eq. 12) in the most stable isomers of Ar_n (Lennard-Jones potential), Be_n and Li_n (DFT, Ref. [9]).

$n =$	7	8	9	10	11	12	13	14	15	16	17	18	19	20
Ar	0.0	0.0	0.0	0.1	0.4	0.9	1.0	1.0	1.0	1.0	1.0	1.9	2.0	2.0
Be	0.0	0.0	0.0	0.0	0.0	0.0	0.0	0.0	0.8	0.8	0.8	1.0	1.0	1.0
Li	0.0	1.0	0.8	0.0	0.8	0.3	1.0	2.0	2.0	2.0	2.0	2.0	3.0	3.1

3.5 Size evolution

The atomization energy (AE) of Be_n clusters are shown in Table I. There is a very sharp rise in AE/n from $n=2$ to $n=4$, a slower rise from $n=4$ to $n=10$, and a gradual rise typical of metal clusters for $n \geq 10$. In the range $n=2$-8, the mean nearest-neighbour interatomic distance d_{avg} varies as follows: 2.40, 2.15, 2.02, 2.00, 1.97, 1.92, and 1.95 Å. For $n > 8$, d_{avg} stays almost constant (between 1.97Å and 2.05Å) which is again typical for metal clusters. The trends in AE/n and d_{nn} signal a transition from van der Waals to metallic bonding in the range $n=2$-7. This is accompanied by a change in the effective configuration of the Be atoms from $1s^22s^2$ to something closer to $1s^22s2p$. The increase in $mean(c)$ is mainly responsible for the slower increase of AE for $n > 8$. The jellium shell closings at $n =4$, 10, 17 and 20 ($n_e=8$, 20, 34, 40) match precisely the local maxima in the stability functions:

$$D_1(n) = AE(n) - AE(n-1)$$
$$D_2(n) = 2AE(n) - AE(n-1) - AE(n+1)$$

This is not a coincidence. Maxima in the HOMO-LUMO gap and IEs (Fig. 4) also occur at $n =4$, 10, 17 and 20, showing the closed shell nature of the electronic structure at those sizes. There is a good correlation between HOMO-LUMO gap and IE, as is often the case in metal clusters[18].

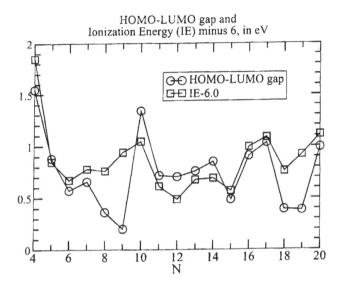

Fig. 4. HOMO-LUMO gap and ionization energies (IE) of the most stable clusters. We subtracted 6 eV from the IE to allow an easy comparison to HOMO-LUMO gaps.

4   Conclusion

The minimum energy structures that we found agree with those of previous DFT studies with few exceptions. Generally, these structures can be summarized as being: (a) maximally compact for $n=3$-7, (b) cage-like for $n=8$-14, and (c) compact hcp fragments for $n=15$-20. We suggest that elements with a large absolute hardness have a higher propensity to form cage-like structures. Short runs (fewer than 3000 energy evaluations) of the TSDS algorithm successfully generated the known best structures at all sizes except $n=16$, 19 where it found structures 0.2 eV higher in energy. The global minima have higher spin states for $n=6,9$ and maybe others in the range $n=2$-9[2] and possibly even larger clusters. We found low-lying triplet states for Be_8 (+0.01 eV) and Be_{19} (+0.16 eV), and a low-lying quintet (+0.04 eV) for Be_7. Since energy differences are small, a reinvestigation of Be_{6-9} and Be_{19} in various spin states with a higher level of theory, would be desirable. The rapid changes in mean interatomic distances, 2p orbital population, and atomization energies show a nonmetal-to-metal transition in Be_n from $n=2$ to 7 roughly. At larger sizes, properties evolve in ways that are typical of metal clusters. Many of the results we obtained through our extensive geometry optimizations at the DFT level agree with the simple jellium model of electronic structure in metal clusters, namely: clusters with 4, 10, 17, and 20 atoms have a larger HOMO-LUMO gap and enhanced stability; Be_4, Be_{10}, and Be_{20} are quasi-spherical; and the overall shape (oblate or prolate) of a majority of the clusters is in line with the ellipsoidal jellium predictions.

References

[1] J. Wang, G. Wang and J. Zhao, J. Phys.:Condens. Matter. 13, L753 (2001).

[2] S. Srinivas and J. Jellinek, J. Chem. Phys. 121, 7243 (2004).

[3] M.K. Beyer, L.A. Kaledin, A.L. Kaledin, M.C. Heaven, and V.E. Bondybey. Chem. Phys. 262. 15 (2002).

[4] R. Kawai and J. H. Weare, Phys. Rev. Lett. 65, 80 (1990).

[5] V.E. Bondybey, Chem. Phys. Lett. 109, 436 (1984).

[6] J. Cheng and R. Fournier, Theor. Chem. Acc. 112, 7 (2004).

[7] A. St-Amant and D. R. Salahub, Chem. Phys. Lett. 169, 387 (1990). M.E. Casida, et al., deMon-KS version 3.2 (deMon software, 1998).

[8] S. H. Vosko, L. Wilk and M. Nusair, Can. J. Phys. 58, 1200 (1980).

[9] R. Fournier, J. Cheng and A. Wong, J. Chem. Phys. 119, 9444 (2003).

[10] R. Fournier, J. Chem. Phys. 115, 2165 (2001).

[11] H. Kietzmann, J. Morenzin, P.S. Bechthold, G. Ganteför. W. Eberhardt, D.-S. Yang, P. Hackett, R. Fournier, T. Pang, and C. Chen, Phys. Rev. Lett. 77, 4528 (1996); R. Fournier, T. Pang, and C. Chen, Phys. Rev. A 57, 3683 (1998).

[12] S. Chekmarev, Phys. Rev. E. 64, 036703 (2001); C. Tsai and K. Jordan, J. Phys. Chem. 97, 11227 (1993).

[13] W. A. De Heer, Rev. Mod. Phys. 65, 611 (1993).

[14] C. Kittel. Introduction to Solid State Physics, (1986, John Wiley & Sons, Inc.).

[15] W. A. DeHeer, Rev. Mod. Phys. 65, 611 (1993).

[16] M.M. Morrell, R.G. Parr, and M. Levy, J. Chem. Phys. 62, 549 (1975).

[17] R.G. Parr and W. Yang, Density Functional Theory of Atoms and Molecules (1989, Oxford University Press).

[18] M.B. Knickelbein, Annu. Rev. Phys. Chem. 50, 79 (1999).

Brill Academic Publishers
P.O. Box 9000, 2300 PA Leiden
The Netherlands

Lecture Series on Computer and Computational Sciences
Volume 5, 2006, pp. 77-85

Dissociative and Associative Attachment of CO, N_2, and NO to Iron Clusters Fe_4, Fe_4^-, and Fe_4^+

G. L. Gutsev,[1] M. D. Mochena,[1] C. W. Bauschlicher Jr.[2]

[1] Department of Physics, Florida A&M University, Tallahassee, Florida 32307
[2] Mail Stop 230-3 NASA Ames Research Center, Moffett Field, CA 94035

Abstract: The lowest energy states of NFe_4N, NFe_4O, Fe_4N_2, Fe_4NO, and CFe_4O, along with their singly negatively and positively charged ions, are optimized using density functional theory with generalized gradient approximation for the exchange-correlation functional (DFT-GGA). It is found that NO attaches dissociatively, independent of the charge on the Fe_4 cluster, while N_2 attaches dissociatively to Fe_4 and Fe_4^-, but associatively to Fe_4^+. CO attaches associatively independent of the cluster charge. The results of these computations, along with the results of previous calculations, are used for evaluating the energetics of $Fe_4A+B \rightarrow Fe_4C +D$, where A, B, C, and D are C, O, N, their dimers, or NCO. A strong dependence on the order of attachment of reagents to the Fe_4 cluster is observed. For example, the $Fe_4CO+O_2 \rightarrow Fe_4O+CO_2$ is highly exothermic (-4.48 eV), while the complimentary reaction $Fe_4O_2+ CO \rightarrow Fe_4O+CO_2$ is endothermic (+0.43 eV).

Keywords: density functional theory, iron clusters, dissociation of N_2, NO, CO; charged 3d-metal clusters, antiferromagnetic states.

PACS: 31.15 Ew; 31.70 Dk; 36.40 Cg, Qv, Wa

1. Introduction

Reduction of NO and oxidation of CO are among the most important problems in environmental chemistry. The simplest conversion reaction is

$$NO+CO \rightarrow 1/2N_2+CO_2 \qquad (1)$$

and is accomplished in car exhausts using catalysts containing 4d- and 5d-metals, such as Rh or Pt. The reaction cycle can be broken in several major steps that include CO and NO adsorption, NO dissociation, N_2 desorption, CO oxidation, and CO_2 desorption. There are also a number of concomitant channels yielding N_2O, NCO, CN, and N_2O. Reaction (1) was studied [1] theoretically using a Pt surface as a catalyst; this work considered only the major reaction steps. Recent experimental efforts were devoted to investigating reaction (1) sponsored by Au/TiO_2 catalysts [2, 3], where gold particles are of a nanometer size (1-6 nm). The latter work [3] reported the observation of NCO species in the infrared (IR) spectra. A related theoretical study [4] of NO attachment to a number of Au_n clusters has shown that the NO attachment to these clusters is associative.

Another important reaction is the oxidation of carbon monoxide

$$CO + 1/2O_2 \rightarrow CO_2. \qquad (2)$$

Shi and Ervin [5] studied the catalytic oxidation of CO by oxygen and found that small platinum cluster anions Pt_n^- (n=3–6) are able to provide the whole oxidation cycle under thermal conditions. A Fourier-Transformed IR (FTIR) spectroscopy study [6] of the oxidation of CO on Au/TiO_2 catalysts has shown the oxidation to be strongly dependent on the adsorption order. In particular, the oxidation is almost completely inhibited if oxygen is pre-adsorbed. Corresponding theoretical studies were devoted to the adsorption of CO [7,8], as well as, co-adsorption of CO and O_2 on neutral [9] and negatively charged [10] gold clusters.

Reactions (1) and (2) catalyzed by 3d-metal clusters received less attention despite the fact that 3d-metal nanoclusters of Fe, Co, Ni are widely used as supported catalysts for production of carbon single- and multi-walled nanotubes [11]. Iron clusters are used also for the gas-phase production of single-walled carbon nanotubes in the HipCo process [12]. The number of iron atoms in a typical catalyst particle, generated in the HipCo process from $Fe(CO)_5$, ranges from ~10 to ~300. Even smaller iron clusters, such as Fe_4^+, are capable [13] of transforming ethylene into benzene in the gas phase under

[1] Corresponding author. E-mail gennady.gutsev@famu.edu

low-pressure conditions. On the theoretical side, interactions of neutral and charged Fe_n clusters with CO were considered [14] for n=1-6 and the catalytic oxidation of CO via reaction (2) was modeled [15] using Fe_4, Fe_4^-, and Fe_4^- clusters. It was found that this reaction sponsored by iron clusters is highly exothermic and has no barrier if CO is pre-adsorbed on a cluster.

Both experimental and theoretical data on interactions of iron particles with NO and N_2 are scarce and restricted to particles consisting of one or two Fe atoms. $Fe(N_2)_n^+$ clusters were probed [16] using collision induced dissociation, and the Fe^+-N_2 bond strength is found to be 0.56±0.06 eV. Reactions of laser ablated iron atoms with nitrogen studied using matrix isolation IR [17] and products included NFeN and FeNN isomers, as well as, Fe_2N and $Fe_2(N_2)$ species. – Density functional theory (DFT) computations were used to help identify species trapped in the matrices. In a recent DFT study [18] of the $M(N)_2$ and $M_2(N)_2$ species, where M is a 3d-metal, no isomers with dissociative attachment of N_2 was reported for $Fe(N)_2$ and $Fe_2(N)_2$. IR spectra of $M(NO)_n$, where M is a 3d-, 4d-, and 5d-atom, along with the results of corresponding DFT calculations were reviewed by Citra and Andrews [19]. No inserted NFeO isomer is reported [19,20].

The aim of this work is to evaluate the energetics of reaction (1) and related reactions sponsored by the Fe_4, Fe_4^-, and Fe_4^+ catalysts. We optimize different isomers of neutral and charged clusters NFe_4N, Fe_4NN, NFe_4O, Fe_4NO, and CFe_4O. Using these results, along with our previous results for Fe_4CO [14], OFe_4O [15], Fe_4C [21], Fe_4O [22], and Fe_4N [23] studied at the same level of theory, allows the calculation of the energetics for Fe_4 reactions involving N_2, NO, CO, CO_2, N_2O, NCO, CN, and N_2O. Since the reactivity of iron clusters is likely to depend on the cluster charge, we optimize singly negatively and positively charged clusters in addition to the neutral ones.

2. Computational Details

The Gaussian 98 program [24] was used. We have used the 6-311+G* basis set [25]: (15s11p6d1f)/[10s7p4d1f] for Fe and (12s6p1d)/[5s4p1d] for C, O and N. Our previous study [mm25a] of bare iron clusters showed that results obtained using many of the DFT-GGA methods included in Gaussian 98 are rather similar; however, the BPW91 vibrational frequencies appear to be less sensitive to the quality of the grid used in the numerical integration than some of the other functionals. On this ground, we choose the BPW91 method, where the exchange-correlation functional is comprised of the Becke's exchange [27] and Perdew-Wang's correlation [28].

The geometry of each cluster was optimized without imposing any symmetry constraints. Optimizations were performed for the spin multiplicities ranging from 1(2) to 15(16) for species with even (odd) numbers of electrons. Each geometry optimization was followed by the calculation of the harmonic vibrational frequencies using analytical second derivatives, in order to confirm that the optimized geometry corresponds to a minimum. Our reported electron affinities and ionization energies are computed as the differences in total electronic energies corrected for the zero-point vibrational energies (ZPVE) for each state at its equilibrium geometry and therefore correspond to adiabatic values. We compute atomic spin densities using Mulliken [29] approach.

3. Geometrical Structures

Optimized structures of the Fe_4+N_2 series are presented in Fig. 1. As is seen, dinitrogen attaches dissociatively in the ground states of NFe_4N^- and NFe_4N, while it attaches associatively in the ground state of $Fe_4N_2^+$. The ground-state spin multiplicities in the series NFe_4N^-, NFe_4N, and $Fe_4N_2^+$ are 8, 9, and 12, respectively, which can be compared to the ground-state spin multiplicities [26] of 16, 15, and 12 in the bare Fe_4^-, Fe_4, and Fe_4^+ clusters, respectively. That is, dissociative attachment reduces drastically the spin multiplicity of the corresponding iron clusters, while associative attachment does not affect their spin multiplicity. The lowest energy isomers of $Fe_4N_2^-$ and Fe_4N_2 with associative N_2 adsorption are high-spin and are above the corresponding ground states by 0.09 and 0.27 eV, respectively. Such small energy differences between the dissociative and associative absorption of N_2 helps explain the small N_2 binding energies for Fe_4 and Fe_4^-, see below. Note that the excess spin density of one iron atom is coupled anti-parallel to the excess spin densities of three other Fe atoms in the states whose spin multiplicity is smaller than or equal to 10. Such states are called as antiferromagnetic and marked in the figures with "AF".

NO dissociates on the Fe_4 clusters independent of their charge states, see Fig. 2. There is a competition between low-spin AF and high-spin ferromagnetic (FM) states. The ground state of

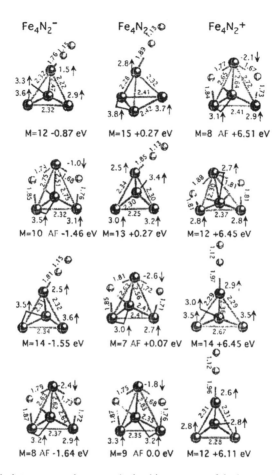

Figure 1. Geometrical structures and excess spin densities at atoms of the lowest energy states formed by associative and dissociative attachment of N₂ to Fe₄⁻, Fe₄, and Fe₄⁺. Bond lengths are in Å; M denotes the spin multiplicity 2S+1 and AF denotes antiferromagnetic.

NFe₄O⁺ is AF while NFe₄O⁻ and NFe₄O possess FM ground states. However, the lowest AF states in the latter two species are above their corresponding ground states by only 0.11 and 0.09 eV, respectively. The isomers with associative attachment of NO are all high-spin and are 1.66, 1.77, and 1.68 eV above the ground state of the anion, neutral, and cation, respectively.

Carbon monoxide attaches associatively to form the high-spin ground states of Fe₄CO⁻, Fe₄CO, and Fe₄CO⁺, see Fig. 3. Their lowest energy isomers with dissociative attachment are above the corresponding ground states by 0.49, 0.32, and 0.88 eV, respectively. As in the previous case, the AF and FM states with associative attachment of CO are close in total energy.

According to experimental findings, CO dissociates on supported catalysts Rh/Al₂O₃ [30] or Ni/MgO [31]. It is not known if CO dissociates on iron clusters either in the gas phase or deposited on a substrate. According to the results of the present calculations, if CO dissociates on Fe clusters, the clusters must contain more than four Fe atoms. In a larger iron cluster, the sum of binding energies of C and O to the cluster may exceed the binding energy of CO plus the binding energy of CO to the iron cluster.

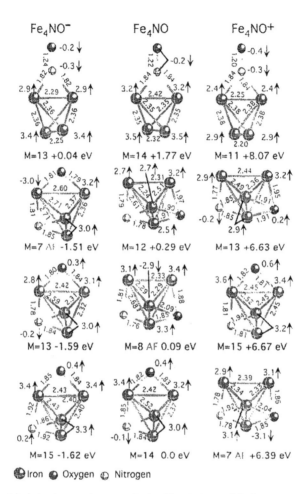

Figure 2. Geometrical structures and excess spin densities at atoms of the lowest energy states formed by associative and dissociative attachment of NO to Fe₄ and its ions.

4. Electron Affinities, Ionization Energies, and Thermodynamic Stability

Our computed adiabatic electron affinities (EA) and ionization energies (IE) of NFe₄N, NFe₄O, and Fe₄CO are compared with those of Fe₄O, Fe₄N, Fe₄C and Fe₄ in Table 1.

Table 1. Adiabatic electron affinities (EA) and ionization energies (IE) of Fe₄X computed at the BPW91/6-311+G* level.

	NFE₄N	NFE₄O	FE₄CO	FE₄O	FE₄N	FE₄C	FE₄
AE, eV	1.64	1.61	1.95	1.60[a]	1.16	1.28	1.76[b]
IE, eV	6.07	6.37	6.06	6.04	6.04	6.52	5.71

[a] Experiment: 1.70±0.02 eV [22];
[b] Experiment: 1.80±0.05 eV [22].

As is seen, the EA or IE energies of all of the species are relatively similar. Experimental data are known for the EA of Fe₄ and Fe₄O [22] and our BPW91/6-311+G* computed values are in good agreement with experiment, which suggests that our computed values for all species should be reasonably accurate.

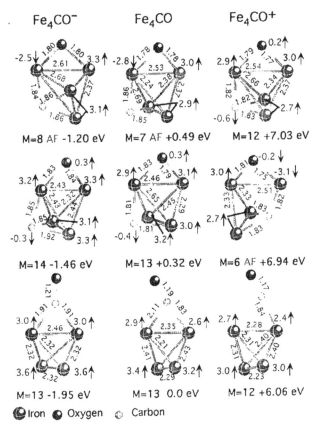

Figure 3. Geometrical structures and excess spin densities at atoms of the lowest energy states formed by associative and dissociative attachment of CO to Fe₄ and its ions.

Table 2 presents fragmentation energies of NFe₄N, NFe₄O, Fe₄CO, and their ions. In general, fragmentation channels of an anion (cation) are more (less) endothermic than the corresponding channels of the neutral species. The channels corresponding to desorption of NO and N₂ from the anions are two exceptions.

Desorption of N₂ is the least endothermic channel in the table, despite the dissociative adsorption in NFe₄N. The loss of the first N via the channel NFe₄N→ Fe₄N + N requires 5.23 eV, while the second N loss requires 5.71 eV [23]. Our computed atomization energy N₂ → 2N is 9.94 eV (experimental value is 9.76 eV [32]). Thus while both of the N atoms in NFe₄N are strongly bound, the high thermodynamic stability of N₂ results in a small energy assocated with the loss of N₂.

Desorption of NO is significantly more endothermic than desorption of N₂, which is due to the smaller NO atomization energy of 6.93 eV (experimental value is 6.51 eV [32]) and the larger binding energy for oxygen than nitrogen; compare NFe₄O→Fe₄N + O with NFe₄N→Fe₄N + N in Table 2. CO possesses the largest atomization energy of 11.18 eV (experimental value is 11.11 eV [32]). The combination of the strong CO bond and the fact that CO is bound to Fe₄ by 1.76 eV, means that CO is molecularly bound to the cluster, despite the sizable bond strengths for O and C to Fe₄, see Table 3. As shown in Fig. 3, the dissociative structure is only 0.32 eV higher than the associative one, thus, to dissociatively absorb CO, requires a change in the cluster that would either weaken the binding of CO to the cluster, increase the binding of C and/or O to the cluster, or both.

Table 2. Fragmentation energies (in eV) of neutral and charged Fe_4CO, Fe_4N_2, and Fe_4NO

CHANNEL	BPW91	CHANNEL	BPW91	CHANNEL	BPW91
$NFe_4N \rightarrow Fe_4 + N_2$	1.00	$NFe_4N \rightarrow Fe_4 + N_2$	0.87	$Fe_4N_2^+ \rightarrow Fe_4^+ + N_2$	0.62
$\rightarrow Fe_4N + N$	5.23	$\rightarrow Fe_4N + N$	5.70	$\rightarrow Fe_4N^+ + N$	5.15
$NFe_4O \rightarrow Fe_4 + NO$	4.68	$NFe_4O \rightarrow Fe_4 + NO$	4.53	$NFe_4O^+ \rightarrow Fe_4^+ + NO$	4.03
$\rightarrow Fe_4N + O$	5.90	$\rightarrow Fe_4N^- + O$	6.35	$\rightarrow Fe_4N^- + O$	5.55
$\rightarrow Fe_4O + N$	5.60	$\rightarrow Fe_4O^- + N$	5.61	$\rightarrow Fe_4O^- + N$	5.25
$Fe_4CO \rightarrow Fe_4 + CO$	1.76	$Fe_4CO \rightarrow Fe_4 + CO$	1.93	$Fe_4CO^+ \rightarrow Fe_4^+ + CO$	1.41
$\rightarrow Fe_4C + O$	5.88	$\rightarrow Fe_4C + O$	6.53	$\rightarrow Fe_4C^+ + O$	6.29
$\rightarrow Fe_4O + C$	6.92	$\rightarrow Fe_4O + C$	7.28	$\rightarrow Fe_4O^+ + C$	6.91

5. Reactivity of Fe_4 and its Ions

The energies of reactions involving Fe_4 are collected in Table 3. The reaction channels are given in complimentary pairs and ordered according to increasing the endothermic character of the lowest energy channels.

Table 3. Energetics of different reactions involving N_2, CO, NO, and O_2 with Fe_4.

	REACTION	ENERGY (EV)
Reactions 3-4	$Fe_4CO + O_2 \rightarrow Fe_4O + CO_2$	-4.48
	$Fe_4O_2 + CO \rightarrow Fe_4O + CO_2$	+0.43
Reactions 5-6	$Fe_4CO + NO \rightarrow Fe_4N + CO_2$	-2.97
	$Fe_4NO + CO \rightarrow Fe_4N + CO_2$	-0.06
Reactions 7-8	$Fe_4N_2 + O_2 \rightarrow Fe_4O + N_2O$	-1.72
	$Fe_4O_2 + N_2 \rightarrow Fe_4O + N_2O$	+3.95
	$Fe_4CO + NO \rightarrow Fe_4O_2 + CN$	-0.58
	$Fe_4NO + CO \rightarrow Fe_4O_2 + CN$	+2.34
	$Fe_4CO + NO \rightarrow Fe_4O + NCO$	-0.41
	$Fe_4NO + CO \rightarrow Fe_4O + NCO$	+2.50
	$Fe_4N_2 + NO \rightarrow Fe_4N + N_2O$	-0.24
	$Fe_4NO + N_2 \rightarrow Fe_4N + N_2O$	+3.47
	$Fe_4N_2 + NO \rightarrow Fe_4N + N_2O$	-0.20
	$Fe_4NO + N_2 \rightarrow Fe_4N + N_2O$	+3.47
	$Fe_4CO + CO \rightarrow Fe_4C + CO_2$	-0.08
	$Fe_4NO + NO \rightarrow Fe_4O + N_2O$	+0.16
	$Fe_4N_2 + O_2 \rightarrow Fe_4N + NO_2$	+0.22
	$Fe_4O_2 + N_2 \rightarrow Fe_4N + NO_2$	+5.89
	$Fe_4NO + O_2 \rightarrow Fe_4O + NO_2$	+0.49
	$Fe_4O_2 + NO \rightarrow Fe_4O + NO_2$	+2.60
	$Fe_4CO + NO \rightarrow Fe_4C + NO_2$	+2.06
	$Fe_4NO + CO \rightarrow Fe_4C + NO_2$	+4.99
	$Fe_4NO + NO \rightarrow Fe_4N + NO_2$	+2.10
	$Fe_4N_2 + CO \rightarrow Fe_4N + NCO$	+2.13
	$Fe_4CO + N_2 \rightarrow Fe_4N + NCO$	+2.88
	$Fe_4N_2 + CO \rightarrow Fe_4NO + CN$	+2.46
	$Fe_4CO + N_2 \rightarrow Fe_4NO + CN$	+3.22
	$Fe_4N_2 + CO \rightarrow Fe_4C + N_2O$	+2.68
	$Fe_4CO + N_2 \rightarrow Fe_4C + N_2O$	+3.43
	$Fe_4NO + NO \rightarrow Fe_4 + 2NO$	+2.88

The first entry presents the $Fe_4CO + O_2 \rightarrow Fe_4O + CO_2$ reaction [reaction (3)], which is highly exothermic (-4.38 eV) and proceeds without energy barrier [14]. When coupled with the $Fe_4O + CO \rightarrow Fe_4 + CO_2$ reaction, it represents Fe_4-catalyzed oxidation of CO, i.e. reaction (2). The complimentary $Fe_4O_2[OFe_4O] + CO \rightarrow Fe_4O + CO_2$ reaction [reaction (4)] is endothermic -by +0.44 eV. That is, the reactivity depends on the order of molecular attachment to the metal cluster, as it was observed experimentally for the oxidation of CO by O_2 on Au/TiO_2 catalysts [6]. The large difference between these two reactions can be traced to the strong Fe_4–O bonds; one Fe_4–O bond is formed in reaction 3 while one is lost in reaction 4.

The difference in fragmentation energies for the channels $Fe_4CO + NO \rightarrow Fe_4N + CO_2$ (5) and $Fe_4NO + CO \rightarrow Fe_4N + CO_2$ (6) is smaller than for (3) and (4), but still sizable. The difference naturally arises from the much larger binding energy of NO–Fe_4 binding energy than CO–Fe_4 binding energy. These reactions, when coupled with a reaction that would convert Fe_4N into $Fe_4 + 1/2N_2$, yield a catalytic cycle for reaction (1).

Curiously enough, the $Fe_4N_2 + O_2 \rightarrow Fe_4O + N_2O$ channel [reaction (7)], which yields N_2O with a weak N_2–O bond, is exothermic, while the complimentary $Fe_4O_2 + N_2 \rightarrow Fe_4O + N_2O$ channel [reaction (8)] is highly endothermic, see Table 3. This difference is due to the strong Fe_4-O bonding; reaction 7 forms an Fe_4-O bond, while reaction 8 breaks one.

The asymmetry of energies is observed for all other couples of reactions presented in Table 3. There are several exothermic channels including those that yield CN and NCO. The rate of a particular reaction depends on many factors, such as barrier heights of reactions, but this is beyond the scope of the present work, which is aimed at determining which reactions are possible and therefore suitable for more detailed study in the future.

6. Conclusion

The results of our DFT-GGA calculations on the geometrical and electronic structure of the lowest energy states of NFe_4N, NFe_4O, Fe_4N_2, Fe_4NO, and CFe_4O, when combined with the results of our previous computations on Fe_4CO, OFe_4On Fe_4, Fe_4C, Fe_4N, and Fe_4O, allow one to draw several conclusions:

(i) NO attaches dissociatively to the Fe_4^-, Fe_4, and Fe_4^+ clusters, N_2 attaches dissociatively to Fe_4 and Fe_4^- and associatively to Fe_4^+, and CO attaches associatively independent of the cluster charge. This behavior correlates with the increasing bond strength in the series NO, N_2, and CO.

(ii) Energies of bimolecular reactions involving an iron cluster depend strongly on which species attached first to the cluster. Even for homonuclear dimers, the order of attachment matters. For example, the $Fe_4N_2 + O_2 \rightarrow Fe_4N + NO_2$ channel is weakly endothermic (+0.22 eV) while the complimentary $Fe_4O_2 + N_2 \rightarrow Fe_4N + NO_2$ channel is highly endothermic (+5.89 eV).

(iii) Based on our computed energetics, iron clusters should be considered as catalysts for the conversion reaction $NO+CO\rightarrow 1/2N_2+CO_2$.

Acknowledgements

This work was supported in part by the Army High Performance Computing Research Center (AHPCRC) under the auspices of the Department of the Army, Army Research Laboratory (ARL) under Cooperative Agreement number DAAD19-01-2-0014. The content of which does not necessarily reflect the position or the policy of the government, and no official endorsement should be inferred. This work was also partly supported by NASA Ames Research Center through contract NAS2-99092 to Eloret Corporation to G. L. G. We thank Dr. Norbert Müller for providing us with the new version of Ball&Stick software used for plotting individual geometrical structures presented in the figures.

References

[1] A. Eichler and J. Hafner, NO Reduction by CO on the Pt(100) Surface: A Density Functional Theory Study, *Journal of Catalysis* **204**, 118-128 (2001).

[2] M. A. Debeila, N. J. Coville, M. S. Scurrell, and G. R. Hearne, DRIFTS studies of the interaction of nitric oxide and carbon monoxide on Au–TiO_2, *Catalysis Today* **72**, 79-87 (2002).

[3] F. Solymosi, T. Bánsági, and T. S. Zakar, Infrared Study of the NO + CO Interaction over Au/TiO_2 Catalyst, *Catalysis Letters* **87**, 7-10 (2003).

[4] X. Ding, Z. Li, J.Yang, J. G. Hou, and Q. Zhu, Theoretical study of nitric oxide adsorption on Au clusters, *The Journal of Chemical Physics* **121**, 2558 -2562 (2004).

[5] Y. Shi and K. M. Ervin, Catalytic oxidation of carbon monoxide by platinum cluster anions, *The Journal of Chemical Physics* **108**, 1757-1760 (1998).

[6] F. Boccuzzi and A. Chiorino, FTIR Study of CO Oxidation on Au/TiO_2 at 90 K and Room Temperature. An Insight into the Nature of the Reaction Centers, *The Journal of Physical Chemistry B* **104**, 5414-5416 (2000).

[7] H. Häkkinen and U. Landman, Gas-Phase Catalytic Oxidation of CO by Au_2^-, *Journal of the American Chemical Society* **123**, 9704-9705 (2001).

[8] D. W. Yuan and Z. Zeng, Saturated adsorption of CO and coadsorption of CO and O_2 on Au_N^- (N = 2–7) clusters, *The Journal of Chemical Physics* **120**, 6574-6584 (2004).

[9] N. Lopez and J. K. Nørskov, Catalytic CO Oxidation by a Gold Nanoparticle: A Density Functional Study, *Journal of the American Chemical Society* **124**, 11262-11263 (2002).

[10] M. L. Kimble, A. W. Castleman, Jr., R. Mitri, C. Bürgel, and V. Bonac^ic'-Koutecky', Reactivity of Atomic Gold Anions toward Oxygen and the Oxidation of CO: Experiment and Theory, *Journal of the American Chemical Society* **126**, 2526–2535 (2004).

[11] A. P. Moravsky, E. M. Wexler, and R. O. Loutfy, Growth of carbon nanotubes by arc discharge and laser ablation, Chapter 3 in *"Carbon nanotubes. Science and applications"* (Editor: M. Meyyappan, CRC Press LLC, Boca Raton, 2005).

[12] . Nikolaev, M. J. Bronikowski, R. K. Bradley, F. Rohmund, D. T. Colbert, K. A. Smith, and R. E. Smalley, Gas-phase catalytic growth of single-walled carbon nanotubes from carbon monoxide, *Chemical Physics Letters* **313**, 91-97 (1999).

[13] P. Schnabel, M. P. Irion, and K. G. Weil, Evidence for low-pressure catalysis in the gas phase by a naked metal cluster: the growth of benzene precursors on iron (Fe_4^+), *The Journal of Physical Chemistry* **95**, 9688-9694 (1991).

[14] G. L. Gutsev and C. W. Bauschlicher, Jr. Structure of neutral and charged Fe_nCO clusters (n = 1–6) and energetics of the $Fe_nO + CO \rightarrow Fe_nC + CO_2$ reaction, *The Journal of Chemical Physics* **119**, 368-3690 (2003).

[15] G. L. Gutsev and C. W. Bauschlicher, Jr. Oxidation of carbon monoxide on small iron clusters, *Chemical Physics Letters* **380**, 435-444 (2003).

[16] B. L. Tjelta and P. B. Armentrout, Gas-Phase Metal Ion Ligation: Collision-Induced Dissociation of $Fe(N_2)_x^+$ (x = 1-5) and $Fe(CH_2O)_x^+$ (x = 1-4), *The Journal of Physical Chemistry A* **101**, 2064-2073 (1997).

[17] G. V. Chertihin, L. Andrews, and M. Neurock, Reactions of Laser-Ablated Iron Atoms with Nitrogen Atoms and Molecules. Matrix Infrared Spectra and Density Functional Calculations of Novel Iron Nitride Molecules, *The Journal of Physical Chemistry* **100**, 14609-14617 (1996).

[18] S. E. Weber, B. V. Reddy, B. K. Rao, and P. Jena, Chemically induced changes in the magnetic moments in transition metal monomers and dimers, *Chemical Physics Letters* **295**, 175-180 (1998).

[19] L. Andrews and A. Citra, Infrared Spectra and Density Functional Theory Calculations on Transition Metal Nitrosyls. Vibrational Frequencies of Unsaturated Transition Metal Nitrosyls, *Chemical Reviews* **102**, 885-912 (2002).

[20] C. Blanchet, H. A. Duarte, and D. R. Salahub, Density functional study of mononitrosyls of first-row transition-metal atoms, *The Journal of Chemical Physics* **106**, 8778-8787 (1997).

[21] G. L. Gutsev and C. W. Bauschlicher, Jr. Interaction of carbon atoms with Fe_n, Fe_n^-, and Fe_n^+ clusters (n=1–6), *Chemical Physics* **291**, 27-40 (2003).

[22] G. L. Gutsev, C. W. Bauschlicher, Jr., H.-J. Zhai, and L. S. Wang, Structural and electronic properties of iron monoxide clusters Fe_nO and Fe_nO^- ($n = 2$–6): A combined photoelectron spectroscopy and density functional theory study, *The Journal of Chemical Physics* **119**, 11135-11145 (2003).

[23] G. L. Gutsev, M. D. Mochena, and C. W. Bauschlicher, Jr., to be submitted.

[24] *Gaussian 98*, Revision A.11, M. J. Frisch, et. al. Gaussian, Inc., Pittsburgh PA, 1998.

[25] K. Raghavachari and G. W. Trucks, Highly correlated systems. Excitation energies of first row transition metals Sc–Cu, *The Journal of Chemical Physics* **91**, 1062-1065 (1989).

[26] G. L. Gutsev and C. W. Bauschlicher, Jr. Electron Affinities, Ionization Energies, and Fragmentation Energies of Fe_n Clusters ($n = 2$-6): A Density Functional Theory Study, *The Journal of Physical Chemistry A* **107**, 7013-7023 (2003).

[27] A. D. Becke, Density-functional exchange-energy approximation with correct asymptotic behavior, *Physical Reviews A* **38**, 3098-3100 (1988).

[28] J. P. Perdew and Y. Wang, Accurate and simple analytic representation of the electron-gas correlation energy, *Physical Reviews B* **45**, 13244-13249 (1992).

[29] R. S. Mulliken, Electronic Population Analysis on LCAO-MO Molecular Wave Functions. IV. Bonding and Antibonding in LCAO and Valence-Bond Theories, *The Journal of Chemical Physics* **23**, 2343-2346 (1955).

[30] M. Frank, S. Andersson, J. Libuda, S. Stempel A. Sandell, B. Brena, A. Giertz, P.A. Brühwiler, M. Bäumer, N. Mårtensson, and H.-J. Freund, Particle size dependent CO dissociation on alumina-supported Rh: a model study, *Chemical Physics Letters* **279**, 92-99 (1997).

[31] U. Heiz, F. Vanolli, A. Sanchez, and W.-D. Schneider, Size-Dependent Molecular Dissociation on Mass-Selected, Supported Metal Clusters, *Journal of the American Chemical Society* **120**, 9668-9671 (1998).

[32] P. J. Linstrom and W. G. Mallard, Eds., NIST Chemistry WebBook, NIST Standard Reference Database Number 69, March 2003, National Institute of Standards and Technology, Gaithersburg MD, 20899 (http://webbook.nist.gov).

Brill Academic Publishers
P.O. Box 9000, 2300 PA Leiden
The Netherlands

*Lecture Series on Computer
and Computational Sciences*
Volume 5, 2006, pp. 86-96

Recent progress in the computational study of transition metal doped Si clusters

Ju-Guang Han[1] and Frank Hagelberg[1]

The Computational Center for Molecular Structure and Interactions,
Jackson State University, Jackson, MS 39217, U.S.A.

Abstract: Computational investigations on silicon clusters (Si_n) in combination with atomic transition metal (TM) impurities are reviewed in this contribution. Emphasis is placed on studies that focus on the size evolution features of $TMSi_n$, such as the critical ligand number for the transition from exohedral to endohedral equilibrium geometry. Geometric, energetic, electronic and magnetic characteristics of $TMSi_n$ are discussed in the size region of $n \leq 20$. It is pointed out that selected $TMSi_n$ systems with $n = 12$ and $n = 16$ emerge from present computational research as the most promising candidates for building blocks of novel nanomaterials.

Keywords: Silicon, transition metals, clusters.

1. Introduction

Studies of small atomic and molecular clusters continue to be an extremely active area of current research. The properties of clusters depend sensitively on both their size and composition, and differ in general substantially from those of the respective bulk phase. In particular, numerous computational and experimental studies have been performed on small silicon clusters [1]. Silicon is the most important semiconducting material in the microelectronics industry. If current miniaturization trends continue, device sizes will soon approach the dimensions of atomic clusters [2]. In this context, silicon clusters are of particular relevance, as they may be employed not only as model systems for investigating localized effects in the condensed phase, but also as building blocks for developing new materials with tunable properties.

In recent years, mixed silicon-metal clusters [3-18] have attracted particular attention. These composites may be viewed as microscopic counterparts of materials of high importance to modern electronic devices, as the controlled manipulation of silicon-metal contacts is an essential facet of microelectronic engineering. Moreover, pure silicon clusters are not suitable as building blocks for novel materials since they are chemically reactive due to the existence of dangling bonds. Metal atom doped silicon clusters, on the other hand, may tend to form closed-shell electronic structures that are of higher stability than the pure species and represent a new class of endohedral clusters encapsulating metal atoms. The geometric rearrangement induced by an endohedrally connected metal atom in a silicon cluster and the impact of the metal impurity on the silicon cluster size evolution are among the primary questions to be addressed by experimental as well as computational research related to these structures. Within this effort, there will be a natural emphasis on transition metal atoms due to the flexibility and variability of their valence shell configurations and, correspondingly, the large range of their possible bonding patterns.

In the following, we will review the recent progress in the research related to silicon clusters with transition metal atom impurities. More specifically, we will give a very condensed account of the recent experimental findings in this field and subsequently highlight the theoretical efforts to understand the characteristic growth patterns of mixed silicon-metal clusters as well as their electronic, geometric, energetic and magnetic properties.

---

[1] Corresponding authors. E-mail: jghan@ustc.edu.cn , or E-mail: hagx@ccmsi.us

2. Experimental progress

In a pioneering series of experiments S. Beck [7] generated mixed transition metal silicide clusters of composition $TM@Si_nH_x$ (TM = Cu, Mo, W) by use of a laser vaporization supersonic expansion technique. These units were found to be more stable towards photofragmentation than pure Si clusters of similar size. Scherer et al. [5] produced mixed transition metal silicides by time-of-flight mass spectroscopy and studied the electronic states of CuSi, AgSi, and AuSi dimers by measuring their laser absorption spectra. In addition, the VSi and NbSi dimers have been investigated by matrix-isolated ESP spectroscopy [19].

Very recently, Hiura *et al.* [4] produced $TM@Si_nH_x^+$ (TM= Cr, Mo, W, Ir, Re, Hf, Ta; $n \leq 18$.) clusters in an ion trap. These units were generated by allowing the respective transition metal cation to react with silane (SiH_4) molecules. For each examined TM species, a characteristic maximum Si ligand number N was identified, further, the cation $TM@Si_N^+$ was found to be completely dehydrogenated, suggesting a high degree of both TM and Si bond saturation and correlated stability of the complex as a whole. In a further mass spectrometric measurement, Ohara et al. [6] used a double-rod laser technique to vaporize both components, TM (TM=Ti, Hf, Mo and W) and Si, and letting the atomic species react with each other. In these experiments, the anions MSi_{16}^- and MSi_{15}^- were detected with higher abundance than their neighboring species, and the transition metal turned out to be encapsulated in Si_n frames with larger ligand number than 15. From photoelectron spectroscopy, information was gained about the threshold detachment energy which gives an upper limit for the adiabatic electron affinity (EA). Along similar lines, the geometric and electronic structure of terbium-silicon clusters ($TbSi_n$ ($6 \leq n \leq 16$)) were investigated [6]. From trends observed in the electron affinities (EAs), the $TbSi_n^-$ clusters were subdivided into three groups of (I) $6 \leq n \leq 9$, (II) n = 10, 11, and (III) $n \geq 12$. This information combined with data on the adsorption reactivity toward H_2O allowed for the conclusion that a Tb atom is encapsulated inside a Si_n cage at $n \geq 10$.

Very recent spectroscopic work focused on chromium-doped Si_n clusters [20]. Specifically, the photoelectron spectra of anionic systems composed of Si_n in combination with one Cr atom were detected for $CrSi_n^-$ with n = 8 –12. From the measurement of vertical detachment energies, enhanced stability was found for the unit $CrSi_{12}$.

3. Theoretical progress.

In the following, we will give an overview of the main results that have emerged from the computational treatment of $TMSi_n$ systems so far. We distinguish between the size regions $n \leq 13$, as described under (1) and n > 13, discussed under (2). The research surveyed in the first subsection focuses mainly on the modification of small silicon clusters induced by an added TM impurity, as well as the evolution of $TMSi_n$ equilibrium geometries with special emphasis on the transition from exohedral to endohedral ground state structures. Efforts subsumed under (2) mostly aim at identifying composites of pronounced stability ('magic clusters') and providing a theoretical explanation of $TMSi_n$ abundances as recorded by mass spectrometric experiment.

1. $TMSi_n$ ($n \leq 13$)

The computational work done on transition metal – silicon clusters in this size regime may be subdivided into two categories. Firstly, systematic studies on systems with $n \leq 6$ and on selected systems with $n \leq 9$. These investigations aim mostly at the elucidation of the TM – Si bond in smaller clusters of the form $TMSi_n$ for varying choices of TM. Secondly, research on the size evolution of geometric and associated electronic and energetic properties on the broader scale of $1 \leq n \leq 12$ or $1 \leq n \leq 13$. We include in this category investigations that do not lead up to n = 12 or 13 but focus on issues related to cluster growth patterns such as the threshold size for the transition from exohedral to endohedral ground state equilibrium structures. Under (a) and (b), we summarize the main findings from the computational analysis of clusters in both these categories. Under (c), we highlight the recent discussion on the unit $TMSi_{12}$ which experiment has proven to be endohedral for TM = W [4].

(a) Case studies on smaller $TMSi_n$ ($n \leq 9$).

Scherer et al. [5] have studied the electronic states of CuSi, AgSi, and AuSi dimers by using CASPT2 method [21]. In addition, the bond energies of the VSi and NbSi dimers were reported [22,23]. For the systems MSi_n (M=Cr, Mo, W; n=1-6) [24-27], the relative stabilities and the charge-transfer mechanism operative within MSi$_n$ clusters were discussed, taking into account various spin configurations, at the B3LYP/LanL2DZ level [28-30]. From this study, internal electron transfer within TMSi$_n$ (TM = Mo, W) clusters in their equilibrium ground structures proceeds from Si atoms to W or Mo, i.e. the transition metal behaves as an electron acceptor. This pattern seems to be rooted in the tendency of Mo (W) to attain a completely filled 4d^{10} (5d^{10}) configuration. CrSi$_n$ (n=1-3,6) clusters, however, show a reversal of this trend.

The most stable TMSi$_n$ (TM = Mo, W; n=1-6) isomers were found to be spin singlets. For these systems, the spin S was systematically varied from S = 0 to S = 2 and, in some cases, to S = 3. From these investigations, the cluster stability turned out to be correlated with the spin of the system, decreasing monotonically with increasing spin. Similarly, the natural charge on the TM species was seen to be spin dependent. In the case of MoSi$_n$ with 1 < n < 7, electron transfer proceeds from the Si$_n$ subsystem to the Mo atom for S = 0, 1, and in the opposite direction for S = 2, 3. Analogous observations were made for WSi$_n$ with 1 < n < 5. For n =5, 6, no charge transfer reversal was found at S = 2. The case of S =3 has not been examined.

In response to experimental investigations of Si$_n$ clusters in combination with a Ir metal atom [4], which represent the first direct evidence for the existence of polyatomic iridium silicides, a computational study on IrSi$_9^+$ was performed [31]. The latter species is the smallest among the endohedral transition metal – silicon cluster cations identified in the ion trap experiment by Hiura et al. [4]. The B3LYP/LanL2DZ study described in ref. 31 discusses several plausible D$_{3h}$ endohedral cage geometries for the IrSi$_9^-$ species. These, however, were shown to distort. A stable isomer emerged from inserting the Ir impurity into the C$_{2v}$ cage of Si$_9$ whose symmetry was lowered to C$_s$ upon geometric relaxation. This resulting endohedral cluster was found to exceed the stability of various substitutional surface geometries generated from the equilibrium ground state structure of Si$_{10}$ by a substantial margin.

(b) Size evolution studies on TMSi$_n$ (1 ≤ n ≤ 13).

Efforts to understand the evolution pattern of TMSi$_n$ in the size range n ≤ 12 or 13 have been made for CuSi$_n$ (4 ≤ n ≤ 12) [32], TaSi$_n$ (1 ≤ n ≤ 13) [18] and ReSi$_n$ (1 ≤ n ≤ 12) [15]. The following paragraphs will give a survey of the computational findings obtained so far on these three types of composites.

Various studies have been devoted to small clusters of the composition CuSi$_n$ (n ≤ 6) [14, 33, 34, 35]. The systems CuSi$_n$ (n=4, 6) [33,34] were investigated by use of the DFT and quantum Monte Carlo methods. According to B3LYP studies [33], the electron transfer in Si$_n$Cu (n=4,6) [33] proceeds from Cu to Si atoms. From population analysis, the 3d shell of the Cu atom is only slightly altered in CuSi$_n$, in contrast to MSi$_n$ (M=Cr, Mo, W). The bonding nature in Si$_n$Cu was analyzed by correlating the HOMO of Si$_n$Cu to the LUMO of the corresponding Si$_n$ cluster. From this analysis, a dominant s-p or p-p bonding was found for the Cu-Si interaction as well as a weak d-p bonding. This bonding scheme differs from the interaction of 3d metals on silicon surfaces or 3d impurities in bulk silicon, where the bonding mechanism involves predominantly the overlap of Si(3p) and Cu(3d) orbitals. The relative energies, binding energies, and adsorption energies of three CuSi$_4$ and two CuSi$_6$ isomers have been computed by means of the fixed-node diffusion Monte Carlo (FNDMC), CASSCF, and B3LYP DFT methods [34]. Comparison with earlier Hartree-Fock (HF) and B3LYP DFT investigations of these systems [33] confirms the suitability of the DFT-B3LYP method for the prediction of the most stable CuSi$_4$ isomer, while for adsorption energies, the CASSCF method compares more favorably with FNDMC than B3LYP DFT. In addition, the small mixed species CuSi, Cu$_2$Si and CuSi$_2$ have been investigated [35] by valence ab initio calculations using energy-adjusted pseudopotentials.

In an attempt to elucidate the size evolution of CuSi$_n$ (n ≤ 12), a systematic DFT–B3LYP investigation has been performed [32] on CuSi$_n$ with n = 4, 6, 8, 10, 12. For each of these species, a variety of isomers has been identified and subjected to comparative analysis. In particular, numerous adsorption and substitution sites of the Cu impurity were described for n ≤ 8 while no stable center sites were found for n < 10. The case of CuSi$_6$ manifests the electron donor function of the Cu impurity, as the Si$_6$ subsystem adopts the C$_{2v}$ equilibrium structure of Si$_6^-$. It turned out that the stabilities of CuSi$_n$ (n=8,10) can be well related to those of Si$_n$. The Si frameworks remain nearly unchanged upon addition of Cu which is located at substitutional sites in many isomers of CuSi$_n$ (n=8,10). The obtained results are in keeping with mass spectrometric observations [7]. In particular, the high abundance of CuSi$_{10}$, as found experimentally, is attributed to both the enhanced stability of CuSi$_{10}$ over neighboring clusters and the existence of a large number of low-lying isomers. In addition, CuSi$_n$ cations and anions (n = 8, 10) were studied [32]. The cluster $CuSi_{12}$ is the smallest in the $CuSi_n$ series reported in [32] for which an endohedral ground state equilibrium structure is proposed. We comment on this species in further detail below in the context of a general discussion on $TMSi_{12}$.

Comparative investigations were performed on $ScSi_n$, YSi_n aand $CuSi_n$ (n = 1-6) clusters by use of the B3LYP method [14,36]. As seen from the examined equilibrium geometries in ref. 14, the structures identified for the most stable isomers of $TMSi_n$ are usually different for TM = Sc and Cu, showing different growth patterns of these two cluster series. On the basis of the calculated MSi_n (M=Cr,Mo,W Cu, Sc; n=1-6) equilibrium geometries, one concludes that the growth-path of the MSi_n clusters strongly depends on the nature of the transition metal impurity. While electron transfer is found to proceed from TM to the Si_n framework in all $TMSi_n$ clusters with M = Cu, Sc, it is more pronounced for TM = Sc than for TM = Cu. Bonding analysis of these species reveals that strong hybridization exists between Sc d and Si orbitals in $ScSi_n$, while the d shell of Cu in $CuSi_n$ remains nearly closed and contributes little to the Cu-Si bonding. On the basis of the optimized geometries, various energetic properties were calculated for the most stable isomers of MSi_n(M=Cu, n=1-6, 8, 10; M=Sc, n=1-6) including the binding and fragmentation energies, vertical and adiabatic ionization potentials, and electron affinities. Both the binding and fragmentation energies indicate that MSi_2, MSi_5 (M = Cu, Sc) and $CuSi_{10}$ have enhanced stability and could possibly be produced with high abundance in mass spectra.

The geometric structures, stabilities and electronic properties of $TaSi_n$ (n=1-13) clusters were investigated by a relativistic density functional theory method (RDFT) in conjunction with the generalized gradient approximation (GGA) [18]. Figure 1 displays the most stable structures identified in this research. The results of this study can be summarized as follows: (1) The architecture of most stable structures of $TaSi_n$ (n=1-6) resembles that of Si_{n-1}, with the exception of $TaSi_3$. Analogous observations were made for the $CuSi_n$ (n=1-6) series [12,37]. With increasing n, the Ta atom is seen to move gradually from an exohedral to an endohedral site of the lowest-energy $TaSi_n$ (n=1-13) isomers. The same phenomenon is observed for $ReSi_n$[15] clusters (see below). (2) The Ta-Si interaction is much weaker than that between neighboring Si atoms, so the structure of the Si_n framework in $TaSi_n$ (n=1-6) is dominated by the Si-Si interactions, and the Ta atom in low-lying $TaSi_n$ (n=1-11) clusters is always adsorbed to a cluster surface site. However, the Ta atom is encapsulated in the Si frame with n=12. (3) When the silicon number increases from 1 to 13, the net Mulliken population and Hirshfeld charge of the Ta atom of $TaSi_n$ vary from positive to negative. If n is 12 or 13, the transfer proceeds from Si to Ta, if n is between 1 and 11, from Ta to Si. (4) As documented by the average binding and fragmentation energies, the units $TaSi_n$ (n=2, 3, 5, 7, 10, 11, 12) show enhanced stabilities as compared to their respective neighbors. (5) The HOMO-LUMO gaps are markedly size and species dependent. As compared to pure silicon clusters, $TaSi_n$ clusters exhibit a universal narrowing of the HOMO-LUMO gap. This feature may call their suitability as building blocks of cluster assembled materials into question.

When comparing the computational results on $TaSi_n$ to the mass spectrometric results of Hiura and coworkers [4], one has to keep in mind that their findings refer to $TaSi_nH_x^-$ cations, showing particularly high abundance for the sizes n=4, 6, 8, 9, 11, 12, and 13. The influence of the positive charge on the equilibrium structures of small $TaSi_n$ units is significant. In the case of larger $TaSi_n$ (n≥12) clusters, the transition metal, although initially in a cationic charge state, will nevertheless be almost neutral after being encapsulated by the Si cages as the positive charges spreads over the whole cluster. These expectations were subjected to quantitative examination in a comprehensive study on the geometric, energetic, and bonding properties of the charged $TaSi_n^-$ (n=1-13) clusters, by use of the ADF program [38]. The results are summarized as follows.

The structures of the $TaSi_n^+$ cations deviate to some extent from those of their neutral counterparts, with especially marked geometric deformations exhibited by the units with n=4 and n=6, as reflected by pronounced differences between the respective VIPs and AIPs. The average of the atomic binding energy was calculated for each $TaSi_n^+$ system. It is found that this quantity increases monotonically as a function of n, while the binding energies of the neutral $TaSi_n$ sequence exhibit a less regular behavior. The small systems show enhanced stability at n=4 and 6 for $TaSi_n^+$, while at n=5 and n=7 for $TaSi_n$. The net Mulliken populations and the corresponding Hirshfeld charges are positive in the size regime n=1-11 both for $TaSi_n$ and $TaSi_n^+$. The positive charge in most of the $TaSi_n^+$ clusters leads to large HOMO-LUMO gaps, indicating chemical stability.

Theoretical investigations of $ReSi_n$ (n=1-12) clusters with doublet, quartet and sextet spin configurations were performed at the UB3LYP/LanL2DZ level [15]. This study includes total energies, equilibrium geometries and stabilities of $ReSi_n$ (n=1-12) clusters, together with fragmentation energies and averaged atomic binding energies as well as natural populations and natural electron configurations. In the most stable $ReSi_n$ (n=1-12) clusters, electron transfer proceeds from the Si constituents as well as from 6s orbital of Re to the 5d orbital of Re. With respect to their natural Re(5d) populations, the most stable $ReSi_n$ clusters with n = 1-12 may be subdivided into three groups, namely n=1,2, n=3-7 and n=8-12 with Re(5d) electronic occupation numbers of about six, seven and eight, respectively, in each case exceeding the 5d shell occupation of the free Re atom which is five. Further, the natural populations of Re(5d) and Re(6s) orbitals for the most stable $ReSi_n$ (n=1-12) clusters correlate with the number of coordinated silicon atoms. It is also observed that the natural population of Re(5d) increases while that of Re(6s) decreases as n goes from 1 to 12. Re acts as an electron acceptor, as charge from the Si constituents is predominantly transferred to the Re(5d) orbitals. This observation explains why the efficiency of semiconductors is degraded after Re is inserted into the Si bulk. It also implies that electrostatic interactions between Re and Si atoms play an important role in the stabilization of the clusters investigated. In particular, the stability of $ReSi_n$ (n=1-12) clusters is impacted by the degree of 5d shell saturation of Re. The most stable $ReSi_n$ (n=2-12) clusters adopt spin doublet configurations. ReSi, however, turns out to stabilize as a spin quartet.

With respect to $ReSi_n$ equilibrium geometries, one finds that Re locates in the most stable $ReSi_n$ (n=1-7) clusters at the surface site of the silicon frame. In the most stable $ReSi_n$ (n=8-12) clusters, however, Re is found to occupy a center position within the silicon frame. Therefore, $Re@Si_8$ turns out to be the smallest endohedral $ReSi_n$ system. The preference of a Re center site in the most stable $ReSi_n$ (n=8-12) systems is in keeping with the available experimental data on $TbSi_x$ (x=6-16) [6]. Locating at a central position, Re in $ReSi_n$(n=8-12) terminates dangling Si bonds with maximal efficiency.

The threshold number of silicon atoms in $TMSi_n$ clusters at which endohedral coordination is favored over adsorption or substitution varies with the type of TM atom. The growth pattern prevailing in the most stable $ReSi_n$ (n=9-12) clusters shows that the preferred structures are sandwich-like. Calculated fragmentation energies and averaged atomic binding energies indicate that the lowest-energy $ReSi_n$ (n=2,9,11,12) clusters are more stable than the remaining systems in this series.

Focusing on $NiSi_n$ units [39], we mention geometry optimizations carried out in the size regime $1 \leq n \leq 8$ at the B3LYP/LanL2DZ level. Calculations of total energies, fragmentation energies, natural populations and natural electron configurations have been performed for these clusters. Related to equilibrium geometry, the main finding of this work is that for n < 7, the Ni atom attaches to the cluster surface, while occupying a center site in $NiSi_8$. As observed by computation for $ReSi_n$ [15] and by experiment for $TbSi_n$ [6], the threshold size for endohedral coordination emerges again as n = 8. Pertaining to spin multiplicities obtained for $NiSi_n$, a spin triplet configuration is found for the most stable NiSi molecule. The same is found for $NiSi_2$ while the MSi_2 clusters with M=Cr, Mo, W, Re and Cu stabilize with lower spin multiplicities. The most stable $NiSi_n$ (n=3-8) clusters are found to be spin singlets. Studies of the electron transfer mechanism in $NiSi_n$ show that for n < 8, electrons are transferred from the Ni atom to the Si atoms, whereas for $NiSi_8$, the opposite electron transfer direction is observed. For the latter system, the electron donation from the Si_8 cage to the metal core is reflected by a sizeable ionic admixture which contributes to the stability of the $NiSi_8$ cluster. Relative stabilities were evaluated on the basis of the fragmentation energies with respect to removing one of the Si atoms from the $NiSi_n$ clusters. The results single out the $NiSi_2$ and $NiSi_8$ clusters as the most stable structures, corresponding to enhanced abundances observed for these species by mass spectroscopy.

For endohedral $FeSi_n$ clusters containing 9 – 11 Si atoms, equilibrium geometries, total energies, ionization potentials, electronic structure, and magnetic properties were calculated using the DFT-GGA method of NRLMOL code[40]. The geometries of pure Si_n clusters are shown to be substantially modified due to the presence of Fe, occupying a center location. The $FeSi_{10}$ cluster is more stable than its neighbors although not all Si atoms are fourfold coordinated. It is worth noting, however, that the stability of $FeSi_{10}$ is consistent with the 18-electron rule. The magnetic moment of Fe is quenched in all studied clusters.

The size evolution of $TM@Si_n$, with TM = Ti, Zr, Hf, has been investigated on the basis of a pseudopotential plane wave approach in the region $8 \leq n \leq 16$. While this series of calculations will receive further consideration in subsection (2), we mention at this place that the critical size for the transition to endohedral geometry was specified to be n = 13 in all three cluster sequences $TM@Si_n$ (TM = Ti, Zr, Hf). For smaller cages, basket – like open structures have been reported as stability maxima [41].

(c) The case $TM@Si_{12}$.

The threshold size for endohedral coordination in MSi_n turned out to be n = 8 for M = Re, Ni and Tb. For M = Cu, however this structural condition is met by n = 12 [32]. In this context, a striking parallel has been drawn between the units $CuSi_{12}$ and WSi_n [13]. The experimentally detected species WSi_{12}^+ (see section II) as well as the respective neutral cluster have been shown by extensive ab initio geometry optimization to adopt the shape of a regular hexagonal Si_{12} prism with the W atom in the center. The analysis of the $CuSi_n$ series [32] yielded a similar geometry as the likely ground state structure of both $CuSi_{12}^+$ and $CuSi_{12}$, namely a Si_{12} double chair arrangement of C_{2h} symmetry enclosing the metal atom impurity. The cage symmetry lowering as one goes from WSi_{12} to $CuSi_{12}$ has been interpreted as a consequence of the internal charge transfer operative in the two compared clusters. Specifically, addition of one electron to 12 Si atoms in a D_{6h} arrangement will give rise to Jahn-Teller distortion of the Si_{12} cage and thus cause the transition of the cage symmetry from D_{6h} to C_{2h}. This case is realized for Cu in Si_{12} which acts as an electron donor and transfers one electron to the cage. W, on the other hand, accepts two electrons from the cage, thus stabilizing Si_{12} in D_{6h} symmetry [13].

These results suggest the systematic importance of Si_{12} cages derived from regular structures with D_{6h} geometry for the architecture of silicon clusters containing metal atom impurities. In a comparative study, the salient features of endohedral $TMSi_{12}$ clusters with TM = Cu, Mo and W were addressed, as well as several cationic and anionic species of these systems, with regard to their geometric, electronic and magnetic structure [13] The interaction between the Si_{12} cage and the enclosed metal impurity is characterized as strongly delocalized bonding for TM = Re, Ta, Ru, Mo, W, associated with substantial electron transfer from the Si_{12} cage to the transition metal impurity. Cu, in contrast, tends to form directed bonds with selected atoms of the cage. Linear extension of the MSi_{12} (M = Mo, W) cells along their principal axes leads to stable units of the form M_2Si_{18} (see Figure 2), suggesting the possibility of a linear continuation of these systems to arrive at silicon nanowires encapsulating a one-dimensional chain of metal atoms.

A computational study of the equilibrium geometries and total energies of Cr enclosed by Si_n clusters reveals that $Cr@Si_{12}$ is more stable than its neighbors [43]. The enhanced stability of $CrSi_{12}$ as well as $FeSi_{10}$ [40, 42] and WSi_{12} [24], is consistent with the 18-electron sum rule commonly used in the interpretation of stability patterns in organometallic complexes [44]. This observation suggests that the 18 electron rule might provide a criterion for magic numbers of Si ligands in $TMSi_n$ clusters. It has been further emphasized that the 6 μ_B magnetic moment of the caged Cr atom, the largest among the 3d transition metal atoms, is completely quenched in $CrSi_{12}$ [43]. This case exemplifies a strong cage-induced effect on the properties of a transition metal atom. The impact of caging may be used in the synthesis of novel cluster based materials.

Sen and Mitas investigated a wide variety of TM impurity atoms encapsulated in a Si_{12} hexagonal prism cage [45]. In this work, geometry optimizations using DFT were complemented by total energy calculations of the obtained equilibrium structures at the level of Quantum Monte Carlo (QMC) computation. The results of this study reflect considerable stability of the $TMSi_{12}$ unit, irrespective of the impurity TM. This observation casts doubt on the hypothesis that the stabilities of $TMSi_n$ clusters are largely determined by a simple 18 electrons counting rule. Further, it has been established for systems with an even number of electrons that the multiplicity of the ground states can be "tuned" between spin singlet and triplet character by varying the TM atom type, while systems with odd numbers of electrons turn out to be spin doublets.

Moreover, the possibility of forming solids with hexagonal structure from selected clusters of the form $TMSi_{12}$ has been explored [45]. On one hand, the stability of $TMSi_{12}$ systems depends but weakly on the TM species. On the other hand, it is recognized that the electronic properties of structurally analogous clusters are determined sensitively by the transition metal atom involved, providing the means of tailoring cluster assembled materials with tunable properties.

2. $TM@Si_n (n>13)$

In the intermediate size range, structural and electronic properties of metal-doped silicon clusters $TMSi_n$ (TM = W, Zr, Os, Pt, Co, etc.) were investigated by ab initio theory [46] for $8 \leq n \leq 20$, adopting the B3LYP/LanL2DZ approach. In this work, geometry optimizations were performed on the basis of some selected highly symmetric Si_n cage structures, defining the initial geometries for both endohedral and exohedral $TM@Si_n$ clusters. The authors compared the size dependence of both the binding and the embedding energy and were able to identify a set of species for which both of these quantities show 'magic' behavior, i.e. are markedly elevated as compared to the neighboring species. Besides two $TMSi_n$ units with n = 12, namely $Os@Si_{12}$ and $W@Si_{12}$, these are: $Zr@Si_{14}$, $W@Si_{15}$ and $Zr@Si_{16}$. The results of this computation suggest maximal abundance for the WSi_n series at n > 12, more specifically at n = 15 or possibly at n = 16, in accordance with the experimental findings of Ohara et al. [47]. It is conjectured that the deviating magic numbers for $TMSi_n$, namely n = 12 from the measurement of Hiura et al. [4] and n = 15, 16 from that of Ohara et al. [47] are related to the different avenues of cluster fabrication followed in these two experiments. Thus, the combination of W^- with silane gas, as employed in [4], may lead to an incomplete reaction between the TM and Si constituents of $TMSi_n$, while this problem is avoided by letting the TM species react with atomic Si.

Isomers of $TMSi_{15}$ with group VIa TM elements, i.e. TM = Cr, Mo, W, and prism-like Si frame geometries are reported in ref. [16]. In this study, stable $TMSi_{15}$ and $TMSi_{15}^-$ units are discussed (TM = Cr, Mo, W), the stability of $TMSi_{15}$ exceeding that of $TMSi_{15}^+$. In keeping with the conclusion drawn in ref. [46], $TM@Si_{15}$ (TM=Cr, Mo, W) clusters are found to be more stable than their counterparts $TMSi_{15}$ with TM located at adsorption sites on the Si_{15} cluster. Two slightly deviating isomers were found for $Mo@Si_{15}$ and $W@Si_{15}$, where the differences between the two structures pertain to the binding energy and the equilibrium geometry. The Mulliken atomic net populations of group VIa TM in both $TM@Si_{15}$ and $TM@Si_{15}^+$ clusters are negative, in accordance with the respective observations made on $TMSi_{12}$ and (TM = Cr, Mo, W), indicating electron transfer from the Si ligands to the TM center.

Pseudopotential plane wave computations using the generalized gradient approximation for the exchange-correlation energy were carried out for various species of the form $TMSi_n$, n > 13 and TM = Fe, Ru, Os, Ti, Zr, Hf [42, 46, 47]. Depending on the size of the transition metal (TM) atom, the silicon matrix was shown to form fullerene-like $Zr@Si_{16}$ and tetrahedral Frank-Kasper shaped $Ti@Si_{16}$ as well as $TM@Si_{14}$, TM = Fe, Ru, Os, cage clusters, the latter adopting cubic form. The term 'fullerene-like' refers to a cage composed of regular pentagonal or hexagonal rings. For a further composite, $Hf@Si_{16}$, the fullerene–like structure was shown to be nearly degenerate with the Frank – Kasper alternative [48].

The embedding energy of the group IVa (Ti, Zr, Hf) and VIIa (Fe, Ru, Os) TM atoms investigated in [42, 46] turned out to be approximately 12 eV due to strong TM-Si interactions that give rise to compact cage structures. This finding is further confirmed by results obtained for systems of the form $TMSi_{15}$ (TM = Cr, Mo, W) [16]. The bonding operative in the endohedral group IVa $TM@Si_n$ clusters has been characterized as predominantly metallic, and the HOMO – LUMO gap amounts to approximately 1.5 eV. However, exceptionally large gaps of about 2.4 eV are obtained for the $TM@Si_{16}$ (TM = Ti, Zr, Hf) Frank-Kasper tetrahedral polyhedron. The latter finding, however, deviates substantially from an available experimental result of 1.90 eV [9] for $Ti@Si_{16}$. The interaction between these systems is weak, making them candidates for building bricks of cluster-assembled materials.

The most stable $TaSi_{16}$ isomer and its cationic counterpart are found to be endohedral structures, stabilizing in a slightly distorted C_{4v} frame. Similar to $TiSi_{16}$ and VSi_{16}^+ clusters, the $TaSi_{16}^+$ cation is a 20 electron system. However, the HOMO-LUMO gaps of $TaSi_{16}$ is predicted to be 1.734 eV [38], which is smaller than the respective experimental result (1.90 eV) for the $TiSi_{16}$ cluster [9].

In addition to the systems mentioned above, $ZrSi_{20}$ has been investigated at the LDA level [11]. From this calculation, an embedding energy of 11.23 eV was found. It is thus in the same range of embedding energies reported for $TM@Si_n$ with n = 14, 16 which suggests a certain persistence of the cage – core bonding features for $TM@Si_n$ with $14 \leq n \leq 20$ and for a variety of transition metal species.

Systems of the form $Re@Si_x$ (x=12,16,20,24,28,32,36,40) [49] with doublet, quartet, and sextet spin configurations were studied at the UHF/LanL2DZ level, supported by vibrational frequency analysis in each case. In this work, equilibrium structures, total energies, stabilities, Mulliken atomic net populations of the Re atom as well as the HOMO-LUMO gaps of $Re@Si_x$ clusters were examined. The results demonstrate that all $ReSi_x$ systems with highly symmetric initial structures undergo slight distortions into geometries of sizeable higher stability but lower symmetry. The Re atom in $Re@Si_x$ (x=12, 16, 20, 24, 28, 32, 36, 40) cages locates at off-center positions of Si_x clusters and acts as an electron acceptor. Correspondingly, an ionic admixture to the bonding between the Re impurity and the Si cage atoms contributes to the stability of Si_x cages. In addition, Si_m cages encapsulating W_n and Ni_n (n=1-5) transition metal clusters were investigated [50], with emphasis on their magnetism, their electronic populations, and equilibrium geometries.

4. Summary

We have given a brief survey of the extensive computational efforts devoted to systems of composition $TM@Si_n$ in the size range $n \leq 40$. These species have been analyzed by means of various quantum chemical *ab initio* and/or Density Functional Theory procedures. With respect to cluster equilibrium geometry, the following main observations are made:

(1) The smaller $TM@Si_n$ systems adopt exohedral, the larger endohedral geometries. The critical size for the transition from the former to the latter structural type varies from n = 8 (as observed e.g. for TM = Ta, Re) to n = 12, as found for TM = Ti, Zr, Hf.

(2) Below the critical size, the geometry of $TM@Si_n$ is largely dictated by the architecture of pure silicon clusters. In particular, the TM species may occupy an adsorption or a substitution site. The respective cluster geometries are thus determined by the Si_n or the Si_{n-1} framework, respectively.

(3) The preferred endohedral geometries identified for $TM@Si_n$ beyond the critical size depend strongly on the nature of TM.

For the prospect of assembling novel nanomaterials with tunable properties from $TM@Si_n$ clusters, 'magic numbers' of Si ligands corresponding to systems of enhanced stability, are of major practical interest. From extended size evolution studies the ligand number 12 has been associated with elevated stability for the series $W@Si_n$, while stability maxima at n = 16 have been obtained for the series $TM@Si_n$ (TM = Ti, Zr, Hf) and again $W@Si_n$, in agreement with available experimental results. Elementary electron counting rules have turned to be too simplistic to account for the observed order of stabilities. The embedding energies of the most stable $TM@Si_n$ isomers were found to be in the order of 10 eV or larger, making them comparable to those of metallofullerenes.

For the smaller ones among the investigated $TM@Si_n$ complexes, the interaction between the TM species and the Si_n frame is characterized by substantial ionic admixtures due to charge transfer between the two cluster subsystems. Electron donating behavior has been established for TM = Cu, while group VIa transition metal atoms as well as Re act, in their most stable spin multiplicities, as electron acceptors. For TM = Ni and Ta, the electron transfer direction has been found to change with the size of the Si_n frame. More specifically, adsorbed or substitutional Ni (Ta) atoms were shown to be electron donors while Si_n encapsulated Ni (Ta) cores turned out to be electron acceptors. A correlation between the electron transfer within $TM@Si_{12}$, with respect to both extent and direction, and the cage symmetry has been described. For larger endohedral systems, such as $TM@Si_{16}$, metallic bonding characteristics have been emphasized.

Studies on the magnetism of $TMSi_n$ clusters have mostly been confined so far to small systems with n < 7. However, for $CrSi_{12}$ it has been shown that the high magnetic moment of the TM species is completely quenched upon implantation into the Si_{12} enclosure.

The computational treatment of $TMSi_n$ is progressing at a fast pace, largely as a consequence of a fruitful collaboration between experiment and theory that has been initialized during recent years. As a result, the salient features of these species, pertaining to their geometries, stabilities, electronic and magnetic properties, are increasingly well understood. In conclusion, it is hoped that the next step, namely the nanotechnological application of these units in the fabrication of novel materials, will be done in the near future.

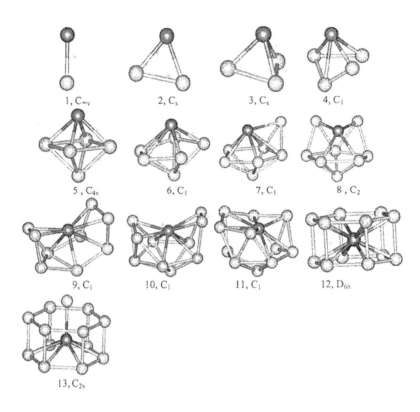

Figure 1 Geometries of the most stable $TaSi_n$ (n=1-13) clusters.

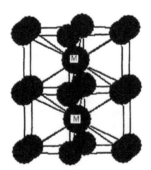

Figure 2, The equilibrium geometries of TM_2Si_{18} (M=Mo,W) clusters.

Acknowledgment

This work is supported by National Natural Science foundation of P. R. China (20173055), by the National Science Foundation through the grants HRD-9805465, NSFESP-0132618 and DMR-0304036, by the National Institute of Health through the grant S06-GM008047, and by the Army High Performance Computing Research Center under the auspices of Department of the Army, Army Research Laboratory under Cooperative Agreement No. DAAD 19-01-2-

References

[1] Ho K. M., Shvartsburg A. A., Pan B., Lu Z. Y., Wang C. Z., Wacker J. G., Fye J., and Jarrold M. F, *Nature*, **392** (1998) 582.

[2] Shvartsburg A. A., Liu B., Jarrold, M. F., Ho K. M., *J. Chem. Phys.* 112 (2000) 4517.

[3] Majumder C., Chiranjib K., *Phys. Rev. B*, 69(2004)115432.

[4] Hiura H.,Miyazaki T., Kanayama T., *Phys. Rev. Lett.*, 86 (2001)1733.

[5] Scherer J. J.,Paul J. B., Collier C. P., Saykally R. J., *J. Chem. Phys.*, 102 (1995) 5190.

[6] Ohara M., Miyajima K., Pramann, A., Nakajima A.,Kaya K., *J. Phys. Chem. A*,106 (2002) 3702; *Chem. Phys. Lett.*371 (2003) 490.

[7] Beck S. M., *J. Chem. Phys.*, 90 (1989) 6306.

[8] Maroulis G., Pouchan C., *Phys.Chem.Chem.Phys.*, 5 (2003) 1992.

[9] Koyasu K., Akutsu M., Mitsui M., Nakajima A., *J. Am. Chem. Soc.*, in press.

[10] Han J. G., Ren Z. Y., Sheng L. S, Zhang Y. W., Morales J. A., Hagelberg F., *J. Mol. Struct. (Theochem).* 625(2003)47.

[11] Jackson K., Nellermoe B., *Chem. Phys. Lett.*,254 (1996) 249.

[12] Xiao, C.; Hagelberg, F.; Ovcharenko, I.; Lester, W. A. *THEOCHEM* (2001), 549, 181.

[13] Hagelberg F., Xiao C., Lester W. A. Jr, Phys. Rev. B, 67(2003)32426.

[14] Xiao C., Abraham A., Quinn R., Hagelberg F. et al, *J. Phys. Chem. A*, 106 (2002) 1380.

[15] Han J. G., Ren Z. Y., Lu B. Z, *J. Phys. Chem. A*, 108 (2004) 5100.

[16] Han J. G., Shi Y. Y., *Chem. Phys.*, 266 (2001) 33.

[17] Han J. G., *Chem. Phys.*, 286 (2003) 181.

[18] Guo P., Ren Z. Y., Wang F., Bian J., Han J. G., Wang G. H., *J. Chem. Phys.*, 121 (2004) 12265.

[19] Harrick Y. M., Weltner W. Jr, *J. Chem. Phys.*, 94 (1991) 3371.

[20] Zheng W., Nilles J. M., Radisic D., Bowen K. H., *J.Chem.Phys.* 122, 71101 (2005).

[21] Turski P., *Chem. Phys. Lett.*, 315 (1999) 115.

[22] Gringerick K. A, *J. Chem. Phys.*,50 (1969) 5426.

[23] Auwera-Mahieu A. V., McIntyre N. S., Drowert J., *Chem. Phys. Lett.* 4 (1969) 198.

[24] Han J. G., Xiao C., Hagelberg F., *Structural Chemistry*,13 (2002) 173.

[25] Han J. G., Hagelberg F., *Chem. Phys.*, 263 (2001) 255.

[26] Han J. G., Hagelberg F., *J. Mol. Struct. (Theochem)*,549 (2001) 165.

[27] Yuan Z. S., Zhu L. F.,Tong X. et al., *J. Mol. Struct. (Theochem)*, 589 (2002) 229.

[28]Lee, C.; Yang, W.; Parr, R. G. *Phys. Rev. B.* 27(1988) 785.

[29] Wadt W. R., Hay P. J., *J. Chem. Phys.*, 82 (1985) 284

[30] Becke, A. D. *J. Chem. Phys.*, 98 (1993) 1372.

[31] Hagelberg F., Xiao C., *Struct. Chem.* 14 (2003) 487.

[32] Xiao C., Hagelberg F., Lester W. A. Jr, *Phys. Rev. B*, 66 (2002) 075425

[33] Xiao, C.; Hagelberg, F., *THEOCHEM.*,529 (2000) 241.

[34] Ovcharenko I.; Lester W. A., Jr.; Xiao C.; Hagelberg F., *J. Chem. Phys.* 114 (2001) 9028.

[35] Plass W., Stoll H., Preuss H., Savin A., *J. Mol. Struct. (Theochem)* 339 (1995) 67.

[36] Xiao C., Blundell J., Hagelberg F., Lester W. A. Jr., *Int. J. of Quant. Chem.*96 (2004) 416.

[37] Hagelberg F., Yanov I., Leszczynski J., *J. Mol. Struct. (Theochem)*487(1999)183.

[38] Guo P., Ren Z., Yang A. P., Han J. G., Wang G. H., *submitted.*

[39] Ren Z., Li F., Guo P., Han J. G., *J. Mol. Struct. (Theochem)*, 718 (2005)165.

[40] Khanna S. N., Rao B. K., Jena P., Nayak S. K., *Chem. Phys. Lett.* 373(2003)433.

[41] Kawamura H.,Kumar V., Kawazoe Y., *Phys.Rev.B* 71, 75423 (2005)

[42] Mpourmpakis G., Froudakis G. E., Andriotis A. N., Menon M., *J. Chem. Phys.*, 119 (2003) 7498.

[43] Khanna S N, Rao B K., Jena P, *Phys. Rev. Lett.*, 89 (2002) 016803.

[44] Pandey R.,Rao B. K., Jena P., Blanco M. A., *J.Am.Chem.Soc.* 123, 3799 (2001).

[45] Sen P., Mitas L., *Phys. Rev. B* 68 (2003) 155404

[46] Lu J., Nagase S., *Phys. Rev. Lett.*, 90 (2003) 115506.

[47] Wang J., Han J. G., *J. Chem. Phys.*, 123 (2005) 064306.

[48] Kumar V., Kawazoe Y., *Phys. Rev. Lett.*, 87 (2001) 045503.

[49] Han J. G., Huang M. J.,Watts J., *submitted.*

[50] Han J. G., *in preparation.*

Brill Academic Publishers
P.O. Box 9000, 2300 PA Leiden
The Netherlands

Lecture Series on Computer
and Computational Sciences
Volume 5, 2006, pp. 97-102

Ab initio studies on the aromaticity of mixed tetramer neutral clusters

Sandeep Nigam, Chiranjib Majumder[1] and S.K.Kulshreshtha

Novel Materials and Structural Chemistry Division,
Bhabha Atomic Research Centre, Trombay, Mumbai-400085

Abstract: Ab initio calculations were performed to asses the aromatic behavior of mixed tetramer neutral cluster (Be_2N_2, Be_2P_2, Mg_2N_2, Mg_2P_2). Harmonic vibrational analysis has been performed to ensure the stability of the optimized geometries. The analysis of structure, vibrational frequencies, and molecular orbitals indicates that all these tetramer favor planar atomic configuration as the lowest energy structure and exhibit the characteristics of aromaticity (planarity and two π- electrons in the delocalized molecular orbital). Other than this, the aromatic character of these clusters has been verified based on established criteria of aromaticity such as chemical (extra stability), and magnetic criteria i.e. by calculating Nuclear Independent Chemical Shift (NICS) at the ring centers. The extra electronic stability of these clusters towards donating or accepting of electrons is also reflected in the calculated large ionization potential and low electron affinity

Keywords: Aromaticity, tetramer cluster.

1. Introduction

Conventionally, aromaticity is related with the cyclic, planar and conjugated molecules with (4n+2) π electron and having specific chemical and structural stability. Aromaticity was traditionally associated with special class of organic molecule such as benzene and its derivatives, which was further extended to include heterosystems and organometallic compounds. However, the criteria used to validate the aromaticity of a chemical compound are controversial, due to the fact that a well-established definition of these concepts has yet to be presented in a quantitative way for general use. There in no direct way to measure aromaticity in a molecule experimentally. In benzene which is a prototype aromatic molecule, the experimental verification has been done by indirect methods i.e, heat of hydrogenation and de-shielded NMR Chemical shift. Recent studies by Li et. al. [1] have extended the concept of aromaticity to include unconventional metal aromaticity. They reported experimental and theoretical evidence of aromaticity in Al_4^{-2} an all metal system. The Al_4^{-2} unit was having square planar shape with two delocalized pi electrons in the highest occupied molecular orbital(HOMO). As, the 4n+2 electron counting rule is satisfied with the two delocalized pi electron, the square planar Al_4^{-2} was proposed to be aromatic. Later various studies proved that Al_4^{-2} has multifold aromaticity (both sigma and pi). In the recent year many articles has been published [2-33] to corroborate the aromatic and anti-aromatic character of small metal and main group element clusters. All most all these studies published in recent years on aromaticity or anti-aromaticity of cluster are mainly concentrated on the charged cluster and very few studies on the neutral cluster are reported. As the charged clusters are relatively unstable as compared to the neutral cluster hence it is desirable to find out stable neutral cluster exhibiting aromatic behavior. In our earlier work[34] we have reported some stable neutral cluster (Al_2Si_2, Al_2Ge_2, Ga_2Si_2, Ga_2Ge_2, Si_3Be, Si_3Mg, Ge_3Be, Ge_3Mg, Al_3P, Al_3As, Ga_3P, and Ga_3As) with 14 *p* electron in the valance shell and their aromatic behavior were established. In this work we have performed ab initio calculation to asses the aromatic behavior of mixed tetramer neutral cluster (Be_2N_2, Be_2P_2, Mg_2N_2, Mg_2P_2,) with 14 *p* electron in the valance shell. The motivation to choose these clusters is to understand the electronic structure and geometric arrangement of isoelectronic tetramer cluster consisting group two and group five elements. As group II and group V elements have S^2 and P^3

---

[1] Corresponding author. E-mail: chmaju@magnum.barc.ernet.in

configuration in their outer most orbital, therefore it is expected that the interaction between these would be weak and can be governed by dispersion force. Harmonic vibrational analysis has been performed to ensure the stability of the optimized geometries. Further to verify the aromatic character of these clusters, conventional criteria of aromaticity such as chemical (extra stability), and magnetic criteria (i.e. Nuclear Independent Chemical Shift (NICS)) has been utilized. Large ionization potential and low electron affinity of the entire cluster studied indicates extra electronic stability of these clusters towards donating or accepting of electrons.

2. Computational Details

Ab-initio molecular orbital theory based on LCAO approach has been employed to elucidate the ground state geometries of these clusters. For this purpose geometry optimization was done using MP2 level of theory. A standard split-valence with polarization functions (6-311+G(d)) was employed as basis set for all these calculations. The core was taken to zero in all calculations. The stability of the lowest energy isomers has been verified from the vibrational frequency analysis at MP2 level[40]. All the calculations were carried out using the GAMESS software [41]. Chemcraft software package has been used to plot the orientations of molecular orbitals. The Nuclear Independent chemical shift (NICS) values were calculated using the gauge-including atomic orbitals (GIAO) method at the MP2 level of theory using the Gaussian 98 program [42].

3. Result and Discussion

The equilibrium geometry all these cluster has been obtained by considering two planar structures viz. cis- and trans- configurations. Three dimensional tetrahedron and other geometries resulted in significantly higher energy as compared to the planer configurations. The difference in the stability between cis and trans isomers can be estimated from the corresponding total energies as listed in table-1. In this table we have summarized the results of the geometrical parameters, total energies, binding energies (B.E.), vertical ionization potentials (VIP) and the vertical electron affinity (VEA). In all the case the trans isomer was found to be more stable in comparison of cis isomer. In case of Mg_2N_2 the even the cis isomer was found to very much higher in energy so not included in the list.

Table-1-Total energies, interatomic separations (Å), binding energy (B.E), vertical ionization potentials (VIP), vertical electron affinity (VEA) and global hardness η for tetramer clusters. The results presented here have been calculated using the *ab initio* molecular orbital theory at the MP2/6-311+G(d) level .Diagonal bond length are not included.

Cluster	Symmetry	Total Energy(a.u.)	B.E. (eV)	N-N/ P-P	M-M	M-N/ M-P	VIP (eV)	VEA (eV)	η (eV)
Be_2N_2	C_{2v}	-138.5560547	9.00	1.26	1.96	1.57,1.63	8.37	0.91	7.46
Be_2N_2	D_{2h}	-138.5655279	9.26	-	-	1.54	7.44	-0.43	7.87
Be_2P_2	C_{2v}	-711.0013276	3.75	2.37	2.72	1.91	7.15	-2.13	9.28
Be_2P_2	D_{2h}	-711.0891579	6.14	-	-	1.98	6.48	-1.57	8.05
Mg_2N_2	D_{2h}	-508.6571718	3.87	-	-	1.92	7.73	1.62	6.11
Mg_2P_2	C_{2v}	-1081.1955769	1.16	2.08	2.73	2.39	3.38	-1.99	5.36
Mg_2P_2	D_{2h}	-1081.2679543	3.13	-	-	2.37	7.58	-0.50	8.08

In table -2 we have listed the binding energy and bond length of dimmers. In order to verify the reliability of the MP2/6-311+G(d) level of calculations, an initial test we have compare the results with the available experimental values and we found a good agreement suggesting the reliability of the computational method applied in this work. As can be seen from the table-2 the Be-N/Be-P bonds are much stronger than the Mg-N/Mg-P that is why beryllium clusters are more stable than the corresponding magnesium clusters.

From the stability point of view, a molecule or cluster is stable if it is resistant to undergo addition reaction with either an electrophile or nucleophile. To satisfy these properties the molecule/cluster should have higher ionization potential as well as low electron affinity. Higher ionization energy and the lower electron affinity of all these clusters further corroborate their stability towards any addition reaction as may be seen from table-1. Both vertical ionization potential and vertical electron affinity were calculated by single point calculation after putting the charge on the optimized geometry of neutral.

Table 2. Dimer energies (experimental values in parehtheses).

Dimer	Mult	B.E.(eV)	Bond Length(Å)
Be-Be	1	0.02(0.05)	2.84
N-N	1	9.51(9.43)	1.12(1.11)
	3	1.25	1.29
P-P	1	4.12(4.85)	1.93(1.89)
	3	0.43	1.98
Mg-Mg	1	0.02(0.02)	4.25(3.89)
Be-N	2	0.58	1.53
	4	1.45	1.60
Be-P	2	0.42	1.77
	4	1.10	2.06
Mg-N	2	-0.36	1.95
	4	0.25	2.07
Mg-P	2	-0.41	2.36
	4	0.33	2.55

The high stability of these clusters is also reflected in their global hardness, η. (η=VIP-VEA) In order to further confirm the stability of the ground state geometries obtained for these neutral clusters we have carried out the frequency analysis of the vibrational energy spectrum at MP2/6-311+G(d) level and the corresponding list of frequencies along with their intensities are summarized in table-3. It is important to note that no imaginary frequency was found for any of these clusters suggesting the stability of the equilibrium geometries.

Table 3. Vibrational frequencies (cm^{-1}) and IR intensities of neutral tetramers calculated in this work at MP2-6-311+G (d) level.

Clusters	Symmetry	Vibrational frequency (IR intensities)			
Be$_2$N$_2$	C$_{2v}$	311.73(1.12)	500.53(1.80)	714.02(0.29)	813.93(0.39)
		933.80(1.94)	1418.60(0.28)		
Be$_2$N$_2$	D$_{2h}$	1115.22(4.24)	1136.47(26.35)	1421.61(1.22)	
Be$_2$P$_2$	C$_{2v}$	135.01(0.01)	159.88(0.07)	567.77(3.06)	892.75(0.06)
		932.83(7.24)			
Be$_2$P$_2$	D$_{2h}$	689.49(1.87)	714.40(10.27)	737.07(10.73)	
Mg$_2$N$_2$	D$_{2h}$	1734.83(43.74)	825.23(18.29)		
Mg$_2$P$_2$	C$_{2v}$	342.68(0.79)	396.11(4.15)	441.16(0.08)	
Mg$_2$P$_2$	D$_{2h}$	426.24(1.91)	429.70(3.54)		

In order to understand the nature of bonding, the spatial orientations of five occupied molecular orbitals (HOMO to HOMO-4) have been worked out for these cluster and representative results are shown in fig. 1. It is clear from this figure that all the clusters have one of the HOMO energy level representing π type molecular orbital where two electrons are delocalized over all four atoms. In case of Be_2N_2 and HOMO-2 which is of π-type and also fully delocalized while HOMO-1 is in the case of Be_2P_2 and Mg_2P_2 as can be seen from the figure.

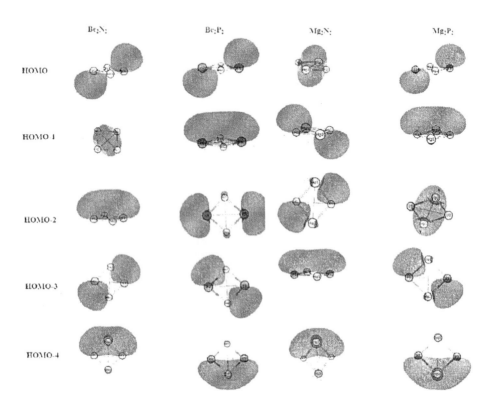

Figure 1: Spatial Orientation of top five occupied molecular orbitals for Be_2N_2, Be_2P_2, Mg_2N_2, Mg_2P_2.

As discussed earlier, NMR chemical shift has been used as the experimental tool to probe aromaticity. Deshielded NMR chemical shift of benzene indicates the diatropic ring current in the molecules. Therefore aromaticity of all these cluster has also been studied by using the Nucleus Independent chemical shift (NICS), method developed by Schleyer and co-workers[35], which is a magnetic criterion that mirrors the ring current. In this method, the nuclear magnetic resonance (NMR) parameters are calculated for a ghost atom, usually placed at the centre of ring, and the NICS value is the negative of the isotropic magnetic shielding constant at the ghost atom. System with negative NICS values are aromatic, since negative values arise when diatropic ring current (shielding) dominates, whereas systems with positive values are antiaromatic because positive value arise when paratropic current (deshielding) dominates. Schleyer et. al. have found the NICS value for benzene to be -9.7 and 27.6 for cyclobutadiene at B3LYP/6-31+G* level[35]. Nonaromatic cyclic system should therefore have NICS values around zero. The more negative the NICS, the more aromatic the system is. In this study we have calculate the NICS (0.0), NICS (0.5) and NICS (1.0), by placing the ghost atom at the ring centre and above by 0.5 Å and 1.0 Å respectively from the four member ring centre. The NICS (0.0) values calculated at the centre of ring, is influenced by σ-bonds, whereas the NICS (0.5), NICS (1.0) values calculated 0.5Å and 1.0Å out of the plane get effected more by the π−system. The results obtained are given in Table-4.

Table 4. NICS values of the cluster

Cluster	Symmetry	NICS(0.0)	NICS(0.5)	NICS(1.0)
Be_2N_2	D_{2h}	-70.29	-30.73	-1.59
Be_2P_2	D_{2h}	8.82	0.33	-6.66
Mg_2N_2	D_{2h}	-66.18	-45.74	-18.57
Mg_2P_2	D_{2h}	-48.68	-38.92	-20.99

These results indicate that all the ring systems studied in the present work are aromatic. In case of Be_2P_2 we found results obtained from the two places are greatly different. NICS (0.0) show positive value but NICS(1.0) was found to be less than zero. This is similar to the observation made by Li et. al.[36] in case of N_4^{-2} and by boldyrev et. al.[37] in case of O_4^{-2}, S_4^{+2}. The reason behind this is, the strong influenced by the local contribution by local sigma bonds. NICS(1.0) value is -6.66 suggesting diatropic ring current by π electrons and revealing the aromatic character of the cluster.

4. Conclusion

We performed a series of *ab initio* calculation on mixed tetramer neutral cluster (Be_2N_2, Be_2P_2, Mg_2N_2, Mg_2P_2) having 14 electrons in their valence shell and all our result clearly show the presence of the global minimum planar structure with trans configuration. All these clusters having 6-p electrons in the outermost orbitals form at least one π-type molecular orbital where two electrons are delocalized over all four atoms. The extra stability of these clusters has been illustrated through their hardness, high IP, low EA. The presence of two π electrons (thus following 4n+2 rule) and appreciable NICS(1.0) values confirmed that these extra stable planar mixed tetramer cluster are aromatic.

Acknowledgments

We are thankful to the members of the Computer Division, BARC, for their kind cooperation during this work. We gratefully acknowledge the help of Dr. Naresh Patwari for providing NICS values for these entire clusters calculated in this work.

References

[1] X.Li, A.K. Kuznetsov, H. Hai-Feng Zhang, A. I. Boldyrev, L. Wang.; *Science*, **291**,859 (2001).
[2] S. Shetty, D. G. Kanhere, S. Pal, *J. Phys. Chem. A*, **108**,628(2004).
[3] A. E. Kuznetsov, A. I. Boldyrev, *Chem. Phys. Lett.*, **388**,452(2004).
[4] J. selius, M. Straka, D. Sundholm, *J. Phys. Chem. A*, **105**, 9939(2001).
[5] A. E. Kuznetsov, K. A. Birch, A. I. Boldyrev, X. Li, H. J. Zhai, L. S. Wang, L. S.; *Science*, **300**, 623(2003).
[6] J. M. Mecero, J. M. Ugalde, *J. Am. Chem. Soc.*, **126**, 3380(2004).
[7] P. W. Fowler, R. W. A. Havenith, E. Steiner, *Chem. Phys. Lett.*,**342**, 85(2001).
[8] P. W. Fowler, R. W. A. Havenith, E. Steiner, *Chem. Phys. Lett.*,**359**, 530(2002).
[9] A. E. Kuznetsov, A. I. Boldyrev, X. Li, L. S. Wang, *J. Am. Chem. Soc.*,**123**, 8825(2001).
[10] A. E. Kuznetsov, A. I. Boldyrev, *Inorg. Chem.*,**41**, 532(2002).
[11] A. E. Kunznetsov, A. I. Boldyrev, *Struct. Chem.*, **13**, 141(2002).
[12] H. Zhai, L. Wang, A. E. Kunznetsov, A. I. Boldyrev, *J. Phys. Chem. A* **106**, 5600(2002).
[13] A. E. Kuznetsov, A. I. Boldyrev, H. Zhai, X. Li, L. Wang,; *J. Am. Chem. Soc.*,**124**, 11791(2002).
[14] C. G. Zhan, F. Zheng, D. A. Dixon, *J. Am. Chem. Soc.*,**124**, 14795(2002).
[15] A. E. Kuznetsov, J. D. Corbett, L. S. Wang, A. I. Boldyrev, *Angew. Chem. Int. Ed.*, **40(18)**, 3369 (2001).
[16] X. Li, H. F. Zhang, L. S. Wang, A. E. Kuznetsov, N. A. Cannon, A. I. Boldyrev, *Angew. Chem. Int. Ed.*, **40(10)**, 1867 (2001).
[17] X. X. Chi, X. H. Li, X. J. Chen, Z. S. Yuang, *J. Molecular structure (Theochem)*, **677**, 21(2004).

[18] Q. Li, L. Gong, Z. M. Gao, *Chem. Phys. Lett.*, **394**, 220(2004).

[19] C. Zhao, K. Balasubramaniam, *J. Chem. Phys.*, **120(22)**, 10501 (2004).

[20] Y. Jung, T. Henine, P.V.R. Schleyer, M. Head-Gordon, *J.Am. Chem. Soc.*, **126**, 3132(2004).

[21] H. M. Tuononen, R. Suontamo, J. Valkonen, R. S. Laitinen, *J. Phys. Chem. A* **108**, 5670(2004).

[22] C. A. Tsipis, E. E. Karagiannis, P. F. Kladou, A. C. Tsipis, *J. Am. Chem. Soc.*,**126**, 12916(2004).

[23] A. E. Kuznetsov, H. J. Zhai, L. S. Wang, A. I. Boldyrev, *Inorg. Chem.*,**41**, 6062(2002).

[24] A. N. Alexandrova, A. I. Boldyrev, H. J. Zhai, L. S. Wang, E. Steiner, P. W. Flower, *J. Phys. Chem. A* 107 1359(2003).

[25] X. Hu, H. Li, W. Liang, S. Han, *Chem. Phys. Lett.*, **397**, 180(2004).

[26] Q. Jin, B. Jin, W. G. Xu, *Chem. Phys. Lett.*, **396**, 398(2004).

[27] R. W. A. Havenith, J. H. V. Lenthe, *Chem. Phys. Lett.*, **385**, 198(2004).

[28] R. W. A. Havenith, P. W. Flower, E. Steiner, S. Shetty, D. G. Kanhere, S. Pal, *Phys. Chem. Chem. Phys.*, **6**, 285(2004).

[29] A. I. Boldyrev, L. S. Wang,*J. Phys. Chem. A* **105**, 10775(2001).

[30] A. N. Alexandrova A. I. Boldyrev, *J. Phys. Chem. A* **107**, 554(2003).

[31] A. E. Kuznetsov, A. I. Boldyrev, *Inorg. Chem.*,**41**, 3596(2002).

[32] H. J. Zhai, L. S. Wang, A. E. Kuznetsov, A. I. Boldyrev, *J. Phys. Chem. A* **106** 5600(2002).

[33] J. M. Matxain, J. M. Ugalde M. D. Towler R. J. Needs *J. Phys. Chem. A* **107**, 10004(2003).

[34] S. Nigam, C. Majumder, S.K. Kulshreshtha. (Communicated)

[35] P. v. R. Schleyer, C. Maerker, A. Dransfeld, H. Jiao and N. J. R., Eikema Hommes, *J. Am. Chem. Soc.*, 118 6317 (1996); P.V.R. Schleyre, H. Jiao, N.V.E. Hommes, V.G. Malkina, O.L.Malkina, *J. Am. Chem. Soc.*,**119**, 12669(1997).

[36] Q. S. Li, L. P. Cheng, *J. Phys. Chem. A* **107**, 2882(2003).

[37] A. I. Boldyrev,.; L. S. Wang, *J. Phys. Chem. A* **109(1)**, 236 (2005) .

[38] H. J. Zhai, A. E. Kuznetsov, A. I. Boldyrev, L. S. Wang, *Chem. Phys. Chem.* 5, 1885(2004) .

[39] L. Todorov, S. C. Sevov, *Inorg. Chem.*,**43**, 6490(2004),.

[40] [M. Haser, J. AlnLof, G. E. Scuseria, *Chem. Phys. Lett.*,**181**, 497(1991).; C. Moller C.; M. S. Plesset, *Phys. Rev.*, **46** 618(1934) ; W. J. Hehre, L. Radom, V. P. R. Schleyer, J. A. Pople, Ab Initio Molecular Orbital Theory (Wiley, New York, 1985).

[41] W. Schmidt, K. K. Baldridge, J. A. Boatz, S. T. Elbert, M. S. Gordon, J. H. Jensen, S. Koseki, N. Matsunaga, K. A. Nguyen, J. S. Su, T. L. Windus, M. Dupuis, J. A. Montgomery *J. Comput. Chem.*, **14**, 1347(1993) .

[42] M.J. Frisch, G.W. Trucks, H.B. Schlegel, G.E. Scuseria, M.A. Robb,J.R. Cheeseman, V.G. Zakrzewski, J.A. Montgomery, R.E. Stratman, J.C. Burant, S. Dapprich, J.M. Millam, A.D. Daniels, K.N. Kudin, M.C. Strain, O. Frakas, J. Tomasi, V. Barone, M. Cossi, R. Cammi, B. Mennucci, C. Pomelli, C. Adamo, S. Clifford, J. Ochterski, G.A. Petersson, P.Y. Ayala, Q. Cui, K. Morokuma, D.K. Malick, A.D.Rabuck, K. Raghavachari, J.B. Foresman, J. Cioslowski, J.V. Ortiz,B.B. Stefanov, G. Liu, A. Liashenko, P. Piskorz, I. Komaromi, R. Gomperts, R.L. Martin, D.J. Fox, T. Keith, M.A. Al-Laham, C.Y. Peng, A. Nanayakkara, C. Gonzalez, M. Challacombe, P.M.W. Gill, B.G. Johnson, W. Chen, M.W. Wong, J.L. Andres, M. Head-Gordon, E.S. Replogle, J.A. Pople, GAUSSIAN-98, Gaussian Inc, Pittsburgh, PA, 1998.

Brill Academic Publishers
P.O. Box 9000, 2300 PA Leiden
The Netherlands

Lecture Series on Computer
and Computational Sciences
Volume 5, 2006, pp. 103-109

On the performance of DFT methods on electric polarizability and hyperpolarizability calculations for the lithium tetramer.

George Maroulis[a]
Department of Chemistry, University of Patras, GR-26500 Patras, Greece
and
Demetrios Xenides
Department of Computer Science and Technology, University of the Peloponnese, GR-22100 Tripolis,
Greece

Abstract: We present a rigorous analysis of the performance of a set of twelve DFT methods on the calculation of the static electric polarizability and hyperpolarizability of the lithium tetramer. Our analysis reveals essential similarities and dissimilarities in the performance of these methods.

Keywords: Lithium tetramer; electric (hyper)polarizability; Density Functional Theory methods.

PACS: 31.20T, 35.20M.

1. Introduction and Theory

Experimental cluster science has made significant progress in recent years in the measurement of the electric properties of metal clusters [1]. Important results have been reported for lithium [2] and sodium [3], copper [4], nickel [5] and niobium [6,7] clusters. The size of the studied systems varies from a few atoms to very large clusters. Understandably enough, theoretical efforts have been limited to small and medium sized molecules [8-13]. The computational cost of the calculations increases dramatically with system size and this is a major factor for such limitations. Consequently, little is known about the performance of computational methods on systems of some size. It is now common experience that highly-predictive **ab initio** calculations cannot be easily extended to large molecules. Density functional theory (DFT) has emerged as a powerful alternative to conventional **ab initio** approaches.

In this paper we turn our attention to the performance of accessible DFT methods on the calculation of the electric polarizability and hyperpolarizability of the lithium tetramer, Li_4. This small but very soft molecule constitutes an ideal testing ground for the performance of quantum chemical methods. Its dipole polarizability is experimentally known [2]. In addition, the dipole polarizability [8,14] and to a lesser extent the hyperpolarizability [8] has been studied theoretically by various research groups. Li_4 is characterized by a very large hyperpolarizability [8] and the same holds also true for organolithium compounds [15].

We follow closely Buckingham's [16] conventions and terminology for the calculation of the dipole polarizability and hyperpolarizability of a tetratomic molecule of D_{2h} symmetry, as Li_4. Particular details about the independent components of the polarizability ($\alpha_{\alpha\beta}$) and hyperpolarizability ($\gamma_{\alpha\beta\gamma\delta}$) tensors of Li_4 can be found in our previous paper [8]. Our calculation of these static properties relies on a finite-field approach presented in some detail elsewhere [17,18]. We give here only the definition of the mean and the anisotropy of the dipole polarizability and the mean of the hyperpolarizability [16].

$$\bar{\alpha} = (\alpha_{xx} + \alpha_{yy} + \alpha_{zz})/3$$

$$\Delta\alpha = (1/2)^{1/2}[(\alpha_{xx}-\alpha_{yy})^2 + (\alpha_{yy}-\alpha_{zz})^2 + (\alpha_{zz}-\alpha_{xx})^2]^{1/2}$$

$$\bar{\gamma} = (\gamma_{xxxx} + \gamma_{yyyy} + \gamma_{zzzz} + 2\gamma_{xxyy} + 2\gamma_{yyzz} + 2\gamma_{zzxx})/5 \tag{1}$$

In our previous work on Li_4 we employed exclusively conventional **ab initio** methods [8]. In this paper we turn our attention to DFT methods. Comprehensive introductions to DFT may be found in

[a] Corresponding author. Electronic address: maroulis@upatras.gr

standard textbooks [19,20]. An essential part of our endeavour is the rigorous analysis of the performance the theoretical methods. In previous work we presented a method that relies on metric considerations and graph-theoretic concepts to introduce similarity, order, classification and clustering in spaces of theoretical descriptions [21]. Our method defines theoretical descriptions (TD) of a molecule as strings of numbers (molecular properties). For each method the set of properties taken into account is $\{\alpha_{xx}, \alpha_{yy}, \alpha_{zz}, \gamma_{xxxx}, \gamma_{yyyy}, \gamma_{zzzz}, \gamma_{xxyy}, \gamma_{yyzz}, \gamma_{zzxx}\}$. Distance ($D_{ij}$) and similarity ($S_{ij}$) between two theoretical descriptions TD_i and TD_j is defined by the Minkowski metric. Clustering of the TD space is then obtained via the construction of the **minimum spanning tree** (MST) and **single linkage cluster analysis** (SLCA) [21,22]. The method has been subsequently applied to various systems [17,18,23].

2. Computational details

The DFT methods used in this work and their major characteristics are given in Table 1. Their application relies on their implementation in the GAUSSIAN 03 program that has been used in all calculations [24].

Table 1. Basic characteristics of widely used DFT methods.

B3LYP	B3:Becke's three-parameter hybrid functional
	LYP:The correlation functional of Lee, Yang, and Parr which includes both local and non-local terms.
	B3: A. D. Becke, *J. Chem. Phys.* **98**, 5648 (1993).
	LYP: C. Lee, W. Yang, and R. G. Parr, *Phys. Rev. B* **37**, 785 (1988); B. Michlich, A. Savin, H. Stoll, and H. Preuss, *Chem. Phys. Lett.* **157**, 200 (1989).
B3P86	P86:The gradient corrections of Perdew, along with his 1981 local correlation functional.
	B3:*as in B3LYP*
	P86: J. P. Perdew, *Phys. Rev. B* **33**, 8822 (1986).
B3PW91	PW91:Perdew and Wang's 1991 gradient-corrected correlation functional.
	B3:*as in B3LYP*
	PW91: K. Burke, J. P. Perdew, and Y. Wang, in *Electronic Density Functional Theory: Recent Progress and New Directions*, Ed. J. F. Dobson, G. Vignale, and M. P. Das (Plenum, 1998); J. P. Perdew, in *Electronic Structure of Solids '91*, Ed. P. Ziesche and H. Eschrig (Akademie Verlag, Berlin, 1991) 11; J. P. Perdew, J. A. Chevary, S. H. Vosko, K. A. Jackson, M. R. Pederson, D. J. Singh, and C. Fiolhais, *Phys. Rev. B* **46**, (1992); J. P. Perdew, J. A. Chevary, S. H. Vosko, K. A. Jackson, M. R. Pederson, D. J. Singh, and C. Fiolhais, *Phys. Rev. B* **48**, (1993); J. P. Perdew, K. Burke, and Y. Wang, *Phys. Rev. B* **54**, 16533 (1996);
B1B95	B1: Becke's one-parameter hybrid functional as defined in the original paper.
	B95: Gradient-corrected correlation functional.
	B1: A. D. Becke, *J. Chem. Phys.* **104**, 1040 (1996).
	B95: A. D. Becke, *J. Chem. Phys.* **104**, 1040 (1996).
B1LYP	**B1:** *as in B1B95*
	LYP:*as in B3LYP*

B98LYP	B98: Becke's 1998 revisions to B97 and it implements equation 2c in Schmider and Becke.
	LYP:*as in B3LYP.*
	B98:A. D. Becke, *J. Chem. Phys.* **107**, 8554 (1997); H. L. Schmider and A. D. Becke, *J. Chem. Phys.* **108**, 9624 (1998).
	LYP:*as in B3LYP*
B98P86	**B98**:*as in B98LYP*
	P86:*as in B3P86*
B98PW91	**B98**:*as in B98LYP*
	PW91:*as in B3PW91*
OLYP	O:Handy's OPTX modification of Becke's exchange functional
	O:N. C. Handy and A. J. Cohen, *Mol. Phys.* **99**, 403 (2001).
	LYP:*as in B3LYP*
OP86	**O**:*as in OLYP*
	P86:*as in B3P86*
OPW91	**O**:*as in OLYP*
	PW91:*as in B3PW91*
VSXC	van Voorhis and Scuseria's τ-dependant gradient-corrected correlation functional.
	VSXC:T. Van Voorhis and G. E. Scuseria, *J. Chem. Phys.* **109**, 400 (1998).
PBE1PBE	The 1997 hybrid functional of Perdew, Burke and Ernzerhof, this functional uses 25% exchange and 75% correlation weighting.
	PBE1PBE:J. P. Perdew, K. Burke, and M. Ernzerhof, *Phys. Rev. Lett.* **77**, 3865 (1996).
mPW1PW91	Modified Perdew-Wang exchange and Perdew-Wang 91 correlation.
	mPW1PW91:C. Adamo and V. Barone, *J. Chem. Phys.* **108**, 664 (1998).

The molecular geometry of the tetramer is defined by the bond lengths R_{Li-Li} = 2.618716 and 3.032824 Å. The orientation, with xz as the molecular plane, is the same as that adopted previously [8]. All calculations were performed with a large, purpose-oriented (15s7p5d) uncontracted basis set consisting of 244 gaussian-type functions. Its construction will be presented in another paper [25].

Atomic units are used throughout this paper. Conversion factors to SI units are: Energy, $1\ E_h$ = 4.3597482 x 10^{-18} J, length, $1\ a_0$ = 0.529177249 x 10^{-10} m, dipole polarizability, $1\ e^2 a_0^2 E_h^{-1}$ = 1.648778 x 10^{-41} $C^2 m^2 J^{-1}$ and dipole hyperpolarizability $1\ e^4 a_0^4 E_h^{-3}$ = 6.235378 x 10^{-65} $C^4 m^4 J^{-3}$. Properties are almost invariably given as pure numbers, $\alpha_{\alpha\beta}/e^2 a_0^2 E_h^{-1}$ and $\gamma_{\alpha\beta\gamma\delta}/e^4 a_0^4 E_h^{-3}$.

3. Results and discussion

We have collected our findings for the interaction dipole moment, the mean and the anisotropy of the polarizability in Tables 2. Electric hyperpolarizabilities are in Table 3. The methods used here are numbered as M1≡B1B95, etc.

Table 2. Dipole polarizability of Li_4 calculated with various DFT methods.

	Method	α_{xx}	α_{yy}	α_{zz}	$\bar{\alpha}$	$\Delta\alpha$
M1	B1B95	590.09	226.52	277.84	364.81	340.82
M2	B1LYP	552.01	229.51	281.63	354.38	299.86
M3	B98LYP	677.11	275.89	333.22	428.74	375.85
M4	B98P86	685.71	278.24	335.84	433.26	381.94
M5	B98PW91	680.70	275.58	332.59	429.62	379.84
M6	OLYP	602.74	234.38	286.34	374.49	345.32
M7	OP86	620.22	237.37	289.45	382.35	359.65
M8	OPW91	622.31	235.95	286.90	381.72	363.57
M9	VSXC	485.30	193.92	245.71	308.31	269.25
M10	PBE1PBE	562.68	231.23	282.51	358.80	309.03
M11	mPW1PW91	566.15	232.88	284.46	361.16	310.71
M12	O3LYP	581.35	232.20	283.60	365.72	326.50

Table 3. Dipole hyperpolarizability of Li_4 calculated with various DFT methods. All values are given as $10^{-3} \times \gamma_{\alpha\beta\gamma\delta}$.

	Method	γ_{xxxx}	γ_{yyyy}	γ_{zzzz}	γ_{xxyy}	γ_{yyzz}	γ_{zzxx}	$\bar{\gamma}$
M1	B1B95	848	1193	494	1065	440	1204	1791
M2	B1LYP	8269	1231	1494	1373	450	1473	3518
M3	B98LYP	15640	2552	3522	3346	983	3980	7666
M4	B98P86	15439	2565	3296	3117	960	3537	7306
M5	B98PW91	14804	2203	2978	2774	839	3277	6753
M6	OLYP	5700	1444	1777	1474	527	1684	3258
M7	OP86	4556	1388	1661	1373	504	1587	2907
M8	OPW91	5265	1260	1538	1326	461	1557	2950
M9	VSXC	6451	998	1143	1161	357	1177	2796
M10	PBE1PBE	6981	1095	1337	1199	401	1312	3048
M11	mPW1PW91	7205	1055	1333	1193	390	1321	3080
M12	O3LYP	6179	1327	1616	1358	483	1522	3170

In Table 4 we give a few selected results for the (hyper)polarizability of Li_4. A more extensive presentation of previous work will be given in another paper [25].

Table 4. Selected theoretical and experimental values for the hyperpolarizability of Li_4.

	$\bar{\alpha}$	$\Delta\alpha$	$10^{-3} \times \bar{\gamma}$
Theory			
B3PW91[a]	333	379	
CCSD(T)[b]	387.01	354.60	2394
CCSD[c]	333.1	233.9	
mPW1PW91[d]	361.16	310.71	3080
Experiment			
Beam deflection[e]	326.6 ± 32.7		

[a] Fuentealba and Reyes [26].
[b] Maroulis and Xenides [8].
[c] Pecul et al. [14].
[d] Present investigation.
[e] Benichou et al. [2].

In Table 5 we give the similarity measures as calculated with the values listed in Tables 2 and 3. The entries in Table 4 refer directly to the theoretical methods, e.g. $S_{12} \equiv S(B1B95, B1LYP) = 0.764$.

Table 5. Similarity measure (S_{ij}) for the performance of the DFT methods on the calculation of the (hyper)polarizability of Li_4.

	M1	M2	M3	M4	M5	M6	M7	M8	M9	M10	M11	M12
M1	1	0.764	0.089	0.132	0.244	0.768	0.793	0.807	0.683	0.807	0.801	0.797
M2	0.764	1	0.219	0.258	0.373	0.861	0.832	0.849	0.735	0.931	0.922	0.918
M3	0.089	0.219	1	0.923	0.815	0.297	0.273	0.245	0	0.170	0.170	0.246
M4	0.132	0.258	0.923	1	0.866	0.338	0.316	0.289	0.030	0.211	0.211	0.287
M5	0.244	0.373	0.815	0.866	1	0.451	0.431	0.407	0.136	0.330	0.331	0.401
M6	0.768	0.861	0.297	0.338	0.451	1	0.945	0.921	0.635	0.842	0.836	0.935
M7	0.793	0.832	0.273	0.316	0.431	0.945	1	0.953	0.614	0.835	0.833	0.911
M8	0.807	0.849	0.245	0.289	0.407	0.921	0.953	1	0.635	0.864	0.864	0.917
M9	0.683	0.735	0	0.030	0.136	0.635	0.614	0.635	1	0.738	0.727	0.689
M10	0.807	0.931	0.170	0.211	0.330	0.842	0.835	0.864	0.738	1	0.982	0.905
M11	0.801	0.922	0.170	0.211	0.331	0.836	0.833	0.864	0.727	0.982	1	0.897
M12	0.797	0.918	0.246	0.287	0.401	0.935	0.911	0.917	0.689	0.905	0.897	1

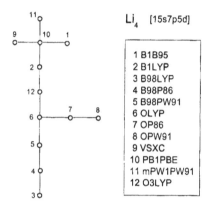

Figure 1. Minimum Spanning Tree (MST) for the space of theoretical descriptions (TD) for Li_4.

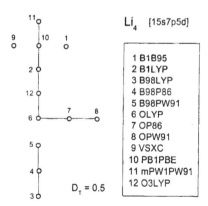

Figure 2. Clustering of TD with a threshold $D_T = 0.5$.

Last, in Figures 1 and 2, we give the minimum spanning tree (MST) constructed for TD = {M_i, i=1,2,...,12} and the clustering produced by removing from the MST by removing all edges above a threshold distance $D_T = 0.5$.

The calculated properties in Tables 2 and 3 show an impressive scatter. For the mean and the anisotropy of the dipole polarizability the VSPX method yields the lowest values. The overestimation of the mean is obvious for the B98LYP, B98P86 and B98PW91 methods. These same methods seem also to overestimate the anisotropy. The results for the dipole hyperpolarizability show clearly an extreme behaviour. This is far worse than that observed for another difficult system, the ozone molecule [27]. The lowest value for the mean hyperpolarizability corresponds to B1B95 while B98LYP, B98P86 and B98PW91 are at the other extreme. Some methods, compared to the conventional **ab initio** values in Table 4, display overall an acceptable predictive capability.

The similarity measures in Table 5 indicate that the two most dissimilar methods are B98LYP and VSXC. M3 ≡ B98LYP is very similar to both M4 ≡ B98P86 and M5 ≡ B98PW91. Other methods are very similar. The highest similarity is S(M10, M11) ≡ S(PBE1PBE, mPW1PW91) = 0.982. Both methods yield a very reliable picture of the electric (hyper)polarizability of the lithium tetramer.

Removing from the MST all edges above an arbitrary threshold $D_T = 0.5$, that is discarding all $D_{ij} > D_T$, produces the clustering shown in Figure 2. The three B98LYP, B98P86 and B98PW91 methods form a distinct cluster. M1 and M9 are separated from all other methods. We also have a large cluster consisting of M2, M6, M7, M8, M10, M11 and M12. All seven methods are very similar to each other. Thus this partitioning of TD,

$$TD = \{M1\} \cup \{M2, M6, M7, M8, M10, M11, M12\} \cup \{M3, M4, M5\} \cup \{M9\} \qquad (2)$$

brings forth significant characteristics of the relative merit of the studies DFT methods.

Adding a last observation at this point, we note that the (hyper)polarizabilities in Table 4 are not strictly comparable as they pertain to different molecular geometries. We are currently investigating this matter as it appears, as preliminary results show, that even small differences in the geometrical parameters of Li_4 has a very strong effect on the calculated molecular properties.

4. Conclusions

We have presented an analysis of the performance of a large set of DFT methods on the calculation of the electric (hyper)polarizability of the lithium tetramer. Our results show that these computationally economical methods show very diverse predictive capability even for such a small system. We have also found that methods as mPW1PW91 or O3LYP are relatively reliable. A more detailed comparison for the properties of Li_4, in which will be also included Møller-Plesset perturbation theory, coupled cluster techniques and the widely used B3LYP and B3PW91 DFT methods will be presented in a future paper. More studies on the behaviour and performance of DFT methods in electric property calculations are now in progress in our laboratory.

Acknowledgement

This work is part of the COST action **D26/0013/02** project of the EEC "Development of Density Functional Theory models for an accurate description of electronic properties of materials possessing potential high non-linear optical properties". DX wishes to express his indebtedness to Dr. Michael Fink, system administrator at the Zentral Informatik Dienst (ZID) of the University of Innsbruck, for specific computer resources allocation.

References

[1] K.D.Bonin and V.V.Kresin, *Electric dipole polarizabilities of atoms, molecules and clusters,* World Scientific, Singapore (1997).
[2] E.Benichou, R.Antoine, D.Rayane, B.Vezin, F.W.Dalby, Ph.Dugourd, M.Broyer, C.Ristori, F.Chandezon, B.A.Huber, J.C.Rocco, S.A.Blundell and C.Guet, Phys.Rev. A 59, R1 (1999).
[3] G.Tikhonov, V.Kasperovich, K.Wong and V.V.Kresin, Phys.Rev. A 64, 063202 (2001).
[4] M.B.Knickelbein, J.Chem.Phys. 120, 10450 (2004).
[5] M.B.Knickelbein, J.Chem.Phys. 115, 5957 (2001).
[6] M.B.Knickelbein, J.Chem.Phys. 118, 6230 (2003).
[7] R.Moro, X.Xu, S.yin, and W. A. de Heer, Science 300, 1265 (2003).
[8] G.Maroulis and D.Xenides, J.Phys.Chem. A 103, 4590 (1999).
[9] P.Calaminici, A.M.Köster, A.Vela and K.Jug, J.Chem.Phys. 113, 2199 (2000).

[10] P.Jaque and A.Toro-Labbé, J.Chem.Phys. 117, 3208 (2003).
[11] G.Maroulis and A.Haskopoulos, Lecture Notes in Computer and Computational Science 1, 1096 (2004).
[12] M.Yang and K.A.Jackson, J.Chem.Phys. 122, 184317 (2005).
[13] M.G.Papadopoulos, H.Reis, A.Avramopoulos, S.Erkoc and L.Amirouche, J.Phys.Chem. B 109, 18822 (2005).
[14] M.Pecul, M.Jaszunski and P.Jørgensen, Mol.Phys. 98, 1455 (2000).
[15] M.G.Papadopoulos, S.G.Raptis and I.N.Demetropoulos, Mol.Phys. 92, 547 (1997).
[16] A.D.Buckingham, Adv.Chem.Phys. 12, 107 (1967).
[17] G.Maroulis, J.Chem.Phys. 108, 5432 (1998).
[18] G.Maroulis, J.Chem.Phys. 118, 2673 (2003).
[19] T.Helgaker, P.Jørgensen and J.Olsen, *Molecular Electronic-Structure Theory*, Wiley, Chichester (2000).
[20] W.Koch and M.C.Holthausen, *A Chemist's Guide to Density Functional Theory*, 2nd Edition Wiley, Chichester (2001).
[21] G.Maroulis, Int.J.Quant.Chem. 55, 173 (1995).
[22] H.Spath, *Cluster analysis algorithms*, Ellis Horwood, Chichester (1980).
[23] G.Maroulis, J.Chem.Phys. 111, 583 (1999).
[24] M. J. Frisch, G. W. Trucks, H. B. Schlegel at al. , **Gaussian 03**, Revision C.02, Gaussian, Inc., Wallingford CT(2004).
[25] G.Maroulis and D.Xenides, in preparation.
[26] P.Fuentealba and O.Reyes, J.Phys.Chem. A 103, 1376 (1997).
[27] G.Maroulis, Comp.Lett. 1, 31 (2005).

Brill Academic Publishers
P.O. Box 9000, 2300 PA Leiden
The Netherlands

Lecture Series on Computer
and Computational Sciences
Volume 5, 2006, pp. 110-115

Interaction of Nitric Oxide and Nitric Oxide Dimer with Silver Clusters

Vitaly E. Matulis[1], O.A. Ivashkevich, V.S. Gurin

Research Institute for Physical Chemical Problems,
Belarusian State University,
Leningradskaya str., 14, 220050, Minsk, Belarus

Abstract: Study of interaction of NO and $(NO)_2$ molecules with silver clusters has been carried out using the hybrid method S2LYP based on density functional theory (DFT). The role of cluster charge and site of adsorption on N–O stretch frequency, adsorption energy and geometry has been investigated. Four cluster models of different size have been used for simulation of $(NO)_2$ adsorption on Ag{111} surface. The pronounced effect of N–N bond shortening in comparison with gaseous $(NO)_2$ has been found due to adsorption of $(NO)_2$ on silver cluster. This phenomenon is important as possible pathway of N–N bond formation in catalytic fragmentation of NO molecule. The calculations showed that the silver octamer is the best candidate for simulation of formation and fragmentation of $(NO)_2$ on Ag{111} surface within the cluster model.

Keywords: Nitric oxide dimer, DFT, silver, vibrational frequencies, adsorption

PACS: 31.15.Ew, 33.15.Dj, 33.15.Fm, 33.20.Ea, 36.40.Jn

1. Introduction

Recently we have developed the exchange-correlation functional denoted hereinafter as S2LYP [1] within the framework of conventional DFT. The suggested functional combines the contributions of Slater and HF exchange and VWN and LYP correlation with adjustable coefficients:

$$\alpha \cdot E_x^S + (1-\alpha) \cdot E_x^{HF} + \beta \cdot E_c^{LYP} + (1-\beta) \cdot E_c^{VWN},$$

where α=0.7; β=0.6; E_x^S, E_x^{HF}, E_c^{LYP} and E_c^{VWN} are the designations of exchange and correlation energy terms. Using this functional we have established the geometries of anionic silver and copper clusters up to decamers [1, 2] and have shown that the developed functional provides high accuracy calculations of electronic characteristics of both copper and silver clusters. It has been shown that some properties, such as geometry, vertical detachment energy and vertical transition energy, are very similar for silver and copper clusters. However, there are considerable distinctions in the properties where d-electrons can play an important role. These distinctions have been investigated by the example of interaction of silver and copper clusters with NO molecule [3].

In the present paper, we focused on interaction of NO molecule with silver clusters. Recently a tendency of NO to form relatively stable neutral dimer $(NO)_2$ during adsorption on silver surface has been observed [4]. Also, the information about stretch frequencies $(NO)_2$ adsorbed on Ag{111} surface is available [4]. Thus, there are two goals in our study. Firstly, to investigate the interaction of NO molecule with small silver cluster and understand how charge of cluster and site of adsorption can influence N–O bond length and stretch frequency. Secondly, to calculate vibrational frequencies of $(NO)_2$ adsorbed on silver clusters of different size and to compare the obtained data with experimental vibrational frequencies of $(NO)_2$ adsorbed on silver surface. The data can be useful for developing cluster model to study the process of formation and fragmentation of $(NO)_2$.

2. Computational details

All calculations have been carried out within DFT with the S2LYP functional [1] and D95V(d) basis set [5] for N and O atoms and LANL2DZ basis set [6] for Ag atoms. For the largest cluster (Ag_{14-8}) used to model silver surface, Ag atoms in the cluster were assigned to two different regions that are

---

[1] Corresponding author. E-mail: Matulis@bsu.by, Vitaly_Matulis@mail.ru

treated differently in terms of the basis sets employed. The Ag atoms closest to the adsorption site, four from the first layer, were treated with the LANL2DZ basis set and the other silver atoms were described by the LANL2MB [6] basis set which differs from LANL2DZ by the use of a minimal basis instead of the double-zeta one to treat the valence electrons. These two different regions are illustrated in Fig. 1 (the silver atoms treated with LANL2DZ basis set are highlighted).

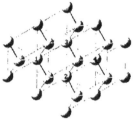

Figure 1: Top view of the Ag_{14-8} cluster used to model the $Ag\{111\}$ surface.

Equilibrium geometries, adsorption energy (E_{ads}) and vibrational frequencies of NO and $(NO)_2$ adsorbed on silver clusters have been calculated. All symmetry allowed geometrical parameters were optimized in order to study the interaction of NO molecule with neutral and charged silver tetramers, while in the case of interaction of $(NO)_2$ with silver clusters simulating $Ag\{111\}$ surface the geometrical parameters of metal clusters were frozen with internuclear distances corresponding to experimental values of bulk silver (2.89 Å).

3. Results and discussion

NO molecule can be considered both as electron donor and acceptor. The π-accepting properties are dominant in NO in contrast to CO molecule. It can be illustrated by the following facts: firstly, the red shift is observed in IR spectra of NO adsorbed on Cu-exchanged ZSM-5 zeolite [7] and in CuNO complex [8]; secondly, the angular structure of CuNO complex [8]. In spite of dominance of π-accepting properties, the general trends can be changed depending on the nature of reactant with NO. To study this phenomenon, we have calculated the geometry and energetic characteristics of complexes of NO with anionic, neutral and cationic silver tetramers. The calculated structures and their relative energies (ΔE) are given in Fig. 2, and the calculated adsorption energy and stretch frequency ($v_{(N-O)}$) of N-O are presented in Table 1. $Ag_4^- - NO$ structures are denoted as (-) and $Ag_4^+ - NO$ structures as (+). Structures I simulate the terminal adsorption of NO at an atom of short diagonal of the rhombic silver tetramer, while structures II simulate the terminal adsorption of NO at long diagonal of the rhombic silver tetramer. Structures III simulate the bridged adsorption. All structures I and II have C_s symmetry and structures III have C_{2v} symmetry except for III(-) which has C_s symmetry. For neutral as well as for charged clusters the terminal adsorption is more preferable than the bridged one. But in the case of cationic clusters the difference is not as large as for anionic and neutral clusters. In this case NO

Table 1: S2LYP calculated properties of complexes of silver tetramers with NO molecule

	I(-)	II(-)	III(-)	I	II	III	I(+)	II(+)	III(+)
$v_{(N-O)}$, cm^{-1}	1630.71	1600.88	1637.35	1873.42	1827.67	1841.08	2043.65	2062.14	1876.36
E_{ads}, kJ/mol	122.56	79.77	57.86	85.88	47.53	38.36	77.36	56.02	66.91

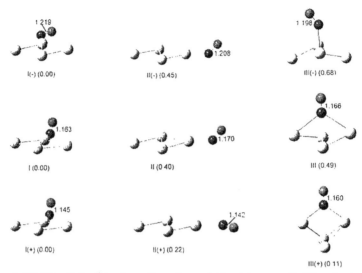

Figure 2: S2LYP optimized structures of complexes of silver tetramers with NO molecule, their relative energies (eV) and N–O bond length (Å).

molecule also influences the structure of cluster stronger than for complexes with anionic and neutral clusters. Table 1 shows that the binding energy of NO molecule increases in the series: neutral – cation – anion, but two exceptions occur. First, for bridged structure of NO complex with cationic tetramer (structure III(+)) the binding energy is larger than for the similar anionic complex. Second, neutral tetramer binds NO molecule stronger than cationic one in the case of structure I. NO reveals π-accepting properties in the reaction with neutral clusters and especially with anions and the partial charge transfer from cluster MO to π-antibonding MO in NO results in a long NO bond and decrease of NO stretch frequency compared to gaseous NO. S2LYP/D95V(d) calculated $v_{(N-O)}$ and $R_{(N-O)}$ for NO molecule are 2076.82 cm^{-1} and 1.151 Å, correspondingly. This trend appears most strongly for terminal adsorption on anionic tetramers. The charge transfer enhances also the binding energy of NO with cluster. On the other hand, in the reaction with cations NO reveals the electron donor property and the partial charge transfer from π-antibonding MO of NO to MO of metal cluster results in the shorter NO bond. But NO stretch frequency remains almost unchanged as compared to the free molecule. It is important to note that there was not observed any charge transfer for structure III(+). Sum of Mulliken atomic charges of NO molecule calculated for structure III(+) is -0.008 (for comparison, the similar value for structure I(+) is 0.155). But owing to rather high overlap population (0.155) between N and two nearest Ag atoms in structure III(+), the overlap population between N and O atoms decreased to the value of 0.407. For comparison, the overlap population between N and O atoms calculated for structure I(+) is 0.435. Thus, the bridged complex of NO with cationic silver tetramer is characterized by long NO bond and decreased NO stretch frequency compared to free NO. Our calculations show that in the case of terminal adsorption the charge of cluster influences the geometry of NO, $v_{(N-O)}$ and E_{ads} more significantly than for the bridged adsorption.

A problem of formation of (NO)$_2$ on metal surface is of great interest because during this process the N–N bond is formed. This is important for catalytic fragmentation of NO with formation of nitrogen and oxygen. Unfortunately, theoretical investigations of mechanism of formation and fragmentation of (NO)$_2$ on transition metal surface is very difficult. DFT model which is very useful for calculation of systems containing transition metal atoms does not give a good results for structure and vibrational frequencies of (NO)$_2$ [9]. On the other hand, multiconfigurational second-order perturbation theory which gives a good results for (NO)$_2$ seems to be too complicate for studying this mechanism within the cluster model. In present investigation we focus on the question how the size of cluster can influence the geometry and vibrational frequency of (NO)$_2$. So, the aim of investigation was to choose the most adequate cluster model for studying the process of formation and fragmentation of (NO)$_2$ with reliable computational cost.

Four cluster models have been used to study geometry and vibrational frequencies of (NO)$_2$ adsorbed on silver surface. The optimized structures of (NO)$_2$ adsorbed on silver clusters are given in Fig. 3. All structures in Fig. 3 have C_s symmetry with symmetry plane along the molecular plane of (NO)$_2$. All chosen clusters can be considered as simulation of bulk Ag{111} surface. We compare the results obtained for small (Ag$_{3-1}$), medium (Ag$_{4-3-1}$ and Ag$_{6-3-1}$) and large (Ag$_{14-8}$) clusters (Fig. 3). Silver octamer, Ag$_8$, is characterized by high stability [1] explained by the electronic shell-closing effect. HOMO-LUMO gap of Ag$_8$ is 1.61 eV, that is about 2.4 times higher than for Ag$_{10}$ (0.67 eV) [1]. For this reason we also did the calculations of vibrational frequencies of (NO)$_2$ adsorbed on Ag$_{10}$, i.e. Ag$_{6-3-1}$, in addition to Ag$_8$, i.e. Ag$_{4-3-1}$. Thus, we can compare the results obtained for these two clusters of nearly the same size. Calculated within the cluster model and experimental stretch frequencies of (NO)$_2$ adsorbed on Ag{111} surface are presented in Table 2.

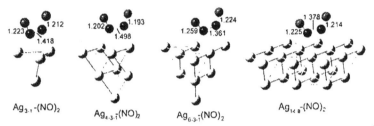

Ag$_{3-1}$-(NO)$_2$ Ag$_{4-3-1}$-(NO)$_2$ Ag$_{6-3-1}$-(NO)$_2$ Ag$_{14-8}$-(NO)$_2$

Figure 3: S2LYP optimized structures of (NO)$_2$ adsorbed on silver clusters (bond length in Å).

Table 2 shows that vibrational frequencies calculated within the above cluster models underestimate the experimental values. The main reason of this is lower stability and higher reactivity of clusters in comparison with the bulk metal. It should be noted that additional error can occur due to inaccurate calculations of the geometry of (NO)$_2$ within DFT model. S2LYP/D95V(d) calculated value of N–N bond (1.8348 Å) is considerably lower than experimental one (2.2630±0.0012 Å). On the contrary, the calculated O$_N$N valence angle (102.53°) is higher than experimental value (97.17±0.05°). However, the calculated and experimental value of N–O bond is in good agreement (1.1558 and 1.1515±0.003 Å, correspondingly).

Table 2: S2LYP calculated within cluster model and experimental stretch frequency of (NO)$_2$ adsorbed on Ag{111} surface

$v_{(NO)_2}$, cm^{-1}	Ag$_{3-1}$-(NO)$_2$	Ag$_{4-3-1}$-(NO)$_2$	Ag$_{6-3-1}$-(NO)$_2$	Ag$_{14-8}$-(NO)$_2$	Exp. [9] Ag{111}-(NO)$_2$
symm	1603.26	1693.60	1553.70	1574.48	1863
asymm	1539.57	1627.80	1367.80	1503.17	1788

The best agreement between the calculated and experimental vibrational frequencies of (NO)$_2$ adsorbed on Ag{111} surface has been observed for the case of Ag$_{4-3-1}$. It should be noted that the deformation of (NO)$_2$ in comparison to the gas phase is minimum for adsorption on silver octamer (Fig. 3). Thus, the interaction of (NO)$_2$ with Ag$_{4-3-1}$ results in a long N–O bond (by 0.04 Å) and a considerable decreased N–N bond (by 0.34 Å)compared to free (NO)$_2$. At the same time, the largest deformations of (NO)$_2$ is observed for Ag$_{6-3-1}$. This result is surprising especially in view of the fact that stability of silver clusters (binding energy per atom) increases with size. But some properties such as vertical detachment energy of anions and HOMO-LUMO gap are very close for silver tetramer and decamer [1]. In this aspect the results of our calculations of vibrational frequencies of (NO)$_2$ within Ag$_{3-1}$ and Ag$_{6-3-1}$ cluster models do not seems too surprising. In addition, the worse agreement with experiment in the case of Ag$_{6-3-1}$ can be explained by the feature of optimized geometry of Ag$_{6-3-1}$-(NO)$_2$ complex. The N–N bond in this complex does not parallel to the cluster surface (Fig. 4) and two N–O bonds have considerably different length (Fig. 3). Moreover, according to our calculations there is no symmetric and asymmetric stretch of N–O bonds in this case. Two vibrational frequencies given in Table 2 correspond two individual stretch of each N–O bond (Fig. 4).
The result obtained within Ag$_{14-8}$ cluster model is also less accurate than for Ag$_{3-1}$. However, the additional error may occur in the first case because of division of silver atoms in the cluster model on

two different regions that are treated differently in terms of the basis set employed in order to make the calculations feasible.

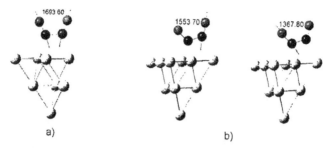

a)   b)

Figure 4: S2LYP calculated displacement vectors and the values of vibrational frequencies (cm^{-1}): a) corresponding to symmetric stretch of $(NO)_2$ adsorbed on Ag_{4-3-1}; b) corresponding to N–O bonds stretch of $(NO)_2$ adsorbed on Ag_{6-3-1}.

4. Conclusions

A series of cluster models simulating NO adsorption on Ag_4 and $(NO)_2$ on $Ag\{111\}$ surface has been calculated using DFT based hybrid method S2LYP. The calculations for complexes of NO with silver tetramers show that the charge of metal cluster significantly influences both N–O bond length and stretch frequency. The site of adsorption affects the above characteristics in less degree, but strongly influences the value of adsorption energy. In the case of terminal adsorption the charge of cluster influences the geometry of NO, $v_{(N–O)}$ and E_{ads} more significantly than for the bridged one.

In the series of $Ag_n–(NO)_2$ structures Ag_{4-3-1} cluster is the best candidate for simulation of formation and fragmentation of $(NO)_2$ on $Ag\{111\}$ surface. It can be explained by the increased stability of Ag_8. It influences the $(NO)_2$ geometry in less degree than the other considered clusters. Tetramer should also be a good candidate for studying the mechanism of $(NO)_2$ reactivity. The comparison of calculated geometry of $(NO)_2$ in free state and on silver clusters showed that the long N–O bond is observed as a result of adsorption. This elongation is larger than found for bridged and terminal adsorption of NO on neutral silver tetramer and close to that found for anionic tetramers. The much more pronounced effect of shortening of N–N bond in comparison with free $(NO)_2$ molecule has been found in the case of adsorption of $(NO)_2$ on silver clusters. This phenomenon is important as possible pathway of N–N bond formation in catalytic fragmentation of NO molecule.

Acknowledgments

This work was supported by the World Federation of Scientists National Scholarship Programme and Belarusian Foundantion for Fundamental Research (Grant No. X03M–083).

References

[1] Vitaly E. Matulis, O.A. Ivashkevich and V.S. Gurin, DFT study of electronic structure and geometry of neutral and anionic silver clusters, *Journal of Molecular Structure (Theochem)* **664–665** 298–308(2003).

[2] Vitaly E. Matulis, O.A. Ivashkevich and V.S. Gurin, DFT study of electronic structure and geometry of anionic copper clusters, *Journal of Molecular Structure (Theochem)* **681** 169–176(2004).

[3] Vitaly E. Matulis and O.A. Ivashkevich, Comparative DFT study of electronic structure and geometry of copper and silver clusters: interaction with NO molecule, *Computational Materiasl Science* **35** 268–271(2006).

[4] W.A. Brown and D.A. King, NO chemisorption and reactions on metal surfaces: a new perspective, *Journal of Physical Chemistry B* **104** 2578–2595(2000).

[5] T.H. Dunning Jr. and P.J. Hay, *Modern Theoretical Chemistry* Editor: H. F. Schaefer III, Plenum, New York), 3(1976), 28.

[6] P. J. Hay and W. R. Wadt, Ab initio effective core potentials for molecular calculations. potentials for K to Au including the outermost core orbitals, *Journal of Chemical Physics* **82** 299–310(1985).

[7] P. Treesukol, J. Limtrakul and T. N. Truong, Adsorption of Nitrogen Monoxide and Carbon Monoxide on Copper-Exchanged ZSM-5: A Cluster and Embedded Cluster Study, *Journal of Physical Chemmistry B* **105** 2421–2428(2001).

[8] M. Zhou and L. Andrews, Reaction of Laser-Ablated Cu with NO: Infrared Spectra and Density Functional Calculations of $CuNO^+$, CuNO, $Cu(NO)_2$, and $Cu(NO)_2^-$ in Solid Neon and Argon, *Journal of Physical Chemistry A* **104** 2618–2625(2000).

[9] R. Sayós, R Valero, J.M. Anglada, Miguel González, Theoretical investigation of the eight low-lying electronic states of the *cis*-and *trans*-nitric oxide dimers and its isomerization using multiconfigurational second-order perturbation theory (CASPT2), *Journal of Chemical Physics* **112** 6608–6624(2000).

Brill Academic Publishers
P.O. Box 9000, 2300 PA Leiden,
The Netherlands

Lecture Series on Computer
and Computational Sciences
Volume 5, 2006, pp. 116-127

The 2D-3D structural transition and chemical bonding in elemental boron nanoclusters

Kah Chun Lau and Ravindra Pandey[1]

Department of Physics
Michigan Technological University
Houghton, MI 49931, USA

Abstract: The rich chemistry of boron compounds are often found dominated by its structural dimensionality and chemical bonding from which some of the qualitative features of boron clusters can easily be extracted. In this article, we review such features to discuss structural properties of B_n clusters. In both small-cluster regime of $n \leq 20$ and large-cluster regime of $n \geq 20$, the preferred topological structures are the result of the interplay between bonding factors related to the delocalized π bonds and the inter-icosahedral and intra-icosahedral bonds. The bulk fragments of boron are also expected to become a competitive isomeric configuration with the increase in the cluster-size, in contrast to 3D spherical cages observed in the large carbon clusters.

Keywords: boron clusters, boron nanostructures

1 Introduction

The rapid developments in science and technology at nanoscale starting in the last decade have encompassed multi-disciplinary areas extending through physics, biology, chemistry, and materials science with promising applications in everyday life. The primary task of both experimental and theoretical studies at nanoscale is to understand the physics and chemistry of objects of few nanometers in size (e.g. 1 - 100 nm), which can be consisted of few to thousands of atoms and may extend to the larger microscopic size before approaching the bulk matter. The physical and chemical properties of a given material at nanoscale are often peculiar, and can vary dramatically with the size. For example, carbon exhibits novel structural and electronic properties in the form of clusters [1, 2], fullerenes [3] and nanotubes [4].

In this reference, boron nanostructures have attracted the attention due to the remarkable properties of the elemental boron which is defined as 'electron-deficient' [5, 6] (i.e. the number of available valence electron is less than the available orbitals in the electronic configuration). In general, the 'electron deficient' nature does not suggest that it is inferior in bonding, but simply that novel structures based on the elemental boron are expected to be adopted. With insufficient electrons to support a structure by conventional '2-electron two-center' bonds, the boron-based compounds generally tend to adopt a novel mechanism to resolve its 'electron-deficiency' through '2-electron multi-center' bonds topologically connected in a complex networks [5, 6]. Thus, the most observed phases of boron crystalline structures have hundreds of atoms per primitive unit cell, and only the simplest elemental α-B_{12} and T_{50}, and thermodynamically stable β-B_{105} rhombohedral phases are reported to have 'simpler' icosahedral-based networks [5, 7, 8, 9, 10, 11]. Similar to its

---

[1]Corresponding author: pandey@mtu.edu

complex bulk structure, a large diversities in the topological configurations of boron nanostructures [12, 13, 14, 15] was to be expected leading to a series of synthesis and characterization studies of clusters [16, 17, 18] nanowires, nanoribbons, nanowhiskers, and nanotubes [19, 20, 21]. Both experimental and theoretical studies find that the existence of nanotubes and clusters are closely related, and can be categorized as a new class of topological structure, in contrast to nanowires and nanoribbons which are more closely related to the boron solids. However, a relatively more subtle question of whether the clusters can be considered as a basic building block of nanotubes has not been fully elucidated. The correlation among the formation and size-dependent structural evolution of boron clusters together with the growth mechanism of boron nanotubes remains to be an active research area.

In this review article, we will focus on the issues related to the size-dependent structural evolution of the boron clusters (B_n, n $\leq$ 100). Specifically, we will discuss 2D-3D structural transition by giving the qualitative arguments relating the structural dimensionality to the bonding features in the boron clusters.

2 Small boron clusters(i.e., B_n, n $\leq$ 15)

The elemental boron clusters have received relatively little attention [22, 23, 24, 25, 26], as compared to its neighboring elemental clusters, such as C, Al and Si. One of the earliest experimental observation of a prominent B_{13}^+ cluster[22] was catalyst for a number of theoretical [27, 28, 29, 30, 31, 32, 33, 34, 35, 36, 37] as well as experimental [23, 24, 25, 26] studies on small B_n (with n $\leq$ 15) clusters. It was predicted that the ground state structural configurations of small boron clusters do not resemble with the fragments of either crystalline or amorphous lattice of the boron. They were found to be planar, convex, or quasi-planar structures[32, 33, 34, 35, 36, 37]. Furthermore, instability of the B_{12} icosahedral cluster was predicted [27], though the bulk boron consists of the B_{12}-icosahedral networks. In order to have a more comprehensive understanding of the small boron clusters, recent theoretical [38, 39, 40, 41, 42, 43] and experimental studies [16, 44, 45, 46, 47, 48] have focussed on structure, bonding, electronic and vibrational properties of both neutral and ionized boron clusters. The stability of previously proposed planar, convex and quasi-planar structures of the neutral and ionized B_n clusters, with n = 3 - 15), has been verified and also confirmed experimentally by the photoelectron spectroscopy measurements. Analogous to hydrocarbons, it was also proposed that the concepts of aromaticity and anti-aromaticity (Figure1), can be applied to explain the cluster stability in conjunction with the planarity found in small boron clusters regime (B_n, where n $\leq$ 15) [46, 47, 48, 16, 49, 50]. Following the Hückel rule which defines aromaticity as $(4n+2)$ and anti-aromaticity as $(4n)$ where n is the integer which defines the number of sets of degenerate bonding orbitals in the molecular orbitals (MOs) diagram. The B_{10}, B_{11}^- and B_{12} clusters possessing six π-electrons are aromatic, while B_{13}^- and B_{14} possessing eight π-electrons are anti-aromatic. B_{15}^- which possess ten π-electrons, is again aromatic. [16]

The electronic structure calculations [16, 29, 30, 31, 32, 33, 34, 35, 36, 37, 42, 43, 44, 45, 46, 47, 48] in the small clusters regime have also shown that the cluster binding energy increases with the size approaching to the cohesive energy of bulk boron around 6.0 eV/atom [51]. On the other hand, the ionization-induced changes in the structural configurations of these small clusters are small. All the lowest-energy geometrical configurations of neutral, anionic and cationic clusters are usually similar, without much of the controversies. It was noticed that in spite of the preference for planarity, some of the common features in the small clusters can be extracted from their predicted stable configurations. For example, the 'electron-deficient' nature of boron is reflected in the preference of a triangular $B - B - B$ unit in these clusters beginning with the the smallest unit of B_3. The photoelectron spectroscopy measurements have also suggested the ground states of $B_6 \leq B_n \leq B_9$ to be cyclic or molecular 'wheel-like' structures [46, 47, 48]. While for $B_{10} \leq B_n \leq B_{15}$

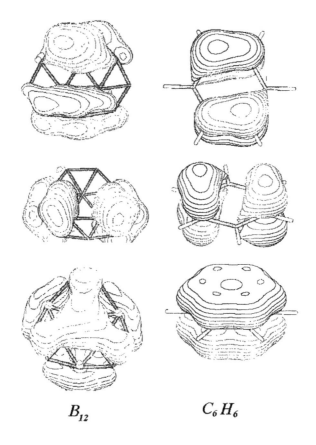

$$B_{12} \qquad C_6H_6$$

Figure 1: Selected occupied π-molecular orbitals of benzene together with those of the B_{12} cluster. [42]

clusters, the lowest-energy structures consist of a combination of B_6, B_7 and B_8 as the basic unit where the planarity prevails [16]. It is attributed to the effective delocalization of the π-electrons in 2D rendering aromaticity and anti-aromaticity in the clusters. The electron-deficiency of boron facilitates the multi-center bonds which effectively cause the delocalization of π and σ bonds [Figure 1] as well as saturate the dangling bonds in such 2D structures [16, 42, 43, 46, 47, 48]. Interestingly, similar arguments can also be used to explain the existence of the highly unusual coordination environments: hepta- and octa-coordinated boron atoms in the ground-state configurations of B_8 and B_9, respectively.[48] It was also suggested that these stable aromatic boron clusters can exhibit chemistry similar to the shown by benzene, such as forming sandwich-type metal compounds[48].

3 Large boron clusters(i.e., B_n, n $\geq$ 15)

In considering the large boron clusters, one can ask the obvious question whether the Hückel rules hold for the larger boron clusters leading to preference of the planarity in the ground state configurations. If planarity is not preferred, then one would like to determine the cluster size where the transition to 3D cages is likely to occur. However, there are relatively fewer experimental or theoretical studies have been performed in the cluster regime of (B_n, n $\geq$15). Recently, Zhai et al. have shown that the π-orbitals appear to be localized or 'fragmented' into different parts of B_{14} and B_{15} clusters. It appears that the Hückel rules which works quite well in explaining the high stability of planarity in the small clusters may not be applicable in the large clusters. The 2D-3D transition in the structural configuration is therefore expected for the cluster regime where the unsaturated dangling bonds in planarity become overwhelming.

For the large boron clusters (e.g. B_{20} [17, 52], B_{24} [18, 53], B_{32} [54], B_{60} [55] and B_{96} [56]), several distinctive shapes of configurations were considered for the electronic structure calculations, namely ring, chain, tubular, spherical cages, convex, quasiplanar, and bulk fragments as shown in Figure 2, instead of performing an exhaustive exploration of all possible isomers on the potential energy surface which is very onerous. The calculated results predict that the large clusters(i.e., B_{24} [18, 53], B_{32} [54] and B_{96} [56]) favor a tubular structure over the planar structure regardless of the charged states of the cluster [18]. Thus, the exact 2D-3D structural transition shown in Figure 3 should occur somewhere in the regime of $B_{15} < B_n < B_{24}$, and indeed the proposed range of the transition has also been suggested through the most recent experimental photoelectron spectra on B_{20} [17]. The calculated results based on density functional theory at the B3LYP/6-311+G* level found the double-ring (tubular) configuration to be the ground state for both B_{20} and B_{20}^-, but analysis of the photoelectron spectra appears to favor the planar structures. In fact, such incongruity can be explained by the difficulties associated with the experimental and computational techniques. Numerically, first principles calculations find the double-ring (tubular) and planar configurations to be degenerate (with $\Delta G = 0.02$ eV). In the case of B_{20}^-, the four low-lying isomers are separated by less than 0.015eV/atom, which is the order of the precision of the quantum chemistry methods employed in the study [17]. On the other hand, experimentally it is known that the production of clusters is mainly controlled by kinematics, and is dependent on experimental techniques employed, as found in the case of C_{20} [57].

In this context, the carbon clusters have been reported to have a very interesting size-dependent structural evolution starting from chains to rings to fullerenes [1]. However, such an evolution is not predicted for the boron clusters where a linear chain or a ring configuration is never found to be the preferred configuration. For example, the monocyclic ring configuration in B_{24} is at 1.00 eV/atom higher than the double-ring configuration [53]. In general, the double-ring configuration in B_{2n} clusters with n $\geq$ 6 is preferred in the staggered arrangements which facilitate the sp^2 hybridization, with the coordination number of four for each B atom. We note that the double-ring without the staggered configuration, and with the coordination number of three for each B atom

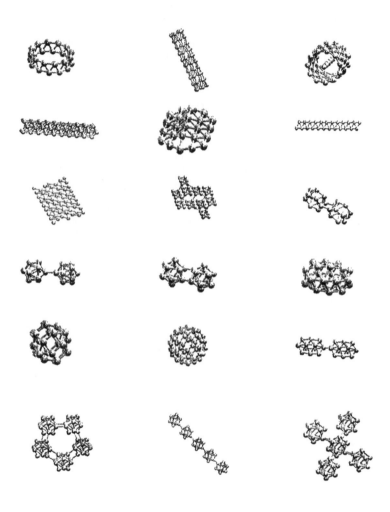

Figure 2: Several distinctive families of the possible configurations proposed in elemental boron clusters: ring, tubular, spherical cages, convex, quasiplanar, and hypothetical boron bulk fragments.

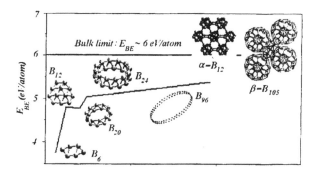

Figure 3: Size-dependent 2D planar to 3D tubular structure transition in elemental boron clusters

found to be less stable [18, 42, 55]. Though both carbon and boron clusters are found to exhibit the 2D-3D structural transition around a 20-atom cluster [17, 57], dissimilar bonding character determine the composition of the 3D configuration. The boron clusters prefer the 3D configuration to be a double-ring (tubular), while the carbon clusters prefer it to be a cage-like configuration. We therefore believe that the stable cage structures, similar to those of C_{20}, C_{32} and C_{36} [1, 2, 58], are not likely to be found for the large boron clusters. Figure 4 shows the size-dependent stability of the 3D configuration relative to the 2D configuration in terms of ΔE_{BE} defined as $E_{BE}(3D)$ - $E_{BE}(2D)$. In the small cluster regime (e.g. B_{12}) where the 2D planarity is preferred, ΔE_{BE} is -0.19eV/atom [42]. When we double the cluster-size to B_{24}, the 3D double-ring configuration gains about 0.26 eV/atom in energy yielding ΔE_{BE} to be 0.07 eV/atom [18]. A similar trend can also be seen in the large clusters regime for B_{32}, B_{60} and B_{96} clusters [54, 55, 56]. As also mentioned in the previous section, the emergence of preference over 2D planarity boron clusters can be comprehended as a consequence of effective charge delocalization from Hückel Rules. Thus, the trend in the stability of the 2D Vs. 3D configurations defined in ΔE_{BE} as shown in Figure 4, can be explained in terms of a competition between the curvature strain (favoring 2D planarity) and elimination of dangling bonds(favoring 3D staggard double-ring) [18, 54].

Figure 5 shows the molecular orbitals (MOs) of the ground state of B_{24} where the notation HOMO-n is used to represent the selected occupied molecular orbitals in these clusters. Analysis of MOs reveals the interesting features of delocalized π, σ, and multi-centered σ bonds between the boron atoms. The highest occupied molecular orbital (HOMO) shows the π bond between the atoms of each ring, while the lowest unoccupied molecular orbital (LUMO) shows a lateral $p - p$ overlap between the atoms of both rings. The HOMO and (HOMO-1) are doubly-degenerate giving rise to an effective delocalization. While the (HOMO-2) and (HOMO-3) orbitals show localized π-bonding in B_1 state, the (HOMO-6) and(HOMO-7) degenerate orbitals show a delocalized π-bonding at both sides of the rings in E state. Besides finding the similar bonding features as benzene in small 2D clusters (Figure 1), a similar feature of fully delocalized benzene-like π bonds between the two staggered rings is achieved in A_1 state of (HOMO-8) orbital.

On the other hand, analysis of MOs of the 2D elongated quasi-planar reveals that the delocalized π bonds between boron atoms appear to be 'fragmented' into different parts of the cluster configuration. Instead of dominant features of delocalized π MOs found in small boron clusters [16, 42, 46, 47, 48], the 2D planar isomer is mainly associated with the more 'localized' orbitals in

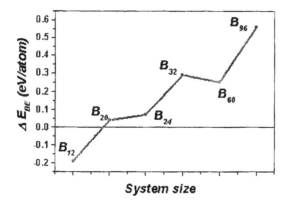

Figure 4: The size dependence of the relative stability of boron clusters (e.g. 2D planarity Vs. 3D double-ring (tubular)). The ΔE_{BE} is defined as $E_{BE}(3D) - E_{BE}(2D)$. The respective values of the energy are taken from the references [17, 18, 42, 54, 55, 56]

this larger cluster regime. Therefore, we may conclude that the absence of delocalized π MOs in the 2D planar configuration in B_{24}, makes the corresponding structure energetically less favorable, due to an increase in the unsaturated dangling bonds with the increase of the size of the cluster. In this conjunction, the presence of delocalized π and multi-centered σ bonds in the double-ring (tubular) structure (e.g. B_{24}), plays a key role in stabilizing this structure, by overcoming the strain energy (or curvature energy) acted on the system.

For the B_n (i.e. $n \geq 30$) clusters, the experimental studies are not available and first principles calculations are rather limited. The reported Hartree-Fock calculations which used the standard STO-3G basis set together with the symmetry-constrained optimization predicted the low-lying stable structures to be quasi-planar and tubular configurations. [54, 56, 59] In the case of B_{32}, the double-ring (tubular) isomer in D_4 symmetry with a diameter of 8.1 Å is predicted to be more stable than C_{2h} quasi-planar and D_{4h} spherical cage by 0.29 and 0.36 eV/atom, respectively. The preferred topological structure of the B_{32} cluster suggested that the interplay between curvature-strain and elimination of dangling bonds determine the stability among these 2D and 3D configurations. A similarly argument can be applied to tubular and quasi-planar configurations of B_{96}. The Hartree-Fock calculations [56] reported that the segments of tubular and quasi-planar sheet turn out to be more stable than the unit cells of α-boron. In B_{60}, density functional theory calculations using the standard STO-3G basis set predict the C_{60}-like spherical cage to be about 1.0 eV/atom less stable in energy relative to the tubular structure of diameter of about 1.53 nm. Similarly, the C_{5v} boron bulk fragment (Figure 2) and the 2D convex (in C_2 symmetry) configurations are at 0.67 and 0.23 eV/atom relative to the tubular isomer.

On the other hand, the bulk fragment (i.e.α-boron unit-cell cluster) of B_{96} is almost degenerate with the 2D quasi-planar sheet, though the tubular isomer with a diameter of 2.35 nm is predicted to be the ground state. Thus, it is noteworthy to point that the bulk fragments of boron can become a competitive isomeric configuration with the increase in the cluster-size, instead of 3D spherical cages observed in carbon clusters. We believe that as the delocalized π MOs which are responsible in eliminating the dangling bonds of the 2D planar boron clusters, expected to be more

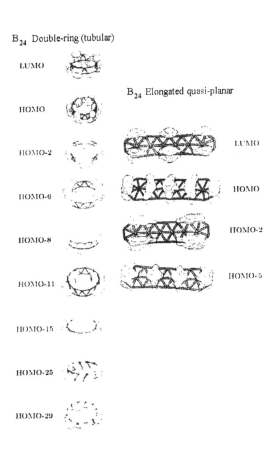

Figure 5: Selected molecular orbitals of the double-ring configuration and 2D elongated quasi-planar configuration of B_{24}. [18]

'fragment' and 'localized' in different parts of the clusters in the so-called boron supercluster regime, making the 2D planarity less favorable in this regime. The emergence of all possible boron bulk fragments based on the B_{12} icosahedral networks, thus cannot be ignored as a probable competitive isomer for large boron clusters. We may therefore conclude that the key role in determining the structural configuration is played by the delocalized π bonds in the small cluster regime, while the inter-icosahedral and intra-icosahedral bonds which coincide with the possible interlink of B_{12} icosahedrons begin to participate in determining the configurations in the large cluster regime of the elemental boron.

4 Summary

The research activities related to elemental boron clusters are comparatively younger than that related to carbon clusters. In this review article, we have presented an overview of the physical and chemical properties of elemental boron clusters, showing the interplay of structural dimensionality and chemical bonding as important factors in building up the structures that were synthesized in experiments or predicted in theoretical studies. The high stability of 2D planarity and aromaticity is anticipated in small clusters regime (e.g. $B_n \leq B_{15}$) suggesting their promising potential applications as a new 'sandwich-type' functional boron nanostructures which are doped with metallic atoms. Besides their potential applications in nanoelectronics, the proposed size-dependent 2D planar to 3D tubular transition beyond B_{20} regime can be regarded as a very promising evidence for the existence of a new 'homo-nuclear' boron nanotubes, which can be used as ultra-light radioactive detectors and neutron capture therapy nanodevices by enriching them with B^{10} isotope, which has a large cross section area for thermal neutron capture.

References

[1] R.O. Jones and G. Seifert, Structure and bonding in carbon clusters C_{14} to C_{24}: chains, rings, bowls, plates, and cages, *Phys. Rev. Lett.* **79** 443-446. 1997.

[2] R.O. Jones, Density functional study of carbon clusters C_{2n} ($2 \leq n \leq 16$) I: structure and bonding in the neutral clusters, *J. Chem. Phys.*, **110** 5189, 1999.

[3] H.W. Kroto, J.R. Heath, S.C.O'brien, R.F. Curl and R.E. Smalley, C_{60}: Buckminsterfullerene, *Nature* **318** 162-163, 1985.

[4] Sumio Iijima, Helical microtubules of grahitic carbon. *Nature* **354** 56-57, 1991.

[5] E.L. Muetterties (Ed): *The Chemistry Of Boron and Its Compounds.* John Wiley, New York. 1967.

[6] E.L. Muetterties (Ed): *Boron Hydride Chemistry.* Academic, New York, 1975.

[7] M. Takeda, K. Kimura, A. Hori, H. Yamashita, and H. Ino, Approximate phase of an icosahedral quasicrystal in a boron-carbon semiconducting system, *Phys. Rev.* B **48** 13159-13161, 1993.

[8] C.L. Perkins, M. Trenary, and T. Tanaka, Direct observation of $(B_{12})(B_{12})_{12}$ supericosahedra as the basic structural element in YB_{66}, *Phys. Rev. Lett.* **77** 4772-4775, 1996.

[9] H. Hubert, B. Devouard, L.A.J. Garvie, M. O'Keeffe, P.R. Buseck, W.T. Petusky and P.F. McMillan, Icosahedral packing of B_{12} icosahedra in boron suboxide (B_6O), *Nature* **391** 376-378, 1998.

[10] N. Vast. S. Baroni. G. Zerah, J.M. Besson, A. Polian, M. Grimsditch. and J.C. Chervin, Lattice Dynamics of Icosahedral α-Boron under Pressure, *Phys. Rev. Lett.* **78** 693-696, 1997.

[11] J. Zhao and J.P. Lu. Pressure-induced metallization in solid boron. *Phys. Rev.* B **66** 092101-92104. 2002.

[12] W.L. Lipscomb: *Boron Hydrides*. W.A. Benjamin, New York. 1963.

[13] E.D. Jemmis, M.M. Balakrishnarajan, P.D. Pancharatna, Electronic requirements for macropolyhedral boranes, *Chem. Rev.* **102**, 93-144 (2002).

[14] E.D. Jemmis and G.J. Elambalassery, Analogies between Boron and Carbon. *Acc. Chem. Res.* **36** 816-824, 2003.

[15] E.D. Jemmis. M.M. Balakrishnarajan, P.D. Pancharatna, A unifying Electron-Counting Rule for Macropolyhedral Boranes, Metallaboranes. and Metallocenes, *J. Am. Chem. Soc.* **123** 4313-4323, 2001.

[16] H.J. Zhai, B. Kiran, J. Li and L.S. Wang, Hydrocarbon analogues of boron clusters-planarity, aromaticity and antiaromaticity, *Nature Materials* **2** 827-833, 2003.

[17] B. Kiran, S. Bulusu. H. Zhai, S. Yoo, X.C. Zeng and L.S. Wang, Planar-to-tubular structural transition in boron clusters: B_{20} as the embryo of single-walled boron nanotubes. *PNAS* **102** 961-964. 2005.

[18] K.C. Lau, M. Deshpande. R. Pati and R. Pandey, A theoretical study of electronic and vibrational properties of neutral. cationic and anionic B_{21} clusters, *Int. J. Quantum Chem.* **103** 866-874, 2005.

[19] C.J. Otten, O.R. Lourie, M. Yu. J.M. Cowley, M.J. Dyer, R.S. Ruoff and W.E. Buhro. Crystalline Boron Nanowire. *J. Am. Chem. Soc.* **124** 4564-4565, 2002.

[20] T.T. Xu. J. Zheng. N. Wu. A.W. Nichollas, J.R. Roth, D.A. Dikin and R.S. Ruoff, Crystalline Boron Nanoribbons: Synthesis and Characterization, *Nano Lett.* **4** 963-968, 2004.

[21] D. Ciuparu. R.F. Klie. Y. Zhu and L. Pfefferle. Synthesis of Pure Boron Single-Wall Nanotubes. *J. Phys. Chem.* B **108** 3967-3969, 2004.

[22] L. Hanley and S.L. Anderson, Production and collision-induced dissociation of small boron cluster ions. *J. Phys. Chem.* **91** 5161-5163. 1987.

[23] L. Hanley, J.L. Whittena and S.L. Anderson, Collision-induced dissociation and ab initio studies of boron clusters ions: determination of structure and stabilities, *J. Phys. Chem.* **92** 5803-5812. 1988.

[24] P.A. Hintz, M.B. Sowa, S.A. Ruatta and S.L. Anderson. Reactions of boron cluster ions (B_n^+. n = 2-24) with N_2O:NO versus NN bond activation as a function of size. *J. Chem. Phys.* **94** 6446-6458. 1991.

[25] M.B. Sowa. A.L. Snolanoff, A. Lapicki and S.L. Anderson. Interaction of small boron cluster ions with HF. *J. Chem. Phys.* **106** 9511-9522. 1997.

[26] S.J. La Placa, P.A. Roland and J.J. Wynne, Boron clusters (B_n, n = 2-52) produced by laser ablation of hexagonal boron nitride, *Chem. Phys. Lett.* **190** 163-168. 1992.

[27] R. Kawai and J.H. Weare, Instability of the B_{12} icosahedral cluster: rearrangment to a lower energy structure, *J. Chem. Phys.* **95** 1151-1159, 1991.

[28] R. Kawai and J.H. Weare, Anomalous stability of B_{13}^+ clusters, *Chem. Phys. Lett.* **191** 311-314, 1992.

[29] A.K. Ray, I.A. Howard and K.M. Kanal, Structure and bonding in small neutral and cationic boron clusters, *Phys. Rev. B* **45** 14247-14255, 1992.

[30] V. Bonacic-Koutecky, P. Fantucci and J. Koutecky, Quantum chemistry of small clusters of elements of group Ia, Ib, and IIa: fundamental concepts, predictions, and interpretation of experiments, *Chem. Rev.* **91** 1035-1108, 1991.

[31] H. Kato, K. Yamashita and K. Morokuma, Ab Initio MO study of neutral and cationic boron clusters, it Chem. Phys. Lett. **190** 361-366, 1992.

[32] I. Boustani, Systematic LSD investigation on cationic boron clusters-B_n^+ (n = 2-14), *Int. J. Quantum Chem.* **52** 1081-1111, 1994.

[33] I. Boustani, Structure and stability of small boron clusters: A density functional study, *Chem. Phys. Lett.* **240** 135-140, 1995.

[34] I. Boustani, Systematic ab initio investigation of bare boron clusters: determination of the geometrical and electronic structures of B_n (n = 2-14), *Phys. Rev. B* **55** 16426-16438, 1997.

[35] A. Ricca and C.W. Bauschlicher, The structure and stability of B_n^+ clusters, *Chem. Phys.* **208** 233-242, 1996.

[36] F.L. Gu, X. Yang, A.C. Tang, H. Jiao and P.V.R. Schleyer, Structure and stability of B_{13}^+ clusters, *J. Comput. Chem.* **19** 203-214, 1998.

[37] J.E. Fowler and J.M. Ugalde, The curiously stable B_{13}^+ cluster and its neutral and anionic counterparts: the advantages of planarity, *J. Phys. Chem. A* **104** 397-403, 2000.

[38] J. Aihara, B_{13}^+ is highly aromatic, *J. Phys. Chem. A* **105** 5486-5489, 2001.

[39] H. Reis and M.G. Papadopoulos, Nonlinear optical properties of the rhombic B_4 cluster, *J. Comp. Chem* **20** 679-687, 1999.

[40] H. Reis, M.G. Papadopoulos and I. Boustani, DFT calculations of static dipole polarizabilities and hyperpolarizabilities for the boron clusters B_n (n = 3-8,10), *Int. J. Quantum Chem.* **78** 131-135, 2000.

[41] A. Abdurahman, A. Shukla and G. Seifert, Ab Initio many-body calculation of static dipole polarizabilities of linear carbon chains and chainlike boron clusters, *Phys. Rev. B* **66** 155423-7, 2002.

[42] K.C. Lau, M. Despande and R. Pandey, A Theoretical Study of Vibrational Properties of Neutral and Cationic B_{12} Clusters, *Int. J. Quantum Chem.* **102** 656-664, 2005.

[43] J. Ma, Z. Li, K. Fan and M. Zhou, Density functional theory study of the B_6, B_6^+, B_6^-, and B_6^{2-} clusters, *Chem. Phys. Lett.* **372** 708-716, 2003.

[44] H.J. Zhai, L.S. Wang, A.N. Alexandrova, A.I. Boldyrev, and V.G. Zakrzewski, Photoelectron Spectroscopy and Ab Initio Study of B_3^- and B_4^- Anions and Their Neutrals, *J. Phys. Chem. A* **107** 9313-9328, 2003.

[45] H.J. Zhai, L.S. Wang, A.N. Alexandrova and A.I. Boldyrev, Electronic structure and chemical bonding of B_5^- and B_5 by photoelectron spectroscopy and ab initio calculations, *J. Chem. Phys.* **117** 7917-7924, 2002.

[46] A.N. Alexandrova, A.I. Boldyrev, H.J. Zhai, L.S. Wang, E. Steiner and P.W. Fowler, Structure and bonding in B_6^- and B_6: Planarity and Antiaromaticity, *J. Phys. Chem. A* **107** 1359-1369, 2003.

[47] A.N. Alexandrova, A.I. Boldyrev, H.J. Zhai and L.S. Wang, Electronic Structure, Isomerism, and Chemical Bonding in B_7^- and B_7, *J. Phys. Chem. A* **108** 3509-3517, 2004.

[48] H.J. Zhai, A.N. Alexandrova, K.A. Birch, A.I. Boldyrev and L.S.Wang, Hepta- and Octaco-ordinate Boron in Molecular Wheels of Eight- and Nine-Atom Boron Clusters: Observation and Confirmation, *Angew. Chem. Int. Ed.* **42** 6004-6008, 2003.

[49] W.N. Lipscomb, Three-center bonds in electron-deficient compounds: The localized molecular orbital approach, *Acc. Chem. Rec.* **6** 257-262, 1973.

[50] R.B. King, Three-Dimensional Aromaticity in Polyhedral Boranes and Related Molecules, *Chem. Rev.* **101** 1119-1152, 2001.

[51] D.R. Lide (Ed): *CRC Handbook of Chemistry and Physics.* CRC Press, Boca Raton, 1995.

[52] M.A.L. Marques and S. Botti, The planar-to-tubular transition in boron clusters from optical absorption, *arXiv:physics* **1** 0504090, 2005.

[53] S. Chacko, D.G. Kanhere and I. Boustani, Ab initio density functional investigation of B_{24} clusters: rings, tubes, planes, and cages, *Phys. Rev. B* **68** 035414, 2003.

[54] I. Boustani, A. Rubio and J.A. Alonso, Ab initio study of B_{32} clusters: competition between spherical, quasiplanar, and tubular isomers, *Chem. Phys. Lett.* **311** 21-28, 1999.

[55] K.C. Lau and R. Pandey, *unpublished results.*

[56] I. Boustani, A. Quandt and A. Rubio, Boron quasicrystals and boron nanotubes: ab initio study of various B_{96} isomers, *J. of Solid State Chem.* **154** 269-274, 2000.

[57] H. Prinzbach, A. Weiler, P. Landenberger, F. Wahl, J. Worth, L.T. Scott, M. Gelmont, D. Olevano and B. Issendorff, Gas-phase production and photoelectron spectroscopy of the smallest fullerene, C_{20}, *Nature* **407** 60-63, 2000.

[58] J.C. Grossman, M.E. Colvin, N.L. Tran, S.G. Louie and M.L. Cohen, Aromaticity and hydrogenation patterns in highly strained fullerenes, *Chem. Phys. Lett.* **356** 247, 2002.

[59] I. Boustani, A. Quandt, E. Hernández and A. Rubio, New boron based nanostructures materials, *J. Chem. Phys.* **110** 3176-3185, 1999.

Brill Academic Publishers
P.O. Box 9000, 2300 PA Leiden,
The Netherlands

*Lecture Series on Computer
and Computational Sciences*
Volume 5, 2006, pp. 128-133

Li and Be clusters: Structure, bonding and odd-even effects in half-filled systems

Ayan Datta and Swapan K Pati[1]

Theoretical Sciences Unit and Chemistry and Physics of Materials Unit,
Jawaharlal Nehru Center for Advanced Scientific Research,
Jakkur PO,
Bangalore-560064, India

Abstract: We compare and contrast the structure and bonding aspects in clusters of alkali and alkaline earth metals: Li and Be respectively. The binding energies for both the clusters increase with increase in cluster size, however, for Be, the binding energies increase much rapidly due to stronger cooperative phenomenon. For the high spin Li clusters, the binding energies are moderate and show a remarkable odd-even effect. Similar oscillations are also observed in their π-electron binding energies. The origin of such effects is traced to the ferromagnetic interactions arising from the unpaired electrons for the high spin clusters. On the contrary, for Be, no such odd-even effects are observed due to absence of unpaired electrons.

Keywords: DFT, spin-frustration, binding energies, ferromagnetic coupling, odd-even oscillation

Mathematics Subject Classification: 31.15.Ew, 36.40.Cg, 36.40.Qv, 36.40.Mr

There is a substantial interest in the chemistry and physics of metal clusters due to their interesting and unusual properties at the nanoscale compared to that in the bulk[1, 2, 3]. The thermal, mechanical, optical and transport properties of these clusters have been a subject of active research from both experimental and computational aspects[4]. Computer modeling of these clusters have been very successful in explaining and predicting new results in this area[5, 6].

For the present work, we consider neutral clusters of Lithium and Beryllium. Li atom has one unpaired electron in the valence orbital ($[He]2s^1$) while Be has no unpaired electrons in the valence orbital ($[He]2s^2$). Li-Li bond in $(Li)_2$ is expected to be formed by sharing unpaired electrons at each atomic sites and should thus have a single bond character. However, for multi-centered interactions like in $(Li)_n$ with n>2, it is not quite clear whether such a simple picture would remain valid. For example, in $(Li)_3$, there are two spin possibilities, high-spin (H.S.): S=3/2 and low-spin (L.S.): S=1/2 configuration. Although the L.S. state corresponds to the ground state, it would be highly frustrated in case of cyclic triangular structure[7]. The picture becomes much more complicated for a multi-atomic cluster. For Be however, such a spin frustration does not exist as the Be atom is diamagnetic. These twin metal clusters thus serve as an excellent model for understanding the role of electronic spins in controlling the structural and bonding aspects in more involved architectures for future electronic devices at the nanoscale.

The geometries for $(Li)_n$ and $(Be)_n$, n=1-8, were fully optimized using the the hybrid Becke 3 Lee-Yang-Parr (B3LYP) gradient corrected approximate density functional procedure at the 6-31G+(d) basis set level[8]. The basis set was further increased to 6-311G+(d,p) level to ensure

---

[1]Corresponding author. Theoretical sciences unit and DST unit on Nanoscience, JNCASR, pati@jncasr.ac.in

basis set convergence. Corresponding to each minimum energy structure, we find that there are several geometrical isomers very close in energy. Several initial guess structures with different symmetries were thus investigated. Additional frequency calculations were performed on these clusters to confirm the ground state geometry and removal of vibrational instabilities. The ground state geometry optimized structures of $(Li)_n$ are shown in Fig. 1.

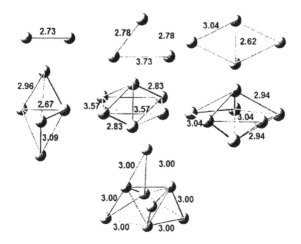

Figure 1: The ground state structures of Li_n, n=1-8 clusters

With the increase in the size of the clusters, these structures become progressively distorted and non-planar. The rhombus geometry in $(Li)_4$, corresponds to the largest planar structure. Further increase in the cluster size leads to formation of closed structures with $(Li)_6$ and $(Li)_7$ being octahedral and pentagonal bi-pyramidal respectively. $(Li)_8$ on the other hand maintains a pyramidal structure. The structure of the $(Li)_6$ cluster is of particular interest. The planar D_{6h}, benzene like structure exists as a local minimal structure and its binding energy is 73.7 kcal/mol compared to the octahedral ground state structure that has a binding energy of 102 kcal/mol.

The ground state for all the systems with n=odd (n=1,3,5 and 7) is an S=1/2 state while for n=even, the stable geometry is associated with pairing of the single unpaired electron in each Li atom suggesting S=0 for the even numbered clusters. However, for the odd clusters, such a spin pairing is geometrically forbidden and the ground state structures have frustrated spin-degeneracy since the unpaired spin can be in any Li atom or is delocalized over the entire cluster.

Fig. 2 shows the ground state structures for the Be clusters. Comparing the geometries in Be and Li clusters of similar sizes, some clear distinctions can be made. While, Li_4 has planar rhombus like structure, the Be_4 cluster has a non-planar tetrahedral structure. The average Be-Be bond lengths are smaller than that of Li-Li bond lengths. Therefore, from the structure itself, it is evident that Be clusters are more compact and stable compared to Li clusters. We have quantitatively calculated the binding energies for these clusters using a dissociation of the type: M_n to nM_1, where M=Li and Be and n stands for the cluster size. Thus, the binding energy for a cluster of size n is defined by $[nE(M_1)-E(M_n)]$, where E is the energy for the corresponding cluster. In Fig. 3, we plot the binding energies for the twin clusters with increase in the size of the system. While, the binding energies for the Li_n clusters increase monotonically with n, the Be_n clusters show a remarkable cooperative phenomena. It increases very slowly from n=2 to

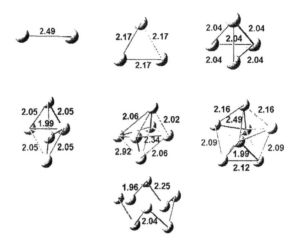

Figure 2: The ground state structures of Be_n, n=1-8 clusters

n=3 but increases rapidly after n=4. In fact for n=2 and n=3, the Li clusters are more stable. However, as n increases, the stability of the Be clusters exceed that for Li. The transition from the planar to non-planar structures after n=4 lead to more compact geometries and also increases the coordination number of the Be atoms and thereby stabilizes the Be clusters.

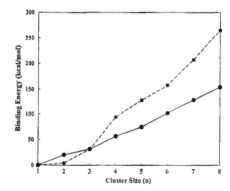

Figure 3: Variation in the binding energies for Li_n (circles) and Be_n (squares) clusters with the increase in the cluster size.

We now specifically consider only the Li clusters since there are many important effects that need special attention. While the even Li_n clusters have an anti-ferromagnetic ground state, the odd membered systems have one unpaired electron in their ground state and thus would certainly possess spin-frustration. This is also true for a single Li atom. However, our previous definition of the binding energy of the Li clusters make no such distinctions. To distinguish the stabilization energies due to different ground states for even and odd membered clusters, we further modify the definition of the B.E as $(B.E)_{odd}=[nE(M_1)-E(M_n)]$ and $(B.E)_{even}= [(n/2)E(M_2)-E(M_n)]$. Note that, for the odd-membered rings, the simplistic dissociation scheme is quite valid as both M_n and M_1 are of paramagnetic nature. However, we specifically use the second formula given above for the even-membered systems as it ensures the diamagnetic nature of the final (M_n) as well as the smallest even membered material (M_2). The variation of the binding energy with the definition above, is shown in Fig. 4, for the Li_n clusters. One clearly observes a remarkable odd-even phenomenon in the binding energies with the odd-membered clusters being more stable than their even-membered congeners.

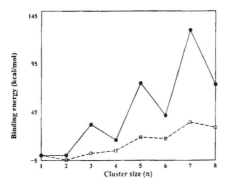

Figure 4: Variation in the binding energies for Li clusters in low-spin (ground state) configuration (circles) and the same in high spin configuration (squares). The binding energies for odd(even)-membered clusters are defined as $\Delta E_n(odd)=nE_1-E_n$ ($\Delta E_n(even)=(n/2)E_2-E_n$) with cluster size, n.

For a proper understanding of such an odd-even oscillation in the binding energies for these Li_n clusters, we also consider the highest spin configurations in these systems. For such a configuration the H.S. geometry does not have any component of π-delocalization and the stability of such clusters involve only the σ-backbone as the π-electrons are already frozen in a H.S. configuration. Therefore, the interactions in these clusters can be formally called as *ferromagnetic bonding* [9, 10]. In Fig. 4, we plot the binding energies for these H.S. structures. Since the odd or even membered rings with H.S. configurations make no such distinction between diamagnetic or frustrated nature, the bindings energies are calculated using the simplistic dissociation scheme discussed previously ($\Delta E_n=nE_1-E_n$) with the energy of Li_n now corresponding to all parallel spin configuration. Note that the H.S. configuration corresponds to the same geometries as with the optimized L.S. configuration and only the spin state is changed. The binding energies for these H.S. clusters also show a similar odd-even effect with larger binding energy slope for the odd membered rings compared to that for the even membered rings. This is quite understandable since for the odd membered systems, the ground state has a doublet spin configuration (S=1/2) with finite magnetization. Thus, the ferromagnetic state involves less destabilization as compared to that for the even membered systems where the ground state is anti-ferromagnetic. One can also notice that for the small dimer, Li_2, with H.S. configuration (S=3/2), the structure is unstable by 4.6 kcal/mol but with the increase in the cluster size, the ferromagnetic structures become progressively stabilized and for the H.S. Li_8 configuration (S=4), the stabilization energy is 28.6 kcal/mol. Although in comparison to the L.S. structures, the binding energies in these ferromagnetic structures are smaller, the moderate binding energies for these ferromagnetic systems suggest that under suitable stabilizing conditions, these H.S. clusters can also be synthesized.

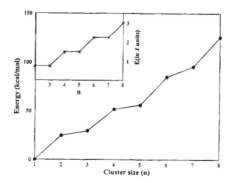

Figure 5: Variation in the π-energies (circles) as a function of increase in the cluster size(n). The inset shows the variation of the Exchange energy (in J units) with n.

These clusters are stabilized through both σ and π electron delocalizations. We quantitatively compute the π-electron contributions to the stability of the structures by performing a σ-π separation analysis. The π electronic energies are calculated as, $E_\pi = E_{GS} - E_\sigma$, where E_{GS} corresponds to the ground state energies for these structures. E_σ actually corresponds to the $E_{H.S.}$ energies as each Li atom has one valence electron and a H.S. configuration for these electrons suggests that these electrons are in all-parallel orientations and so are not involved in delocalization in the π-bonding interactions. Only the remaining core [He] electrons involve in bonding to form the σ-backbone. In Fig. 5, we plot the π-electron energy as the cluster size increases. One again observes a clear odd-even phenomenon with the energies being larger for the even-membered structures compared to the odd-ones.

The advantage of separating out the π-contribution from σ backbone is that one can then consider simple spin-spin interaction models to critically analyze the odd-even effects in these clusters. We use the well-known Heisenberg model[11] with localized π-electronic spin to calculate the interaction between the paramagnetic Li-centers. The interactions for an N site system can be written as:

$$H_{spin-spin} = J \sum_{<ij>} S_i . S_j \qquad (1)$$

where the sum runs over all N pairs. Since, the ground state geometry for these systems have L.S. configuration, we consider anti-ferromagnetic interaction between the electronic spins (positive J). The interaction energy can be calculated as

$$E_{spin-spin} = (J/2)[S_{total}(S_{total} + 1) - N S_1 (S_1 + 1)] \qquad (2)$$

where $S_1 = 1/2$ (spin of a single Li atom). One can further simplify the above equation as: $E_{spin-spin} = (J/2)[S_{total}(S_{total} + 1) - 3N/4]$. We assume that the interactions are isotropic in nature and the interaction between each pair is same (J) for all neighboring pairs. In Fig. 5 (inset), the exchange energy is plotted with the increase in the cluster size. The odd-even oscillation is evident though the magnitude of exchange for the nth and $(n-1)^{th}$ (where n is odd) are same. Note that, although our assumption that J is constant for all the pairs is not entirely correct since the structures for the Li_n clusters are distorted from ideal polygonal structures, the fact that even such a simple model can explain odd-even oscillations for these clusters certainly adds credibility to our calculations. More detailed numerical calculations are underway to take into account different exchange constants between different pairs.

In conclusion, we have have shown that in contrast to Be, clusters of alkali metals like Li show strong odd-even oscillations in their stabilities with larger stabilities in the odd membered cluster family. This is counterintuitive as the odd-membered rings have one unpaired electron compared to that for the even-membered rings where all the valence electrons are paired up and thus one would expect the even-clusters to be more stable. In fact, this is clearly seen for the π-electron energies where the even clusters are more stable. But, the actual stability for these clusters are controlled by the electrons in the σ-backbone as the stability for the H.S. clusters are more in the odd-series. In our opinion this is a very important result because the σ-electrons which are otherwise known only to have backbone effect, take a dominant role in these clusters.

SKP acknowledges CSIR, DST and the DST unit on nanoscience, Govt. of India, for the research grants. AD thanks CSIR for SRF scholarship.

References

[1] (a) Roy L. Johnston, *Atomic and Molecular Clusters.* Taylor & Francis, 2002. (b) Kawazoe. Y.; Kondow, T.; Ohno, K. (Eds.) *Clusters and Nanomaterials*, Springer, 2002. (c) Khanna, Shiv N.; Castleman, Albert W. (Eds.) *Quantum Phenomena in Clusters and Nanostructures.* Springer, 2003.

[2] Selvakannan. P. R.; Mandal. S.; Pasrichha, S.D.; Sastry, M., *Chem. Commun.*, **13**, 1334 (2002).

[3] Porel, S.; Singh, S.; Radhakrishnan, T. P.; *Chem. Commun.*, **18**, 2387 (2005).

[4] Kreibig, U.; Vollmer, M., *Optical properties of metal clusters.* Springer Verlag, Berlin, 1992.

[5] (a) Maroulis, G.; Pouchan, C. *J. Phys. Chem.B.* **107**, 10683 (2003). (b) Datta, A.; Pati, S. K. *J. Phys. Chem.A*, **108**, 9527 (2004). (c) Reis, H.; Papadopoulos, M. G.; *J. Comput. Chem.*, **20**. 679 (1999). (d) Datta, A.; Pati, S. K. *J. Am. Chem. Soc.*, **127**, 3496 (2005).

[6] (a) *Aromaticity and Antiaromaticity*, V. I. Minkin, M. N. Glukhontsev, B. Ya. Simkin, Wiley, NY, **1994**. (b) A. Kuznetsov, K. Birch, A. I. Boldyrev, X. Li, H. Zhai, L. Wang, *Science* **2003**. *300*, 622-625. (c) Z. Chen, C. Corminboeuf, T. Heine, J. Bohmann, P. V. R. Schleyer, *J. Am. Chem. Soc.* **2003**, *125*, 13930-13931.

[7] (a) Degenhardt. C.; Fiebig, M.; Pisarev, R.V.; *Phys. Rev. Lett.*, **88**, 027203 (2002). (b) Diep, H. T. (Ed.) *Frustrated Spin Systems*, World Scientific, 2005. (c) Ong, N. P.; Cava, R. J.; *Science*, **305**, 52 (2004).

[8] (a) Lee, C.; Yang, W.; Parr, R. G., *Phys. Rev. B* **37**, 785, (1988). (b) Schmidt, M. W.; Baldridge. K. K.; Boatz. J. A.; et al. *J. Comput. Chem.*, **14**, 1347, (1993).

[9] S. P. de Visser, D. Danovich, W. Wu, S. Shaik, *J. Phys. Chem. A*, **106**, 4961, (2002).

[10] (a) S. P. de Visser. D. Danovich, W. Wu, S. Shaik. *J. Phys. Chem. A*, **104**, 11223, (2000). (b) S. P. de Visser, D. Danovich, S. Shaik, *Phys. Chem. Chem. Phys.*, **5**, 158, (2002).

[11] *Magnetism: Molecules to Materials IV*, Ed: J. S. Miller and Marc Drillon, Wiley-VCH, Weinheim, 2003.

Brill Academic Publishers
P.O. Box 9000, 2300 PA Leiden,
The Netherlands

Lecture Series on Computer
and Computational Sciences
Volume 5, 2006, pp. 134-144

Clustering of water molecules on model soot particles: an ab initio study.

B. Collignon[a], P.N.M. Hoang[a], S. Picaud[a1], and J.C. Rayez[b]

[a]Laboratoire de Physique Moléculaire - UMR CNRS 6624
Université de Franche-Comté, 16 route de Gray
25030 Besançon Cedex, France
[b]Laboratoire de Physico-Chimie Moléculaire - UMR CNRS 5803,
Université de Bordeaux I, 351 cours de la Libération,
F-33405 Talence Cedex, France

Abstract: Clustering of water molecules on model soot particles is studied by means of quantum calculations based on the ONIOM approach. The soot particles are modelled by anchoring OH or COOH groups on the face side or on the edges of a graphite crystallite of nanometer size. The quantum calculations aim at characterizing the adsorption properties (structure and adsorption energy) of small water aggregates containing up to 5 water molecules, in order to better understand at a molecular level the role of these OH and COOH groups on the behavior with respect to water adsorption of graphite surface modelling soot emitted by aircraft.

Keywords: ab initio calculation , water adsorption , soot

1 Introduction

Aircraft emissions are suspected to play an important role in atmospheric chemistry not only because airplanes are the main source of pollutant molecules at their cruise altitude, but also because soot particles generated by aircraft engines are implied in the nucleation of ice particles in contrails due to their ability to adsorb and condense water molecules. These processes (adsorption and condensation) result in the formation of artificial cirrus clouds[1, 2] that may have a large impact on the chemistry of the upper troposphere/lower stratosphere (UTLS) by providing active surfaces for heterogeneous chemical processes such as, for example, the conversion of HNO_3 to NO_x[3, 4], or the photo-oxidation of adsorbed volatile organic compounds to HO_x[5]. Moreover, these artificial cirrus clouds may also add their contribution to the impact of natural clouds in climate changes by allowing solar radiation to heat the Earth surface and/or by absorbing terrestrial radiation which adds to "greenhouse" warming[6].

Despite this environmental interest, aircraft-generated soot are still poorly characterized, although recent transmission electron microscopy studies have shown that soot is made of nanocrystallites containing graphite-type layers of 20- to 50-nm size[7, 8]. Additional results of Raman spectroscopy revealed that these graphite layers contain a certain number of hydrophilic groups such as carbonyl, carboxyl, phenol and hydroxyl groups[8], and measurements of water adsorption isotherms confirmed that soot particles can acquire a substantial amount of water molecules unlike pure graphite[9, 10].

---

[1]Corresponding author. E-mail: sylvain.picaud@univ-fcomte.fr

From a theoretical point of view, only few studies on this topic have been reported so far, and a theoretical detailed understanding at the molecular level of the water nucleation on soot remains challenging. For example, Tarasevich and Aksenenko used the semiempirical PM3 method to characterize the equilibrium configuration of up to three water molecules with partially oxidized graphite surfaces[11, 12, 13]. and show that vacancies or/and OH and COOH hydrophilic groups can favor the formation of small water aggregates on the graphite surface. Adsorption equilibrium of a much larger number of water molecules has also been studied on partially oxidized graphite surface by means of Grand Canonical Monte Carlo[14, 15, 16] or Molecular Dynamics[17] simulations based on a classical description of the interaction potentials between water and the graphite surface. These works have shown that the water adsorption is strongly dependent on the presence and arrangement of the hydrophilic groups. Although these previous theoretical works have taken into account the influence of hydrophilic groups, a full quantum chemical study on the first steps of the water aggregation around these groups was lacking. Therefore, by using high-level *ab initio* calculations based on the ONIOM method[18], we have recently performed a detailed characterization of the water nucleation mechanism on OH groups anchored either on the face or on the edge of a graphite cluster of nanometer size modelling a soot particle[19]. The corresponding adsorption energy of up to five water molecules has thus been determined, and we have shown that OH acts as a trapping site for the water molecules, leading to the formation of clusters containing up to 3-5 molecules, with mean adsorption energies per water molecule that range between -16.7 and -32.2 kJ/mol on the face, and between -19.3 and -34.2 kJ/mol on the edge of the hydroxylated graphite cluster. The formation of such small water aggregates is in agreement with the interpretation of recent experimental data obtained on different types of soot[8]. These results were compared with those obtained for one single water molecule adsorbed on a COOH group anchored on the graphite cluster[19, 20], and showed that OH is less attractive for one water molecule than COOH, with an adsorption energy for a single H_2O equal to about -38.0 kJ/mol on COOH. Moreover, due to the larger size of the carboxyl group, the adsorption characteristics for one water molecule does not depend on the location of the COOH group on the graphite surface (face or edge site).

In the present work, we extend our comparison between the ability of OH and COOH to adsorb water molecules, by investigating the adsorption of small water aggregates on both kinds of hydrophilic groups anchored on a small graphite cluster (face and edge sites) modelling a soot nanocrystallite. The calculations are based on the ONIOM method, and we especially focus on the nucleation properties of the OH and COOH groups with respect to the water adsorption by calculating the optimized structures of aggregates containing up to 5 water molecules interacting with the partially oxidized graphite surfaces. The corresponding values of the interaction energy are also calculated and compared for these two kinds of hydrophilic groups on both face and edge sites.

The paper is organized as follows. In section 2, we briefly describe the method and summarize the computational details. The results of the quantum study of the interaction between a small water aggregate and the OH groups anchored on the face or on the edge of a small graphite cluster are presented and compared to those obtained when considering a COOH group in section 3. The main conclusions are summarized in section 4.

2   Method and Computational Details

The method used in the present work is similar to the one developed in our previous papers [19, 20]. The graphite-like surface is modelled by means of a $C_{80}H_{22}$ cluster (30 fused benzene rings) that represents a nanometer-size graphite crystallite (Fig 1). The ONIOM method[18] has been used to implement an OH or a COOH group either on the surface (face-oxidized) or on the edges (edge-oxidized) of the graphite cluster. In these calculations, all the boundary C atoms of the cluster have been saturated with hydrogen atoms, except the one that is attached to the hydrophilic group. Then, the structure of water aggregates containing up to five water molecules interacting with the COOH or OH group has been optimized, in order to characterize the behavior of the oxidized graphite surface with respect to water nucleation.

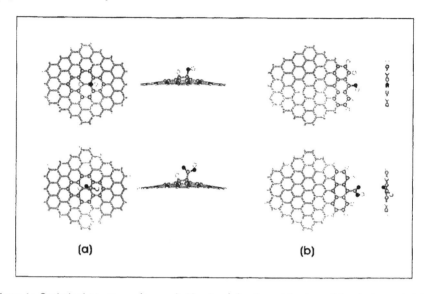

Figure 1: Optimized structures (top and side views) for the oxidized graphite cluster containing an anchored OH or COOH group on its face (a) or on its edge (b). This cluster contains 80 carbon atoms, 22 hydrogen atoms that are used to saturate the edges of the cluster, and the anchored OH+H or COOH+H group (see text). When considering anchoring on the edge, the cluster contains 80 carbon atoms, 21 hydrogen atoms for the saturation of the edges, and the anchored OH or COOH group. The atoms pertaining to the DFT-cluster in the ONIOM calculations are represented by small circles.

To perform geometry optimizations and energy calculations of such a large system, we make use of the two layers ONIOM method[18]. The central part of the system, that contains the water molecules, the hydrophilic (COOH or OH) group and the closest neighboring C and H atoms, is treated with a high-level of accuracy by using Density Functional Theory (DFT) and defines what we call the DFT-cluster, whereas the rest of the system is taken into account with the semiempirical PM3 method[21]. The calculations have been performed with the Gaussian 03 quantum chemistry package[22], by using the B3LYP exchange-correlation functional[23] and the cc-pVDZ basis set[24] in the DFT calculations of most stable geometries. Once the geometry of the system is optimized, the final energy of the water+hydroxylated graphite system is calculated with the larger 6-311++G(2d,2p) basis set for the DFT layer.

On the graphite face, the hydrophilic group (OH or COOH) is placed on one of the two carbons that are located at the center of the cluster, and an additional H atom is added on the surface to saturate the resulting free valence on the neighboring central C atom. The DFT-cluster contains the four fused benzene rings around the C atom that is bound to the OH group, and the rest of the graphite cluster is treated with the PM3 method (Fig. 1a). When characterizing adsorption on the

Table 1: Mean adsorption energy per molecule ($\Delta E_{\text{ads}}/n$) and the corresponding incremental association energy (ΔE_{inc}) above the defective graphite surface for small water aggregates containing n H_2O molecules. Values are given for an OH or a COOH group located on the surface or on the edge of the graphite cluster. Energies are given in kJ/mol.

group	n	$\Delta E_{\text{ads}}/n$ (face)	ΔE_{inc} (face)	$\Delta E_{\text{ads}}/n$ (edge)	ΔE_{inc} (edge)
OH	1	16.7	16.7	19.3	19.3
	2	24.8	32.9	26.9	34.5
	3	30.4	41.6	34.2	48.8
	4	30.5	30.8	32.2	26.2
	5	32.2	39.0	33.0	36.2
COOH	1	38.4	38.4	38.1	38.1
	2	40.1	41.8	40.3	42.5
	3	37.4	32.0	37.6	32.2
	4	35.6	30.2	35.3	28.4
	5	34.8	31.6	35.1	34.3

edges of our graphite cluster, only symmetric anchoring site has been considered[19], corresponding to the definition of a symmetric DFT-cluster in our ONIOM calculations, as shown in Fig. 1b. This DFT-cluster thus contains 3 benzene rings arranged in a linear structure. Such a choice of DFT-clusters has been shown to be a good compromise between accuracy and computational time[19, 20].

3   Results and Discussion

First of all, let us mention that the optimized structure for the surface containing the OH or COOH group is characterized by a loss of planarity near the anchored group due to relaxation along the z direction perpendicular to the bare graphite plane (Fig 1a). This originates from the rehybridization of the carbon atoms to which the OH or COOH group and the additional H atom are attached[19, 20]. By contrast, no significant reorganization of the graphite cluster is obtained when the OH or COOH group is anchored on the edge of the cluster. Note however that, whereas the OH group is located in the graphite plane, the COOH group is rotated out of this plane (by an angle θ_{COOH} equal to about 50°) in order to avoid the steric repulsion of the underlying H atoms (i.e. those who are saturating the boundary C atoms)(Fig 1b). On the face-oxidized surface, the COOH group is also rotated by an angle ϕ_{COOH} equal to about 14° with respect to the C-C symmetry axis of the system (i.e. the two carbon atoms bearing the COOH group and the additional H atom).

3.1   Adsorption on the OH group

The adsorption energies for water molecules adsorbed above an OH group anchored on the face side or on the edge of our graphite cluster are given in Table 1. Note that for clarity, these energy values are given as absolute values. Obviously, these energies are in fact negative because they refer to adsorption processes.

When increasing the number n of adsorbed water molecules, the mean adsorption energy per water molecule $\Delta E_{\text{ads}}/n$ increases with n, from 16.7 kJ/mol for one single water molecule up to a nearly constant value of about 30 kJ/mol for an aggregate containing from 3 to 5 water molecules adsorbed on the face-oxidized graphite cluster (Fig. 2). A similar behavior is obtained above the edge-oxidized cluster, with however slightly larger energy values, ranging from 19.3 kJ/mol (single water molecule) up to about 33 kJ/mol (small water aggregate $H_2O_{(n=3.5)}$). This indicates that the water adsorption is favored on the edges with respect to the face of the graphite surface. Such a difference could come from a small steric repulsion effect of the π-conjugated system on the face of the defective graphite surface.

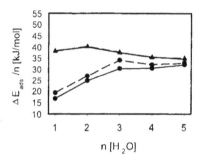

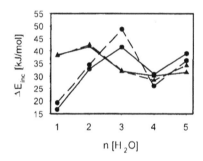

Figure 2: Adsorption and incremental energies in kJ/mol for small aggregates containing n water molecules adsorbed above an OH (circles) or a COOH (triangles) group anchored on the face (full curve) or on the edge (dashed curve) of a graphite cluster.

Another way to characterize the energy behavior with n is to calculate the incremental association energy ΔE_{inc} that corresponds to the energy gained by the system upon the addition of one water molecule. Table 1, together with Fig. 2, clearly show that the maximum gain above the two oxidized clusters is obtained by adding a third water molecule on the OH group, indicating that the saturation of the OH group (defined as the maximum number of water molecules that is necessary to optimize the adsorption energy gain) corresponds to an aggregate containing three water molecules.

These energy results can be related to the adsorption geometry of the water aggregate, especially the formation of hydrogen bonds. For example, the most stable geometry for a single water molecule adsorbed on the OH group on both oxidized clusters is given in Fig. 3. It clearly exhibits the formation of one hydrogen bond between the OH group and the water molecule, in which this OH group acts as a proton donor. In a general way, the geometries of the most stable water aggregates adsorbed on the oxidized graphite cluster are governed by the formation of a hydrogen bonds network that is similar above the face and the edge-oxidized clusters, at least when considering the position of the O atoms with respect to the OH group (Fig. 3). A careful examination of these geometries shows that the saturation of the OH group by three water molecules corresponds to the optimization of the hydrogen bonds network between the water molecules and the defective graphite surface, whereas the energy gain obtained when adsorbing additional H_2O molecules ($n = 4$ and 5) rather comes from optimization of the lateral interactions inside the water aggregate.

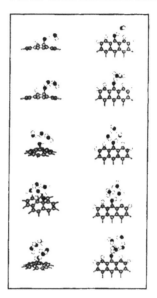

Figure 3: Geometry of the stable structures for small water aggregates adsorbed on a OH group anchored either on the face (left) or on the edge (right) of the graphite cluster. Only a small part of the system around the OH group is shown for clarity. Grey, black and white circles represent C, O and H atoms, respectively, involved in the DFT-cluster. The rest of the system is represented by grey sticks.

Note also that the optimization of this hydrogen bonds network leads to a rotation of the OH group (i.e. ϕ_{OH} increases from 0 to 100°) on the oxidized graphite surface upon water adsorption (see Fig. 3 and Ref.[19]).

3.2 Adsorption on the COOH group

For comparison, we have performed the same calculations for the adsorption of small water aggregates on a COOH group anchored on the face or edge-oxidized graphite cluster. The corresponding mean adsorption energies per water molecules are given in Table 1 together with the incremental association energies. In a general way, the present results demonstrate that the water adsorption on a COOH group does not depend on its anchoring above the graphite cluster, as indicated by the superimposition of the corresponding energy curves in Fig. 2. This feature can be related to the fact that the water molecules are located farther from the underlying graphite surface than above an OH group (Fig. 4). Indeed, when considering the adsorption above an OH group, the water molecule feels the interaction with the underlying atoms of the surface and, as a consequence, larger differences are obtained between adsorption on edge and on face of the corresponding oxidized graphite cluster.

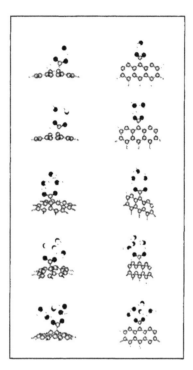

Figure 4: Geometry of the stable structures for small water aggregates adsorbed on a COOH group anchored either on the face (left) or on the edge (right) of the graphite cluster. Only a small part of the system around the COOH group is shown for clarity. Grey, black and white circles represent C, O and H atoms, respectively, involved in the DFT-cluster. The rest of the system is represented by grey sticks. Note that due to the rotation of the COOH group out of the graphite plane, angle views have been selected for the largest water aggregates.

Moreover, for the smallest aggregates ($n = 1, 2$) the adsorption energy is much higher on COOH than on OH groups (Table 1 and Fig. 2). For example, it is equal to 38.4 kJ/mol for a single water molecule, i.e. a value twice larger than above OH, because of the formation of two hydrogen bonds between H_2O and the COOH group, instead of only one in the case of OH (Fig. 4). By contrast, when increasing the size of the water aggregate, the equilibrium configuration and thus the corresponding adsorption energy are rather governed by the lateral interactions between water molecules, and $\Delta E_{ads}/n$ tends to a constant value of about 35 kJ/mol, i.e. a value similar to that obtain above OH.

Examination of the incremental association energy for water adsorbed above the COOH group shows that the maximum gain is obtained for $n = 2$, indicating that only two H_2O molecules are required to saturate this kind of defect (Fig. 2). This is due to the formation of a very stable water cluster above the COOH oxidized surface, each water molecule being tied to the COOH group by a hydrogen bond (one acceptor H-bond above the hydroxyl part of COOH, and one donor H-bond above the carbonyl part). The resulting cluster is also stabilized by a third H-bond between the two water molecules, leading to a hydrogen bonds network very similar to that obtained in a water tetramer, that is one of the most stable small water clusters[25, 26]. It is interesting to note that above an OH group, the saturation is obtained when adsorbing three water molecules, a situation corresponding again to the formation of a square hydrogen bonds network similar to that of the water tetramer (3 adsorbed H_2O + the OH group) (Fig. 5).

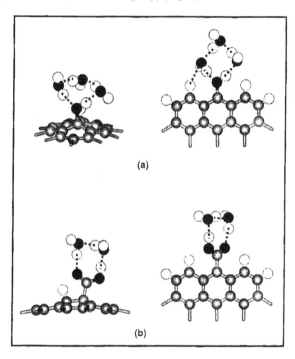

(a)

(b)

Figure 5: Illustration of the hydrogen bond network in the case of the stable water aggregates saturating the OH (a) or the COOH (b) groups anchored either on the face (left) or on the edge (right) of the graphite cluster. Only a small part of the system around the OH and COOH groups is shown for clarity. Grey, black and white circles represent C, O and H atoms, respectively, involved in the DFT-cluster. The rest of the system is represented by grey sticks. The hydrogen bonds within the water aggregate and between the water molecules and the surface are indicated by dotted lines.

As already observed on the OH group, the optimization of the hydrogen bonds network leads to a reorientation of the COOH group on the oxidized graphite surface upon water adsorption (see Fig. 4). For example, the rotation angle θ_{COOH} increases from $50°$ to about $60°$ when the number of water molecules increases from $n = 0$ to $n = 5$ on the edge-oxidized cluster. On a similar way, the COOH group slightly rotates around the C-COOH axis by about $\phi_{COOH} = 11°$ when n

increases from 0 to 3, but ϕ_{COOH} reaches about $90°$ when $n = 4, 5$ in order to better accommodate the additional water molecules near the graphite surface.

Finally, the mean adsorption energy per water molecule is larger on COOH than on OH groups, for all the clusters ($n = 1, 5$) considered in the present calculations, indicating that COOH has a longer range influence on the water nucleation process than OH, although it is saturated with only two water molecules.

4 Conclusions

In this paper, we have studied, by means of *ab initio* calculations based on the ONIOM method, the adsorption of water molecules on OH and COOH groups anchored on the face or on the edges of a graphite cluster modelling nanometer-size graphite crystallites as evidenced in soot particles. Our calculations show that the OH and COOH groups act as nucleation centers for small water aggregates, containing a few number of molecules, with mean adsorption energies per water molecule that depend on the number of hydrogen bonds formed between the water aggregate and the oxidized surface. They indicate that COOH group is more attractive than OH with respect to water adsorption, and evidence a much stronger interaction between water and the oxidized graphite surface than between water and bare graphite surface (6.8 kJ/mol for a single water molecule adsorbed on bare graphite[17, 27, 28]. Such conclusions can be very useful to understand, at a molecular level, the nucleation of water molecules on soot particles, especially those containing carboxylic groups.

However, such groups are rapidly saturated when increasing the coverage, in agreement with the interpretation of recent experimental data obtained on different types of soot[8], and a quite large distribution of such active sites is certainly necessary for a graphite surface to become hydrophilic.

Acknowledgment

This work was supported by the "Agence de l'Environnement et de la Maîtrise de l'Energie (ADEME)" through the PRIMEQUAL2-PREDIT program (No. 04 06 C0047).

References

[1] Y. CHen, S.M. Kreidenweiss, L.M. McInnes, D.C. Rogers, P.J. DeMott, Geophys. Res. Lett. **25**, 1391 (1998).

[2] P.J. DeMott, Y. Chen, S.M. Kreidenweiss, L.M. McInnes, D.C. Rogers, D.E. Sherman, Geophys. Res. Lett. **26**, 2492 (1999).

[3] D.A. Hauglustaine, B.A. Ridley, S. Solomon, S. Hess, S. Madronich, Geophys. Res. Lett. **23**, 2609 (1996).

[4] C.A. Rogaski, D.M. Golden, L.R. Williams, Geophys. Res. Lett. **24**, 381 (1997).

[5] J.P.D. Abbatt, Chem. Rev. **103**, 4783 (2003) and references therein.

[6] M.A. Zondlo, P.K. Hudson, A.J. Prenni, and M.A. Tolbert, Annu. Rev. Phys. Chem. **51**, 473 (2000).

[7] O.B. Popovicheva, N.M. Persiantseva, M.E. Trukhin, G.B. Rulev, N.K. Shonija, Y.Y. Buriko, A.M. Starik, B. Demirdjian, D. Ferry, J. Suzanne, Phys. Chem. Chem. Phys. **2**, 4421 (2000).

[8] O.B. Popovicheva, N.M. Persiantseva, B.V. Kuznetsov, T.A. Rakhmanova, N.K. Shonija, J. Suzanne, and D. Ferry, J. Phys. Chem. A **107**, 10046 (2003).

[9] O.B. Popovicheva, M.E. Trukhin, N.M. Persiantseva, N.K. Shonija, Atmos. Environ. **35**, 1673 (2001).

[10] D. Ferry, J. Suzanne, S. Nitsche, O.B. Popovicheva, N.K. Shonija, J. Geophys. Res. **107**, 4734 (2002).

[11] E.V. Aksenenko and Y.I. Tarasevich, Adsorp. Sci. Technol. **14**, 383 (1996).

[12] Y.I. Tarasevich, A.I. Zhukova, E.V. Aksenenko, and S.V. Bondarenko, Adsorp. Sci. Technol. **15**, 497 (1997).

[13] Y.I. Tarasevich, and E.V. Aksenenko, Colloids Surf., A: Physicochem. Eng. Aspects **215**, 285 (2003).

[14] E.A. Müller, L.F. Rull, L.F. Vega, K.E. Gubbins, J. Phys. Chem. **100**, 1189 (1996).

[15] E.A. Müller, K.E. Gubbins, Carbon **36**, 1433 (1998).

[16] C.L. McCallum, T.J. Bandosz, S.C. McGrother, E.A. Müller, and K.E. Gubbins, Langmuir **15**, 533 (1999).

[17] S. Picaud, P.N.M. Hoang, S. Hamad, J.A. Mejias, and S. Lago, J. Phys. Chem. B **108**, 5410 (2004).

[18] M. Svensson, S. Humbel, R.D.J. Froese, T. Matsubara, S. Sieber, K. Morokuma, J. Phys. Chem. **100**, 19357 (1996).

[19] B. Collignon, P.N.M. Hoang, S. Picaud, and J.C. Rayez, Chem. Phys. Lett. **406**, 430 (2005).

[20] S. Hamad, J.A. Mejias, S. Lago, S. Picaud, and P.N.M. Hoang, J. Phys. Chem. B **108**, 5405 (2004).

[21] J.J.P. Stewart, J. Comput. Chem. **10**, 221 (1989).

[22] M. J. Frisch et al. *Gaussian 03*; Gaussian, Inc., Wallingford CT, 2004.

[23] A.D. Becke, J. Chem. Phys. **98**, 5648 (1993).

[24] D.E. Woon and T.H. Dunning Jr., J. Chem. Phys. **98**, 1358 (1993).

[25] C. Lee, H. Chen, and G. Fitzgerald, J. Chem. Phys. **102**, 1266 (1995).

[26] S.M. Kathmann, G.K. Schenter, and B.C. Garrett, J. Chem. Phys. **111**, 4688 (1999).

[27] E.V. Aksenenko, Y.I. Tarasevich, Adsorp. Sci. Technol. **9**, 54 (1992).

[28] H. Ruuska and T.A. Pakkanen, Carbon **41**, 699 (2003).

Brill Academic Publishers
P.O. Box 9000, 2300 PA Leiden,
The Netherlands

*Lecture Series on Computer
and Computational Sciences*
Volume 5, 2006, pp. 145-153

Electron correlation effects in small iron clusters

G. Rollmann[1] and P. Entel

Theoretical Low-Temperature Physics,
Physics Department, University of Duisburg-Essen, Campus 47048 Duisburg, Germany

Abstract: We present results of first-principles calculations of structural, magnetic, and electronic properties of small Fe clusters. It is shown that, while the lowest-energy isomers of Fe_3 and Fe_4 obtained in the framework of density functional theory within the generalized gradient approximation (GGA) are characterized by Jahn-Teller-like distortions away from the most regular shapes (which is in agreement with other works), these distortions are reduced when electron correlation effects are considered explicitly as within the GGA+U approach. At the same time, the magnetic moments of the clusters are enhanced with respect to the pure GGA case, resulting in maximal moments (in the sense of Hund's rules) of 4 μ_B per atom for the ground state structures of Fe_3 and Fe_4, and a total moment of 18 μ_B for Fe_5. This already happens for moderate values of the Coulomb repulsion parameter $U \sim 2.0$ eV and is explained by changes in the electronic structures of the clusters.

Keywords: Density functional theory, GGA + U, Fe cluster, Magnetic moment

PACS: 31.15.Ew, 36.40.Cg, 36.40.Mr

1 Introduction

Magnetic transition metal (TM) particles are an important ingredient in many state-of-the-art technological applications, ranging from catalysis to ultra-high density magnetic storage devices. In the latter case, miniaturization has already reached a point where particle sizes are so small that quantum effects start to play a role in determining their magnetic properties, which, in turn, show a pronounced size dependence. Therefore, a detailed understanding of the electronic structure of small TM clusters is not only very desirable from a fundamental point of view, but also inevitable if one wants to gain insight into the processes which govern particle formation necessary for the design of new materials with unique properties. One step towards this was taken a decade ago by Billas *et al.* who used a Stern-Gerlach type apparatus in combination with a time-of-flight mass spectrometer in order to measure magnetic moments of isolated TM clusters [1]. These experiments revealed that the magnetic moments of free Fe, Co, and Ni clusters are not just given by simple interpolations between the limiting values of the isolated atoms and the corresponding bulk materials, but rather change non-monotonically with cluster size in an oscillatory fashion. Unfortunately, resolution in cluster size (i.e., number of atoms) was only in the range of 10 %, and so a direct relation between cluster size and magnetic moment could not be established from these data.

In the following years, numerous experimental studies have been undertaken to investigate different properties of small TM clusters. But while such measurements are relatively easy to perform

---

[1] Corresponding author. E-mail: georg@thp.uni-duisburg.de

for clusters deposited on surfaces (whose properties, though, can change drastically upon deposition due to their interaction with the substrate), the opposite is true for isolated clusters. This difficulty can be assigned to their great reactivity and the associated problem to produce particles with a given, well-defined size in high concentrations. Therefore, it may not seem surprising that, from experimental side, still not much is known about geometries, morphologies, and even magnetic properties of small TM clusters. In the case of Fe clusters, which are the subject of the present work, the bond length has only been measured for the dimer [2], and vibrational frequencies have been obtained for Fe_2 and Fe_3 [3]. While properties related to the electronic structure and energetics of the clusters have been obtained quite accurately [4, 5], again only sparse information is available regarding their magnetic moments.

On the other hand, due to the rapid development of computational capacities it has become possible to calculate properties of small atomic clusters from first principles with a high degree of accuracy in quantitative agreement with experiment. Therefore, in the case of Fe clusters, most information about structural and magnetic properties stems from such *ab initio* simulations, mainly based on density functional theory (DFT) [6]. For an overview, we refer to [7, 8] and references therein. It soon became clear, that it is important to go beyond the local density approximation (LDA) and include gradient corrections (GGA) when calculating the exchange and correlation energy. It also became evident that, in order to find the lowest-energy isomers for a given cluster size, it is important to allow for free relaxation of the atoms without imposing symmetry constraints. The reason for this is the presence of degenerate electronic states in highly symmetric clusters originating from the interaction of the d-manifold, giving rise to the Jahn-Teller effect [9], which in turn leads to distorted ground-state geometries with lower symmetry [10]. For Fe_5, even a ground state characterized by a non-collinear magnetization density has been proposed [11]. But it could be shown that this is only a metastable state on the potential energy surface (PES) of the cluster, and that the energy can be lowered when the atoms are allowed to relax freely [12, 13].

Resulting from these different computational schemes, proposed magnetic moments reach from 8 to 10 μ_B for Fe_3, 10 to 14 μ_B for Fe_4, and 14 to 18 μ_B for Fe_5, all related to different geometric arrangements of the atoms and different employed levels of theory [7,10-20]. Recently, two comprehensive investigations (in the framework of DFT) of the PES of Fe_3 and Fe_4 have revealed the true complexity of problem, yielding a high number of local minima close in energy [7]. In the case of the Fe trimer, at least 4 different states have been reported to be situated in a small energy range of less than 100 meV above the ground state. The situation is practically the same for Fe_4, and therefore a definite assignment of the ground states has up to day neither been achieved for Fe_3 nor Fe_4. Despite of this, the spin multiplicities were the same for all these low-lying states, giving rise to the assumption that the ground states of Fe_3 and Fe_4 have magnetic moments of 10 and 14 μ_B, respectively. By similar considerations one is lead to the conclusion that the lowest-energy isomer of Fe_5 possesses a total moment of 16 μ_B within DFT/GGA.

But even when all the aspects mentioned above are considered, a mayor drawback of current implementations of DFT remains in all these calculations: The well-known fact that, within conventional LDA (and also GGA), electron correlation due to intra-atomic Coulomb repulsion of localized d or f electrons is not described very well. Different methods have been proposed to overcome this limitation. Of these, the LDA + U method [21], where a Hubbard-like term U is incorporated into the density functional, has been applied successfully to a variety of problems in strongly correlated systems where ordinary LDA gives qualitatively wrong results. A prominent example are Mott insulators like the 3d TM oxides. In contrast to DFT in the LDA, which predicts metallic behavior or band gaps which are sometimes one order of magnitude too small, the insulating nature with correct band gaps is recovered within the LDA + U approach. For example, for the case of an Fe-based system (antiferromagnetic α-Fe_2O_3), we have shown that this method yields the correct high-pressure phase diagram [23].

Due to this lack in conventional LDA/GGA, one may challenge some of the results achieved for Fe clusters within DFT up to day. Add to that, recent high-level quantum-chemical calculations on the Fe dimer have given some indication that magnetic moments of small Fe clusters are actually larger than the values given above [24]. In this letter, we discuss the influence of electronic correlation on geometric and magnetic properties of small Fe clusters, by explicitly investigating the effect of the size of the parameter U on various properties of selected clusters. In the following section, we give a brief account on the employed computational scheme. Subsequently, we discuss our results for Fe_3, Fe_4, and Fe_5. We conclude by making a prediction concerning the properties of larger clusters and give an outlook for future work.

2   Computational method

In our search for the lowest-energy isomers of Fe_3, Fe_4, and Fe_5, we only have considered triangular geometries for Fe_3, and three-dimensional structures for Fe_4 and Fe_5, respectively, as these were found to be energetically most favorable in previous calculations. For each given arrangement of atoms in the cluster, the total energy was calculated in the framework of DFT [6] in combination with the GGA for the description of exchange and correlation in a functional form proposed by Perdew and Wang [25]. A number of 8 valence electrons was taken into account for each Fe atom, the remaining core electrons together with the nuclei were described by following the projector augmented wave method [26] as implemented in the Vienna *ab initio* simulation package [27]. The electronic wavefunctions were expanded in a plane-wave basis set with an energy cutoff of 335 eV. The clusters were positioned in cubic supercells of 11 Å length periodically repeated in space. The Brillouin zone integration was performed using the Γ-point only. We have allowed for a non-collinear magnetization density as described in [11].

For the GGA + U calculations, we have adopted a version proposed by Dudarev *et al.* [22]. In this implementation, the total energy depends on the difference $U - J$:

$$E_{GGA+U} = E_{GGA} + \frac{U - J}{2} \sum_{m\sigma} (n_{m\sigma} - n_{m\sigma}^2),$$

where $n_{m\sigma}$ is the occupancy of the orbital with magnetic quantum number m and spin σ, and U and J represent the spherically averaged on-site Coulomb interaction and screened exchange integrals, respectively. It can be shown that within this formalism unoccupied d states are shifted towards higher energies by $(U - J)/2$, while the opposite is true for occupied d states. For a comprehensive discussion we refer to the literature [21, 22]. As the value of J was kept constant at $J = 1$ eV in our calculations, the case $U = 1$ eV corresponds here to the pure GGA limit, because in this case $U - J = 0$ eV.

The structural relaxations were performed with the conjugate gradient method, without imposing any symmetry constraint. As initial structures, we have taken different lowest-energy states found in earlier calculations. The geometries were considered to be converged when all forces were smaller than 1 meV/Å. The distortions of the clusters are calculated with respect to a perfectly symmetric cluster with the same average bond length as explained in [12]. For the case of Fe_3 and Fe_4, this simply reduces to the root-mean-square bond length fluctuation.

3   Results for Fe_3

The energetic relationships for the Fe_3 cluster as obtained with different values for the parameter U are shown in **Fig. 1**. The spin multiplicities were varied from 9 to 13, yielding the differently colored curves. Open symbols correspond to equilateral triangular geometries with identical bond

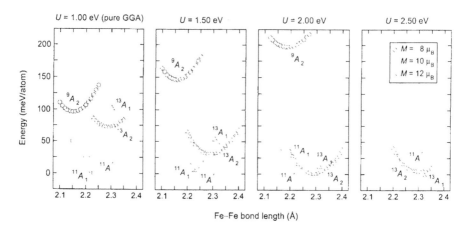

Figure 1: Relative total energy of the different isomers of the Fe_3 cluster as a function of the average bond length, symmetry, and magnetic state for different values of U. The curves were shifted so that $E = 0$ corresponds to the lowest-energy isomer found for a specific value of U. Open symbols refer to equilateral triangles, filled symbols denote energies of relaxed clusters.

lengths (D_{3h} symmetry). For the relaxed clusters, whose energies are given by the filled symbols, the average interatomic distances were used for the Fe–Fe bond lengths.

In the case of conventional GGA ($U = 1.00$ eV), we find that the lowest-energy states of Fe_3 possess magnetic moments of 10 μ_B. When D_{3h} symmetry constraints are imposed, an energy minimum for an Fe Fe bond length of 2.225 A is obtained. But this state is only metastable with respect to a Jahn-Teller distortion, as will be discussed below. When the atoms are allowed to relax freely, we find several states close in energy, of which the $^{11}A_1$ state with one short and two longer bonds emerges as ground state. An $^{11}A'$ state with C_s symmetry is located some 12 meV/atom higher in energy. A detailed discussion of the nature of these states (and also several others), including the influence of the employed GGA functionals, has been given elsewhere [7] and is beyond the scope of the present work. We only note that, although the individual bond lengths differ significantly from one isomer with 10 μ_B to the next, the average interatomic distances are nearly the same (~ 2.23 Å).

In contrast to the case of $M = 10\,\mu_B$, equilateral triangles with spin multiplicities of 9 and 13 are stable with respect to structural deformations. But while the $^9A_2$ state is the ground state in LDA calculations [7,10-11,15-19], it lies much higher in energy when GGA functionals are used. As can be seen from Fig. 1, the $^9A_2$ state may only be lowest in energy for very small interatomic distances. Concerning isomers with a moment of 12 μ_B, we found a $^{13}A_2$ state with identical bond lengths as well as a $^{13}A_1$ state with one long (2.39 A) and two short (2.26 A) bonds. In the former state, two electrons occupy majority spin orbitals, which are higher in energy than empty minority spin orbitals (see Fig. 2), and therefore it is not a ground state for this arrangement of atoms and is irrelevant within DFT. The latter may be identified as the one found previously [7], but it does not play a role in the search for the lowest-energy isomer, as it is located well above in energy.

In spite of the different technical implementations, the results presented here are in very good agreement with those obtained in [7]. The small differences may be ascribed in part to our use of the PAW method compared to the all-electron calculations of the latter. Therefore, it may be worthwhile to investigate the effect of including the Fe 3p electrons to the valence electrons.

Table 1: Structural and magnetic properties of selected isomers of Fe_3 calculated within conventional GGA and GGA + U with different values for U. Magnetic moments are given in μ_B, bond distances in Å, distortions δ in %, and energies in meV/atom.

U (eV)	State	M	Symm.	d_1	d_2	d_3	δ	E
1.00	$^{11}A_1$	10	C_{2v}	2.067	2.301	2.301	4.97	0
	$^{11}A'$	10	C_s	2.143	2.263	2.286	2.80	12
	$^{13}A_1$	12	C_{2v}	2.261	2.261	2.387	2.59	101
1.50	$^{11}A'$	10	C_s	2.149	2.251	2.306	2.91	0
	$^{11}A_1$	10	C_{2v}	2.069	2.306	2.306	5.01	7
	$^{13}A_1$	12	C_{2v}	2.262	2.262	2.398	2.77	53
2.00	$^{11}A'$	10	C_s	2.151	2.253	2.316	3.04	0
	$^{13}A_1$	12	C_{2v}	2.264	2.264	2.412	3.01	14
2.50	$^{13}A_1$	12	C_{2v}	2.266	2.266	2.431	3.35	0
	$^{11}A'$	10	C_s	2.152	2.257	2.327	3.21	27

However, first tests have already revealed that the results are qualitatively unchanged. On the other hand, we have used a plane-wave basis set, which is in the sense superior to localized orbitals that calculated quantities converge smoothly with the cutoff energy. We therefore assume that the major part of difference stems from the use of incomplete basis sets in [7].

When we increase the value of the Hubbard U parameter, we observe that the relative positions

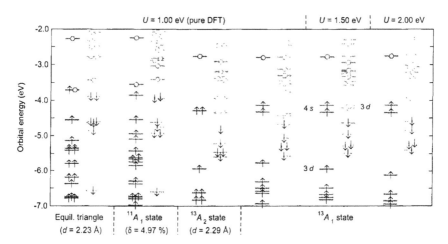

Figure 2: Kohn-Sham eigenvalues (horizontal bars) of selected states of the Fe_3 cluster for conventional GGA and GGA + U with different values for U. Arrows represent electrons (of either spin), circles denote holes.

of the states are shifted. While the $^9A_2$ state becomes energetically unfavorable, states with a total moment of 12 μ_B are lowered. At the same time, the order of $^{11}A_1$ and $^{11}A'$ are reversed, so that the latter becomes the lowest-energy isomer already for $U = 1.50$ eV.

When U is increased to 2.00 eV, the isomers with multiplicities of 11 and 13 are getting practically degenerate, with $^{11}A'$ still being the ground state. For $U = 2.50$ eV, we finally encounter the $^{13}A_1$ state, with a magnetic moment of 12 μ_B and a distortion of 3.4 %, being lowest in energy. We have listed structural and magnetic properties of selected isomers of Fe$_3$ in Table 1.

In order to gain some insight into the mechanisms responsible for the ordering of states, we take a closer look at the electronic structures of the different isomers, but not without bearing in mind that in principle there is no direct physical meaning associated with the calculated one-electron orbitals in DFT. In Fig. 2 we have depicted these energy levels for several isomers and different values of U. As a starting point for the discussion we take the perfect triangle with a moment of 10 μ_B. We note that the highest occupied energy level is doubly degenerate, but occupied with only one electron. This immediately gives rise to a Jahn-Teller distortion leading to the $^{11}A_1$ state, for which the degenerate levels split upon deformation of the cluster. Although the HOMO of Fe$_3$ in the $^{13}A_2$ is also twofold degenerate, there is no reason for a distortion due to the double occupation (promotion of one minority electron to the majority spin manifold). But because of the fact that two unoccupied minority 3d orbitals are lower in energy than the occupied majority 4s orbitals (violation of the aufbau principle), neither this state, nor the $^{13}A_1$ state are ground states for this geometry and are in principle not accessible/relevant within DFT. But when the U parameter is increased, this situation changes. We observe, that occupied majority spin d states are shifted towards lower energies, while the empty minority spin d states are moved upwards. This leads to a state crossing at the Fermi energy for $U \sim 1.50$ eV and to the fact that, from around $U = 2.00$ eV, the aufbau principle is fulfilled and the $^{13}A_1$ is the ground state. As we saw above, it is even the global energy minimum of the Fe$_3$ cluster for $U = 2.50$ eV.

4   Results for Fe$_4$ and Fe$_5$

The energetic relationships for the Fe$_4$ cluster are depicted in Fig. 2. We again begin our discussion with the situation within conventional GGA. When tetrahedral symmetry constraints are imposed, the energy is minimal for a cluster with a magnetic moment of 12 μ_B and interatomic distances of 2.276 Å. This state has been found in previous studies. Ballone and Jones were the first to show that the energy can be lowered when symmetry is broken. They found a state with D_{2d} symmetry (butterfly structure) by molecular dynamics simulations. In our calculation, this isomer (filled circle) has 2 short and 4 longer bonds of 2.20 and 2.32 Å, respectively. Although the lowest-energy isomer of Fe$_4$ (found within DFT/GGA) belongs to the same point group, it is characterized by a magnetic moment of 14 μ_B, 2 long and 4 shorter bonds of 2.54 and 2.23 Å. As in the case of Fe$_3$, there are again several minima found within a small energy range, and for a more comprehensive discussion we refer to [7].

When we increase the value for the Hubbard U, we first observe a similar effect as in the case of the Fe trimer. Low-moment states shifted to higher energies, and the isomers with a moment of 16 μ_B are becoming favorable. But, while in the case of Fe$_3$ the overall situation had not yet changed for $U = 1.50$ eV, we here get already the high-moment state lowest in energy among all perfect tetrahedra. For a value of $U = 2.00$ eV, also the lowest-energy isomer of Fe$_4$ carries a moment of 16 μ_B or 4 μ_B per atom.

A further discussion of the different states will not be given here. Instead, we would like to finish our remarks by presenting a result for the Fe$_5$ cluster. It turns out that, while the ground state found within conventional DFT has a multiplicity of 17, this value is increased to 19 already for $U = 1.50$ eV. The associated distortion of the cluster is reduced from 4.6 to 3.0%.

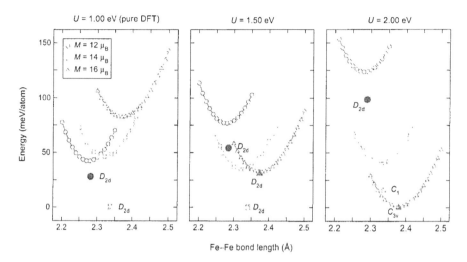

Figure 3: Total energy of the Fe_4 cluster as a function of cluster size, symmetry, and total magnetic moment for different values of U. The curves were shifted so that $E = 0$ corresponds to the lowest-energy isomer found for a specific value of U. Open symbols refer to perfect tetrahedral cluster, filled symbols denote energies of relaxed clusters.

5 Conclusion

We have shown that the order of states of small Fe clusters (namely, Fe_3 and Fe_4) changes drastically compared to conventional GGA when electronic correlation effects are considered explicitly. Total magnetic moments of the lowest-energy isomers are by 2 μ_B higher, yielding values of 12 and 16 μ_B for Fe_3 and Fe_4, respectively. This was explained to be due to the shift of one-electron Kohn-Sham levels which depends on the magnitude of U. While the situation is not so clear for the trimer, where even for $U = 2$ eV no definite assignment of the ground state could be made, the lowest-energy isomer of Fe_4 was found to be a nearly perfect tetrahedron with a total moment of 16 μ_B already for $U = 2$ eV. A similar behavior was encountered for Fe_5. We expect this trend observed for the small clusters to continue as the number of atoms is increased, and therefore predict the calculated moments of larger Fe clusters to be higher (by at least 2 μ_B) when electron correlation is explicitly taken into account. In order to justify reasonable choices of U, we emphasize that it is inevitable to perform further investigations of other properties related to the electronic structure of these clusters, like ionization potentials, electron affinities, and binding energies, as these have been obtained in part to good accuracy in experiments.

Acknowledgment

This work has been supported by the German Science Foundation through the SFB 445 *"Nano-Particles from the Gasphase: Formation, Structure, Properties"*. The calculations have been performed at the Regional Computer Center of the University of Cologne (RRZK).

References

[1] I.M.L. Billas, J.A. Becker, A. Châtelain, and W. A. de Heer, Magnetic moments of iron clusters with 25 to 700 atoms and their dependence on temperature, *Phys. Rev. Lett.* **71** 4067-4070(1993).
I.M.L. Billas, A. Châtelain, and W.A. de Heer, Magnetism of Fe, Co and Ni clusters in molecular beams, *J. Magn. Magn. Mater.* **168** 64-84(1997).

[2] P.A. Montano and G.K. Shenoy, EXAFS study of iron monomers and dimers isolated in solid argon, *Solid State Commun.* **35** 53-56(1980).
H. Purdum, P.A. Montano, and G.K. Shenoy, Extended x-ray-absorption-fine-structure study of small Fe molecules isolated in solid neon, *Phys. Rev. B* **25** 4412-4417(1982).

[3] M. Moskovits and D.P. DiLella, Di-iron and nickeliron. *J. Chem. Phys.* **73** 4917-4924(1980).
T.L. Haslett, K.A. Bosnick, S. Fedrigo, and M. Moskovits, Resonance Raman spectroscopy of matrix-isolated mass-selected Fe$_3$ and Ag$_3$, *J. Chem. Phys.* **111** 6456-6461(1999).

[4] D.G. Leopold and W.C. Lineberger, A study of the low-lying electronic states of Fe$_2$ and Co$_2$ by negative ion photoelectron spectroscopy, *J. Chem. Phys.* **85** 51-55(1986).
D.G. Leopold, J. Almlöf, W.C. Lineberger, and P.E. Taylor, A simple interpretation of the Fe$_2^-$ photoelectron spectrum, *J. Chem. Phys.* **88** 3780-3783(1988).

[5] E.A. Rohlfing, D.M. Cox, A. Kaldor, and K.H. Johnson, Photoionization spectra and electronic structure of small iron clusters, *J. Chem. Phys.* **81** 3846-3851(1984).
E.K. Parks, T.D. Klots, and S.L. Riley, Chemical probes of metal cluster ionization potentials, *J. Chem. Phys.* **92** 3813-3826(1990).
S. Yang and M.B. Knickelbein, Photoionization studies of transition metal clusters: Ionization potentials for Fe$_n$ and Co$_n$, *J. Chem. Phys.* **93** 1533-1539(1990).
L.S. Wang, H.S. Cheng, and J. Fan, Photoelectron spectroscopy of size-selected transition metal clusters: Fe$_n^-$, $n = 3 - 24$, *J. Chem. Phys.* **102** 9480-9493(1995).
L.S. Wang, X. Li, and H.F. Zhang, Probing the electronic structure of iron clusters using photoelectron spectroscopy, *Chem. Phys.* **262** 53-63(2000).

[6] P. Hohenberg and W. Kohn, Inhomogeneous electron gas, *Phys. Rev.* **136** B864-B871(1964).
W. Kohn and L.J. Sham, Self-consistent equations including exchange and correlation effects *Phys. Rev.* **140** A1133-A1138(1965).

[7] S. Chrétien and D.R. Salahub, Kohn-Sham density-functional study of low-lying states of the iron clusters Fe$_n^+$/Fe$_n$/Fe$_n^-$ ($n = 1 - 4$), *Phys. Rev. B* **66** 155425(2003).
G.L. Gutsev and C.W. Bauschlicher, Jr., Electron affinities, ionization energies, and fragmentation energies of Fe$_n$ Clusters ($n = 2 - 6$): A density functional theory study, *J. Phys. Chem. A* **107** 7013-7023(2003).

[8] G. Rollmann, S. Sahoo, and P. Entel, Structure and magnetism in iron clusters (Eds: S.N. Sahu and P.K. Choudhury), *Proc. Indo-US Workshop "Nanoscale Materials: From Science to Technology"*, Nova Science, New York, 2005, in print.

[9] H.A. Jahn and E. Teller, Stability of polyatomic molecules in degenerate electronic states. I. Orbital degeneracy. *Proc. Roy. Soc. (London)* **A161** 220-235(1937).

[10] M. Castro, The role of the Jahn-Teller distortions on the structural, binding, and magnetic properties of small Fe$_n$ clusters, $n \leq 7$, *Int. J. Quantum Chem.* **64** 223-230(1997).

[11] D. Hobbs, G. Kresse, and J. Hafner, Fully unconstrained noncollinear magnetism within the projector augmented-wave method, *Phys. Rev. B* **62** 11556-11570(2000).

[12] G. Rollmann, S. Sahoo, and P. Entel, Structural and magnetic properties of Fe-Ni clusters, *Phys. Status Solidi A* **201** 3263-3270(2004).

[13] G. Rollmann, P. Entel, and S.Sahoo, Competing structural and magnetic effects in small iron clusters, *Comput. Mater. Sci.* **35** 275–278(2005).

[14] H. Tatewaki, M. Tomonari, and T. Nakamura, The band structure of small iron clusters from Fe_1 to Fe_6, *J. Chem. Phys.* **88** 6419-6430(1988).

[15] M. Castro and D.R. Salahub, Density-functional calculations for small iron clusters: Fe_n, Fe_n^+, and Fe_n^- for $n \leq 5$, *Phys. Rev. B* **49** 11842-11852(1994).

[16] P. Ballone and R.O. Jones, Structure and spin in small iron clusters, *Chem. Phys. Lett.* **233** 632-638(1995).

[17] M. Castro, C. Jamorski, and D.R. Salahub, Structure, bonding, and magnetism of small Fe_n, Co_n, and Ni_n clusters, $n \leq 5$, *Chem. Phys. Lett.* **271** 133-142(1997).

[18] T. Oda, A. Pasquarello, and R. Car, Fully unconstrained approach to noncollinear magnetism: application to small Fe clusters, *Phys. Rev. Lett.* **80** 3622-3625(1998).

[19] O. Diéguez *et al.*, Density-functional calculations of the structures, binding energies, and magnetic moments of Fe clusters with 2 to 17 atoms, *Phys. Rev. B* **63** 205407(2001).

[20] Ž. Šljivančanin and A. Pasquarello, Supported Fe nanoclusters: evolution of magnetic properties with cluster size, *Phys. Rev. Lett.* **90** 247202(2003).

[21] V.I. Anisimov, J. Zaanen, and O.K. Andersen, Band theory and Mott insulators: Hubbard U instead of Stoner I, *Phys. Rev. B* **44** 943-954(1991).

[22] S.L. Dudarev, G.A. Botton, and S.Y. Savrasov, C.J. Humphreys, and A.P. Sutton, Electron-energy-loss spectra and the structural stability of nickel oxide: An LSDA+U study, *Phys. Rev. B* **57** 1505-1509(1998).

[23] G. Rollmann, A. Rohrbach, P. Entel, and J. Hafner, First-principles calculation of the structure and magnetic phases of hematite, *Phys. Rev. B* **69** 165107(2004).

[24] O. Hübner and J. Sauer, Confirmation of $^9\Sigma_g^-$ and $^8\Sigma_u^-$ ground states of Fe_2 and Fe_2^- by CASSCF/MRCI, *Chem. Phys. Lett.* **358** 442-448(2002).
C. W. Bauschlicher, Jr. and A. Ricca, Can all of the Fe_2 experimental results be explained?, *Mol. Phys.* **101** 93-98(2003).

[25] J.P. Perdew and Y. Wang, Accurate and simple analytic representation of the electron-gas correlation energy, *Phys. Rev. B* **45** 13244-13249(1992).

[26] P.E. Blöchl, Projector augmented-wave method, *Phys. Rev. B* **50** 17953-17979(1994).
G. Kresse and D. Joubert, From ultrasoft pseudopotentials to the projector augmented-wave method, *Phys. Rev. B* **59** 1758-1775(1999).

[27] G. Kresse and J. Furthmüller, Efficient iterative schemes for *ab initio* total-energy calculations using a plane wave basis set, *Phys. Rev. B* **54** 11169-11186(1996).
G. Kresse and J. Furthmüller, Efficiency of ab-initio total energy calculations for metals and semiconductors using a plane-wave basis set, *Comput. Mater. Sci.* **6** 15-50(1996).

Brill Academic Publishers
P.O. Box 9000, 2300 PA Leiden
The Netherlands

*Lecture Series on Computer
and Computational Sciences*
Volume 5, 2006, pp. 154-159

A theoretical study on size-dependent properties of rock-salt ZnS clusters

Sougata Pal, Biplab Goswami and Pranab Sarkar [1]

Dept. of Chemistry, Visva-Bharati University
Santiniketan- 731235, India

Abstract: We present the results of our theoretical calculation on structural, electronic and optical properties of rock-salt ZnnSn clusters as a function of size of the clusters. We have focused on the variation of Mulliken populations, electronic energy levels, band gap and stability as a function of size for rock-salt derived ZnS clusters. We have also compared the structural and electronic properties of rock-salt derived clusters with those of zinc-blende and wurtzite clusters, previously studied.

Keywords: rock salt ZnS clusters, DFTB method, structural, electronic and optical properties

PACS: Nos. 73.22.Dj, 61.46.+w, 36.40.-c, 78.67.Bf

1. Introduction

Compound semiconductor nanocrystals (quantum dots) are exciting class of materials whose electronic and optical properties can be manipulated by changing their size or composition. When the size of the crystallites are of the order of a few nanometer or even less, the photo generated carriers i.e. electrons and holes, feel the spatial confinement. As a consequence of this the electronic energy levels shift to the higher energy. This leads to increase in the HOMO-LUMO gap. However, the extent of the increase in the band gap with size depends on the specific type of the semiconductor material and also very much on the crystal structures. Because of their unique optical and electronic properties, nanocrystals are likely to play a key role in the emerging new field of nanotechnology, the applications of which ranges from optoelectronic devices to biological fluorescence marking [1-4]. Zinc sulfide, the material of the present study, both in its doped and undoped forms, is an important phosphorescent material having a direct band gap of 3.7 eV. Recently it has been reported that ZnS doped with transition metal ions such as manganese is an efficient light emitting material. The insertion of such dopants in the nanometer-sized ZnS matrix, may exhibit interesting magneto-optical properties[5]. ZnS quantum dots have also used as photo-catalysts, especially for reactions involving water pollutants[6]. The photocatalytic activity of these colloids is enhanced by varying the size of the nanocrystals owing to the shift of the valence and conduction bands[7]. Zinc sulfide at room conditions adopts two different crystalline modifications namely zinc-blende and wurtzite. In addition to these crystal structures, ZnS may have rocksalt structure which are stable at high pressure[8]. The rocksalt phase has been reported to be stable to 45 GPa. Desgreniers et. al [9] showed that initial room condition phases of ZnS, zincblende and wurtzite, transform unambiguously to the rocksalt structure at 12 GPa and at room temperature. Recently, we have studied the structural, electronic properties of both zinc-blende and wurtzite clusters by employing density-functional tight-binding (DFTB) method[10,11]. The objective of this paper is to present the theoretical results of size-dependent structural, electronic and optical properties of rock salt ZnS clusters and to compare the properties with those of zinc-blende and wurtzite ZnS clusters thereby we also identify the crystal structure specific properties.

---

[1] Corresponding author, E. Mail: pranab_69@yahoo.co.in

2. Theoretical Method

We use the parametrized density-functional method of Seifert et al[10,11]. In this method, the single particle wavefunctions are expanded in set of atomic orbitals, $\Psi_k(r) = \sum_m C_{km} \Phi_m(r)$, which in turn are obtained from self-consistent calculations on the isolated atoms. The coefficients C_{km} are obtained from the secular equation $HC_k = \varepsilon_k . O.C_k$. The total single-particle potential $V_{eff}(r) = \sum_m V_m(r - R_m)$ is written as a superposition of the potential from the isolated atoms, and we assume that $\langle \Phi_k | V_m | \Phi_l \rangle$ vanishes unless at least one of the functions Φ_k and Φ_l is centered on R_m. The binding energy of the system of interest is written as a difference between the orbital energies (ε_i) calculated above and those of the isolated atoms (ε_{im}), augmented with pair potentials,

$$E_{bin} = \sum_i \varepsilon_i - \sum_m \sum_i \varepsilon_{im} + \frac{1}{2} \sum_{m1 \neq m2} U_{m1,m2} (|R_{m1} - R_{m2}|).$$

The above-mentioned Hamilton matrix elements as well as the pair potentials U are obtained from calculations on the isolated diatomics. Accordingly, by construction the method is accurate for the two-atomic systems. To test its applicability for larger systems, we calculate the structural properties (e.g. lattice constants, bond lengths, bulk modulus etc.) of the infinite crystals. We obtain values for ZnS which are in good agreement with the available experimental values. This approach then can also be used for the intermediate systems i.e. for finite clusters is then an assumption. The systems we considered were obtained by cutting out a sphere from the infinite periodic crystal with rocksalt structure. By putting the center of the sphere on the center of a nearest- neighbour bond, we obtain stoichiometric clusters and subsequently let them relax to closest local energy minimum whereby all atoms in the cluster are allowed to move. The properties we shall analyze, include the Mulliken gross population for the individual atoms as functions of the radial distance, density of states, spatial distribution of HOMO/LUMO, bandgap and stability for rocksalt derived clusters as function of size.

3. Results and Discussions

Figure 1 shows the Mulliken gross population as a function of the radial distance. From the figure it is clear that similar to our findings[12] for zinc-blende and wurtzite clusters the gross populations are markedly different from the neutral atoms. However for zinc-blende and wurtzite clusters there is a small electron transfer from zinc to sulphur in the inner region whereas in the outer region we can define a surface region characterized by an increased electron transfer and having thickness 2 – 2.5 Å. But for rocksalt clusters it is clearly seen from the figure that there is electron transfer from zinc to sulphur almost throughout the whole region of the clusters. So rocksalt derived clusters are more ionic in character compared to its corresponding zinc-blende and wurtzite derived clusters.

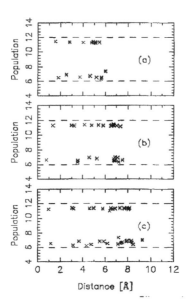

Figure. 1. Radial distribution of Mulliken gross populations of Zinc and Sulfide atoms for rocksalt clusters of different sizes: (a) Zn30S30 (b) Zn55S55 (c) Zn75S75.The horizontal dashed lines mark the values for neutral atoms, i.e., 6 for S and 12 for Zn .

In figure 2 we have shown the density of states, obtained by broadening the individual electronic levels slightly with Gaussians, for two representative rocksalt derived structures. It is observed that the states below the Fermi energy arrange into separate bands. The bands corresponding to sulfur 4s functions lies in the range between -18 and -17 eV, the one corresponding to Zn 3d in the range -12 to -10 eV and the uppermost occupied band between -9 to -6 eV is formed mainly due to S 3p and partly Zn 4s functions. This observation is exactly the same as for zinc-blende and wurtzite clusters.

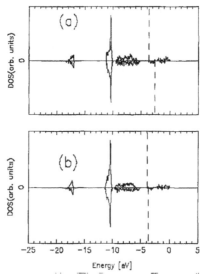

Figure 2. Density of states (DOS) for different rocksalt clusters of two different sizes: (a) Zn30S30 (b) Zn75S75. The upper part of each panel is representing the relaxed and the lower part unrelaxed structures, respectively. The vertical dashed lines mark the Fermi energy. Notice that the different panels have different scales on the y axis.

In order to arrive at a qualitative description of the distribution of the various orbitals, we define a radial density as follows. With Nij being the Mulliken gross population for the jth atom and ith orbital we define the density   with   being a chosen fixed constant. Subsequently, we calculate the spherical average of this density which are shown in figure 3. From the figure it is seen that LUMO is located at the surface while HOMO is in the inner part of the cluster. This finding for rocksalt structure is different from that of the zinc-blende and wurtzite clusters where LUMO is the surface state while HOMO is delocalized throughout the whole cluster. Analyzing the two orbitals in detail, we found that the LUMO has dominant contributions from the outer zinc atoms. As LUMO is the surface state, it energy depends sensitively on the cluster size. The surface localization of the LUMO has the consequence that HOMO and LUMO has different spatial distribution within the cluster. This difference in spatial distribution of HOMO and LUMO is important for low energy transitions and is in agreement with the recent experimental results on related CdSe semiconductor [13].

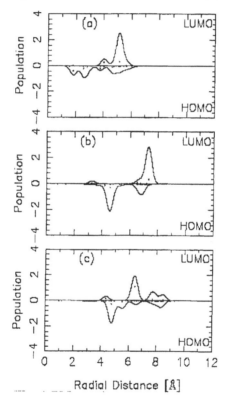

Figure 3. The schematic representation of the radial distribution of the HOMO and LUMO for the same clusters as in fig.1.

The sensitivity of the LUMO to the surface variation is illustrated in figure 4 (upper half) in which we have plotted the HOMO, LUMO energies as a function of the cluster size for rocksalt clusters. The results show that the dependence of energy of the HOMO on cluster size is more or less smooth whereas the same for LUMO is irregular and oscillating which is clear indication that the LUMO is the surface states. The lower part of the figure shows the variation of total energy (dashed line) as well as HOMO-LUMO energy gap (solid line) per ZnS pair of rocksalt clusters. From the figure it is seen that the band gap values increases with decreasing cluster size, a manifestation of so called quantum confinement effect. The variation of both total energy per pair and band gap value are more or less

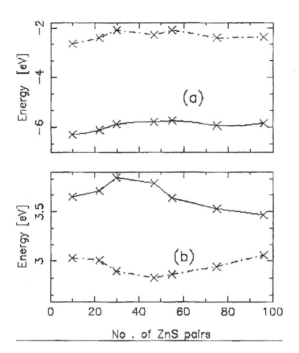

Figure 4. (a) HOMO (lower curve) and LUMO (upper curve) energies as well as (b) HOMO-LUMO gap (solid curve) and relative total energy per ZnS pair (shifted by an additive constant) (dashed curve) for rocksalt derived clusters as functions of the number of ZnS pairs.

4. Results and Discussions

By employing the DFTB method we have calculated the electronic structure of ZnS clusters of rocksalt modification as a function of size. The study of Mulliken population suggests that the clusters are largely ionic in character as opposed to zinc-blende and wurtzite modifications of ZnS which are largely covalent. The band gap increase with decreasing cluster size. For the cluster size studied here, LUMO is the surface state and HOMO is located in the inner part of the clusters which is different from that of zinc-blende and wurtzite clusters where LUMO is the surface states but HOMO is delocalized over the whole clusters.

Acknowledgments

The authors would like to thank the UGC, New Delhi, for the financial support through research grant [F12.30/2003(SR)].

References

1. V. L. Colvin, M. C. Schlamp and A. P. Alivisatos, Light-emitting diodes made from Cadmium Selenide nanocrystals and a semiconducting polymer. Nature, **370**, 354-357(1994).

2. W. U. Huynh, J. J. Dittmer and A. P. Alivisatos, Hybrid Nanorod-Polymer Solar Cells. Science, **295**, 2425-2427(2002).

3. W. C. W. Chan and S. M. Nie, Quantum Dot Bioconjugates for ultrasensitive Nonisotropic Detection. Science, **281**, 2016-2018(1998).

4. M. Bruchez, M. Moronne, P. Gin and S. Weiss, A. P. Alivisatos, Semiconductor Nanocrystals as Fluorescent Biological Labels. *Science*, **281**, 2013-2016(1998).

5. P. Calandra, A Longo and V. T. Leveri, Synthesis of ultra-small ZnS Nanoparticles by Solid-Solid Reaction in the confined Space of AOT Reversed Micelles. *J. Phys. Chem. B*, **107**, 25-30(2003).

6. R. N. Bhargava, D. Gallaghar, X. Hong and N. Nurmikko, Optical Properties of manganese-doped nanocrystals of ZnS. *Phys. Rev. Lett.* **72**, 416-419(1994).

7. T. A. Kennedy, E. R. Glaser, P. B. Klein and R. N. Bhargava, Symmetry and electronic structure of the Mn impurity in ZnS nanocrystals. *Phys. Rev. B*, **52** R14356-R14359(1995).

8. Y. Zhou, A. J. Campbell and D. L. Heinz, Equations of State and optical properties of the high pressure phase of Zinc Sulfide. *J. Phys. Chem. Solids*, **52**, 821-825(1991).

9. S. Desgreniers, L. Beaulieu and I. Lepage, Pressure-induced structural changes in ZnS. *Phys. Rev. B*, **61**, 8726-8733(2000).

10. G. Seifert, D. Porezag and Th. Frauenheim, Calculations of Molecules, Clusters, and Solids with a Simplified LCAO-DFT-LDA Scheme. *Int. J. Quantum Chem.*, **58**, 185-192(1996).

11. D. Porezag, Th. Frauenheim, Th. Kohler, G. Seifert and R. Kaschner, Construction of tight-binding like potentials on the basis of density-functional theory: Applications to Carbon. *Phys. Rev. B*, **51**, 12947-12957(1995).

12. S. Pal, B. Goswami and P. Sarkar, Size-dependent properties of Zn_mS_n clusters-a density functional tight-binding study. *J. Chem. Phys.* **123**, 044311-9(2005).

13. E. Lifshitz, I. Dag, I. Litvin and G. Hodes, Optically Detected Magnetic Resonance study of Electron/Hole Traps on CdSe Quantum Dot surfaces. *J. Phys. Chem.* **102**, 9245-9250(1998).

Brill Academic Publishers
P.O. Box 9000, 2300 PA Leiden,
The Netherlands

*Lecture Series on Computer
and Computational Sciences*
Volume 5, 2006, pp. 160-168

Enhancement of fullerene stabilities from excited electronic states[1]

Zdeněk Slanina[2],*, Filip Uhlík[§], Shyi-Long Lee[¶], Ludwik Adamowicz[♣], and Shigeru Nagase[*]

*Department of Theoretical Molecular Science, Institute for Molecular Science
Myodaiji, Okazaki 444-8585, Japan

[§]Department of Physical and Macromolecular Chemistry, Charles University
Albertov 6, CZ-128 43 Prague 2, Czech Republic

[¶]Department of Chemistry and Biochemistry
National Chung-Cheng University, Chia-Yi 62117, Taiwan

[♣]Department of Chemistry, University of Arizona
Tucson, AZ 85721-0041, USA

Abstract: There is one factor in relative stabilities of isomeric fullerenes that has rarely been studied so far – contribution of excited electronic states. The contribution is clearly defined by the electronic partition function, supposing the related excitation energies can be evaluated. As temperatures in fullerene synthesis are high, the term should be taken into account. In this report the problem is studied on four isomeric systems. The first system is the set of five IPR (isolated pentagon rule) isomers of C_{78}, relatively well known from experiment. The second system studied is a model set of four isomers of $Mg@C_{72}$ (not yet isolated species). The third case consists of seven IPR isomers of C_{80}. The last set is formed by six C_{74} cages. The electronic excitation energies are computed by limited configuration interaction (CI) approach, mostly with the ZINDO semiempirical method. Isomers of $Mg@C_{72}$ are evaluated by means of the single-excitation CI or CI-Singles (CIS) in the standard LanL2DZ basis set. It is found that the electronic partition function can cause significant changes in the computed equilibrium relative concentrations of isomers at high temperatures. Metallofullerenes are more likely candidates for such enhanced effects.

Keywords: Fullerenes and metallofullerenes; electronic excited states; Jahn-Teller effect; Gibbs energy

PACS: 31.15.Ew; 36.40.Cg; 74.70.Wz

1 Introduction

Very high temperatures of fullerene synthesis should also produce significant populations of excited electronic states, thus implying non-negligible electronic partition functions. This interesting aspect is one of the substantial features of fullerene and metallofullerene syntheses and it can have some significant consequences for computed fullerene-related thermodynamics or kinetics. Still, the aspect has rarely been treated so far. The excited electronic states can be evaluated by means of

---

[1]Dedicated to the memory of Prof. Dr. Jaroslav Koutecký (1922–2005).
[2]Corresponding author, e-mail: zdenek@ims.ac.jp.

(limited) configuration interaction (CI) approach [1] or time-dependent density functional theory (DFT) response theory [2]. For systems of fullerene dimensions, the semiempirical (CI based) ZINDO method developed by Zerner *et al.* [3, 4, 5, 6] represents a useful, more practical option.

In this paper, numerical illustrations are presented on four interesting fullerene and metallo-fullerene systems [7, 8, 9, 10, 11, 12, 13. 14. 15, 16, 17, 18, 19, 20, 21, 22, 23, 24, 25, 26, 27, 28, 29, 30, 31, 32], namely C_{78}, $Mg@C_{72}$, C_{80}, and C_{74} isomeric sets. There are five [7] isolated-pentagon-rule (IPR) satisfying isomers for C_{78} [8, 9, 10, 11, 12, 13. 14, 15, 16] but only three were originally observed in experiments while the fourth species was reported [15] only recently. On the other hand, $Mg@C_{72}$ is a model. not yet isolated system belonging to an interesting class of C_{72} related species [17, 18, 19, 20, 21, 22, 23]. C_{80} is represented by seven [7] topologically possible IPR structures. The C_{80} IPR structures were also computed several times [24, 25, 26, 27, 28, 29, 30], and two of them also isolated [31, 32]. Moreover, C_{80} cages are well known from some metallo-fullerenes [33, 34, 35, 36]. C_{74}, like C_{72}, exhibits just one IPR structure, however, there are several C_{74} non-IPR cages with a relatively low energy [37]. The present paper deals with the role of the electronic excited states in evaluation of the cage stabilities.

2 Calculations

For C_{78}, our previously optimized structures [16] are used here. The geometry optimizations were first carried out with the semiempirical method SAM1 [38] and re-optimized at the *ab initio* Hartee-Fock (HF) SCF level in the standard 3-21G basis set (HF/3-21G) using the Gaussian program [39]. The separation energetics was refined with the B3LYP treatment in the standard 6-31G* basis set (B3LYP/6-31G*), and the ZINDO electronic excitations energies were empl
partition function q_{el}.

The four-membered $Mg@C_{72}$ isomeric system is treated here based on
puted data set [21, 22]. The computations were performed with a parame:
MNDO method known as MNDO/d. The limited single-excitation CI treatment
LanL2DZ basis sets (CIS/LanL2DZ) was carried out in order to obtain the electronic   ...5
energies for the electronic partition function q_{el}.

The C_{80} IPR structures treated here are of the SAM1 origin [26, 27] and the electronic excitations energies were generated by the ZINDO method. Finally, six C_{74} cages [37] were optimized at the B3LYP/3-21G level while the separation energetics was derived from the B3LYP/6-31G* approach and q_{el} is again based on the ZINDO method.

The computed energy, structural, vibrational, and electronic data are combined for the construction of isomeric partition functions and evaluations of the relative Gibbs free energies [41] converted into the relative concentrations (mole fractions) x_i as the final output. The rotational-vibrational partition functions are of the rigid rotator and harmonic oscillator quality, and no frequency scaling is considered. The geometrical symmetries of the optimized cages were determined by a procedure with a variable precision of the coordinates [26]. Chirality contribution [42] was considered accordingly. The electronic partition function q_{el} was constructed by a direct summation.

3 Illustrative Examples

The IPR isomers of C_{78} exhibit the D_3, C_{2v}, C_{2v}, D_{3h}, and D_{3h} symmetries. Fig. 1 depicts their computed equilibrium mole fractions, evaluated with and without the electronic partition functions. At the highest temperatures the difference is in some cases about five percent points. When the electronic partition function is included, structure **5** in particular increases its presence while the relative concentration of structure **2** is reduced. The changes at high temperatures are ...

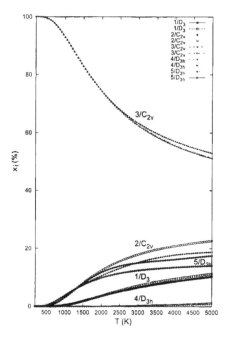

Figure 1: Mole fractions x_i of five IPR isomers of C_{78} – the ZINDO electronic partition function q_{el} (the full and empty symbols refer to the calculations with and without q_{el}, respectively).

negligible. Generally, after inclusion of the electronic excited states, some relative concentrations will increase while others will have to decrease as their sum must be the same.

The $Mg@C_{72}$ structures considered here are closely related to the $Ca@C_{72}$ cages [17]: the IPR structure (**a**), two non-IPR structures each with one pair of connected pentagons (**b**, **c**), and a structure with one heptagon (**d**). It turns out that the **d** structure exhibits particularly low excited states. Fig. 2 presents the equilibrium mole fractions of the $Mg@C_{72}$ isomers computed with and without the CIS/LanL2DZ electronic partition functions. The effects of the excited states are somewhat larger than in the C_{78} case.

There is an interesting issue concerning the triplet electronic states - one could consider the electronic partition function based either on both singlet and triplet electronic excited states or just on singlet electronic excited states. It can be argued that the singlet-only approach could produce more realistic results. The basic reason is that it could be expected that the fullerene triplet species, after condensation in the form of soot, will in the end polymerize and form insoluble solids (supposing that the triplet states will have sufficiently long life time). If the equilibrium gas-phase isomeric mixture is cooled down and condenses, the high-temperature gas-phase mole fractions are effectively frozen. If the triplet-state isomers can be removed by some mechanism during the condensation, the singlet-state isomers should still keep their high-temperature concentration ratios and those should be the values that would be found by a chemical analysis of the soot.

It can be shown that all what is needed to get the observed values is just to cross out the triplets from the very beginning of the computational treatment. Thus, we can limit the calculations only to the isomers in the singlet electronic states as long as we are interested in comparison with

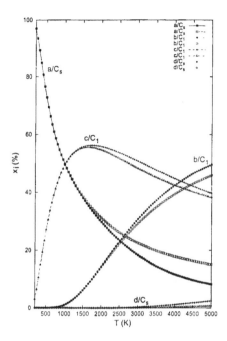

Figure 2: Mole fractions x_i of four isomers of Mg@C_{72} – the CIS/LanL2DZ electronic partition function q_{el} (the full and empty symbols refer to the calculations with and without q_{el}, respectively).

the observed concentration ratios derived from the condensed-phase products. However, low-lying triplet states also imply reduced production yields as they are scaled down owing to the part of the cages that were converted into the polymeric material. The issue of the singlet-triplet versus singlet-only partition functions is illustrated in the two following examples.

Fig. 3 deals with the interplay of seven IPR isomers of C_{80}. The **C** structure (D_{5d} symmetry) comes as the species located lowest in the potential energy while the **A** structure (D_2 symmetry) is the second lowest in the SAM1 computations. Thus, at very low temperatures the ground-state structure **C** should be prevailing. However, relatively soon after a temperature of 1000 K the **A** species reaches equimolarity with the **C** species, and also other species become gradually significant. There is a temperature interval in which the **A** isomer is the most populated species. The temperature interval is wider and the two isomers are better separated when just the singlet electronic excited states are included into the electronic partition function q_{el} while all the triplet states are ignored. Incidentally, this singlet-only partition function gives a better agreement with the available experiments [31, 32] as the **A** (D_2) cage is in fact produced [32] in larger amounts. It is however true that the computational picture is also sensitive to the separation energetics and its evaluation at higher levels of theory would be still desirable.

C_{74} is represented here by six cages [37] - Fig. 4: D_{3h} (IPR), C_2 (5/5 fusion), C_1 (5/5 fusion), C_1 (5/5 fusion), C_1 (5/5 fusion & 7-ring), C_1 (5/5 fusion & 7-ring). Shinohara *et al.* [43] recently recorded electronic spectrum of C_{74} anion and suggested that the cage could have D_{3h} symmetry. Moreover, low triplet states were computed [44] for the C_{74} IPR cage. Fig. 4 shows that although the IPR species is indeed prevailing, the picture is sensitive to the triplet

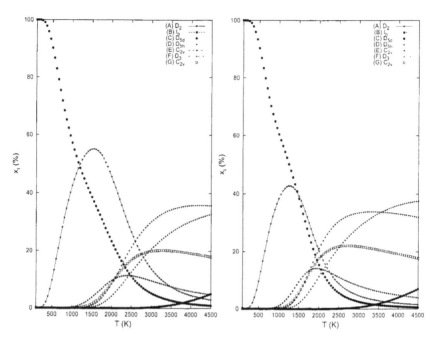

Figure 3: Mole fractions x_i of seven IPR isomers of C_{80} from the SAM1 data and the ZINDO electronic partition partition q_{el} with the singlet (left) and the singlet and triplet excitation energies (right).

states inclusion/suppression.

In overall, the computations suggest that at high temperatures electronic excited states can make some significant contribution into thermodynamics. It is likely that, after an extended search, some isomeric system can be pointed out with especially pronounced changes in the relative isomeric concentrations upon inclusion of the electronic partition function. Metallofullerenes are more likely candidates for such enhanced effects though calculations of their vibrational and electronic spectra still represent a challenging problem [45]. However, even pristine fullerenic isomers can show interesting effects, for example if Jahn-Teller distortions are involved.

Acknowledgment

The reported research has been supported by a Grant-in-aid for NAREGI Nanoscience Project, and for Scientific Research on Priority Area (A) from the Ministry of Education, Culture, Sports, Science and Technology of Japan, by the National Science Council, Taiwan-ROC, and by the Czech National Research Program 'Information Society' (Czech Acad. Sci. 1ET401110505).

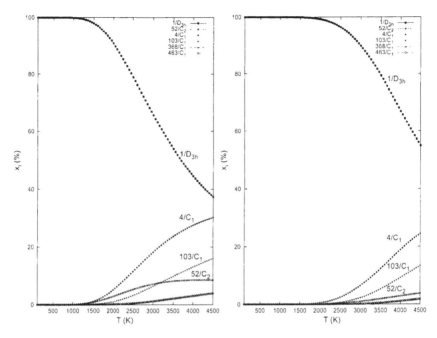

Figure 4: Relative concentrations of six C_{74} isomers based on the B3LYP/6-31G* energetics and the ZINDO electronic partition function q_{el} with the singlet (left) and the singlet and triplet excitation energies (right).

References

[1] W. J. Hehre, L. Radom, P. v. R. Schleyer and J. A. Pople, Ab Initio Molecular Orbital Theory, J. Wiley Inc., New York, 1986.

[2] M. E. Casida, C. Jamorski, K. C. Casida and D. R. Salahub, Molecular excitation energies to high-lying bound states from time-dependent density-functional response theory: Characterization and correction of the time-dependent local density approximation ionization threshold, J. Chem. Phys. 108, 4439-4449 (1998).

[3] R. Bendale, J. Stanton and M.C. Zerner, Structure and spectroscopy of Jahn-Teller distorted C_{60}^+, Chem. Phys. Lett. 194, 467-471 (1992).

[4] Q. Teng, S. Feng, C. Sun and M.C. Zerner, Theoretical predictions of the structures and electronic spectra of $C_{60}NH_2^+$ with comparisons with the isoelectronic molecules $C_{60}O$ and $C_{60}CH_2$, Int. J. Quantum Chem. 55, 35-45 (1995).

[5] R. Bendale, D. Baker and M.C. Zerner, Calculations on the electronic structure and spectroscopy of C_{60} and C_{70} cage structures, Int. J. Quantum Chem. S25, 557-568 (1991).

[6] R. D. Bendale and M. C. Zerner, Electronic structure and spectroscopy of the five most stable isomers of C_{78} fullerene, J. Phys. Chem. 99, 13830-13833 (1995).

[7] P. W. Fowler and D. E. Manolopoulos, An Atlas of Fullerenes. Clarendon Press, Oxford, 1995.

[8] F. Diederich, R. L. Whetten, C. Thilgen, R. Ettl, I. Chao and M. M. Alvarez, Fullerene isomerism - isolation of C_{2v}-C_{78} and D_3-C_{78}, Science 254, 1768-1770 (1991).

[9] P. W. Fowler, R. C. Batten and D. E. Manolopoulos, The higher fullerenes - a candidate for the structure of C_{78}, J. Chem. Soc., Faraday Trans. 87, 3103-3104 (1991).

[10] D. Bakowies, A. Geleßus and W. Thiel, Quantum-chemical study of C_{78} fullerene isomers, Chem. Phys. Lett. 197, 324-329 (1992).

[11] K. Kikuchi, N. Nakahara, T. Wakabayashi, S. Suzuki, H. Shiromaru, Y. Miyake, K. Saito, I. Ikemoto, M. Kainosho and Y. Achiba, NMR characterization of isomers of C_{78}, C_{82} and C_{84} fullerenes, Nature 357, 142-145 (1992).

[12] Z. Slanina, J.-P. François, D. Bakowies and W. Thiel, Fullerene C_{78} isomers - temperature-dependence of their calculated relative stabilities, J. Mol. Struct. (Theochem) 279, 213-216 (1993).

[13] R. Taylor, G. J. Langley, A. G. Avent, T. J. S. Dennis, H. W. Kroto and D. R. M. Walton, ^{13}C NMR-spectroscopy of C_{76}, C_{78}, C_{84} and mixtures of C_{86}-C_{102} - anomalous chromatographic behaviour of C_{82}, and evidence for $C_{70}H_{12}$, J. Chem. Soc., Perkin Trans. 2 1029-1036 (1993).

[14] M. Saunders, R. J. Cross, H. A. Jiménez-Vázquez, R. Shimshi and A. Khong, Noble gas atoms inside fullerenes, Science 271, 1693-1697 (1996).

[15] K. Yamamoto, Abstract no. 1489, The 200th ECS Meeting, ECS, San Francisco, 2001.

[16] F. Uhlík, Z. Slanina and E. Ōsawa, C_{78} IPR Fullerenes: Computed B3LYP/6-31G*//HF/3-21G Temperature-Dependent Relative Concentrations, Eur. Phys. J. D 16, 349-352 (2001).

[17] K. Kobayashi, S. Nagase, M. Yoshida and E. Ōsawa, Endohedral metallofullerenes. Are the isolated pentagon rule and fullerene structures always satisfied?, J. Am. Chem. Soc. 119, 12693-12694 (1997).

[18] T. S. M. Wan, H.-W. Zhang, T. Nakane, Z. Xu, M. Inakuma, H. Shinohara, K. Kobayashi and S. Nagase, Production, isolation, and electronic properties of missing fullerenes: Ca@C_{72} and Ca@C_{74}, J. Am. Chem. Soc. 120, 6806-6807 (1998).

[19] M. D. Diener and J. M. Alford, Nature, Isolation and properties of small-bandgap fullerenes. 393, 668-671 (1998).

[20] Z. Slanina, X. Zhao, F. Uhlík and E. Ōsawa, Non-IPR fullerenes: C_{36} and C_{72}, Electronic Properties of Novel Materials - Science and Technology of Molecular Nanostructures (Editors: H. Kuzmany, J. Fink, M. Mehring and S. Roth), AIP, Melville, 179-182 (1999).

[21] Z. Slanina, X. Zhao, X. Grabuleda, M. Ozawa, F. Uhlík, P. M. Ivanov, K. Kobayashi and S. Nagase, Mg@C_{72}: MNDO/d Evaluation of the Isomeric Composition, J. Mol. Graphics Mod. 19, 252-255 (2001).

[22] Z. Slanina, F. Uhlík, L. Adamowicz, K. Kobayashi and S. Nagase, Electronic excited states and stabilities of fullerenes: Isomers of C_{78} and Mg@C_{72}, Int. J. Quantum Chem. 100, 610-616 (2004).

[23] Z. Slanina, K. Ishimura, K. Kobayashi and S. Nagase, C_{72} Isomers: The IPR-satisfying cage is disfavored by both energy and entropy, Chem. Phys. Lett. 384, 114-118 (2004).

[24] S. J. Woo, E. Kim and Y. H. Lee, Geometric, electronic, and vibrational structures of C_{50}, C_{60}, C_{70}, and C_{80}, Phys. Rev. B 47, 6721-6727 (1993).

[25] K. Nakao, N. Kurita and M. Fujita, Ab-initio molecular-orbital calculation for C_{70} and 7 isomers of C_{80}, Phys. Rev. B 49, 11415-11420 (1994).

[26] M.-L. Sun, Z. Slanina, S.-L. Lee, F. Uhlík and L. Adamowicz, AM1 computations on 7 isolated-pentagon-rule isomers of C_{80}, Chem. Phys. Lett. 246, 66-72 (1995).

[27] M.-L. Sun, Z. Slanina, S.-L. Lee, F. Uhlík and L. Adamowicz, The IPR isomers of C_{80}: SAM1 computations, Physics and Chemistry of Fullerenes and Their Derivatives (Editors H. Kuzmany, J. Fink, M. Mehring and S. Roth), World Sci. Publ., Singapore, 63-66 (1995).

[28] K. Kobayashi, S. Nagase and T. Akasaka, A theoretical study of C_{80} and $La_2@C_{80}$, Chem. Phys. Lett. 245, 230-236 (1995).

[29] Z. Slanina, S.-L. Lee and L. Adamowicz, C_{80}, C_{86}, C_{88}: Semiempirical and ab initio SCF calculations, Int. J. Quantum Chem. 63, 529-535 (1997).

[30] F. Furche and R. Ahlrichs, Fullerene C_{80}: Are there still more isomers? J. Chem. Phys. 114, 10362-10367 (2001).

[31] F. H. Hennrich, R. H. Michel, A. Fischer, S. Richard-Schneider, S. Gilb, M. M. Kappes, D. Fuchs, M. Bürk, K. Kobayashi and S. Nagase, Isolation and characterization of C_{80}, Angew. Chem., Int. Ed. Engl. 35, 1732-1734 (1996).

[32] C.-R. Wang, T. Sugai, T. Kai, T. Tomiyama and H. Shinohara, Production and isolation of an ellipsoidal C_{80} fullerene, J. Chem. Soc., Chem. Commun. 557-558 (2000).

[33] K. Kobayashi, S. Nagase and T. Akasaka, Endohedral dimetallofullerenes Sc-2@C-84 and La-2@C-80.

[34] K. Kobayashi and S. Nagase, Structures and electronic states of endohedral dimetallo-fullerenes: $M_2@C_{80}$ (M=Sc, Y, La, Ce, Pr, Eu, Gd, Yb and Lu). Chem. Phys. Lett. 262, 227-232 (1996).

[35] Y. F. Lian, S. F. Yang and S. H. Yang, Revisiting the preparation of $La@C_{82}$ (I and II) and $La_2@C_{80}$: Efficient Production of the "Minor" isomer $La@C_{82}$ (II), J. Phys. Chem. B 106, 3112-3117 (2002).

[36] K. Kobayashi and S. Nagase, Structures and electronic properties of endohedral metallo-fullerenes, theory and experiment, Endofullerenes - A New Family of Carbon Clusters (Editors T. Akasaka and S. Nagase), Kluwer Academic Publishers, Dordrecht, 99-119 (2002).

[37] Z. Slanina, K. Kobayashi and S. Nagase, $Ca@C_{74}$ isomers: Relative concentrations at higher temperatures, Chem. Phys. 301, 153-157 (2004).

[38] M. J. S. Dewar, C. Jie and J. Yu, SAM1 - the 1st of a new series of general-purpose quantum-mechanical molecular models, Tetrahedron 49, 5003-5038 (1993).

[39] M. J. Frisch, G. W. Trucks, H. B. Schlegel, G. E. Scuseria, M. A. Robb, J. R. Cheeseman, V. G. Zakrzewski, J. A. Montgomery, Jr., R. E. Stratmann, J. C. Burant, S. Dapprich, J. M. Millam, A. D. Daniels, K. N. Kudin, M. C. Strain, O. Farkas, J. Tomasi, V. Barone, M. Cossi, R. Cammi, B. Mennucci, C. Pomelli, C. Adamo, S. Clifford, J. Ochterski, G. A. Petersson, P. Y. Ayala, Q. Cui, K. Morokuma, D. K. Malick, A. D. Rabuck, K. Raghavachari, J. B.

Foresman, J. Cioslowski, J. V. Ortiz, B. B. Stefanov, G. Liu, A. Liashenko, P. Piskorz. I. Komaromi, R. Gomperts, R. L. Martin, D. J. Fox, T. Keith, M. A. Al-Laham, C. Y. Peng, A. Nanayakkara, C. Gonzalez, M. Challacombe, P. M. W. Gill, B. Johnson, W. Chen. M. W. Wong, J. L. Andres, C. Gonzalez, M. Head-Gordon, E. S. Replogle, and J. A. Pople. GAUSSIAN 98, Revision A.7, Gaussian, Inc.. Pittsburgh. PA, 1998.

[40] W. Thiel and A. A. Voityuk, Extension of MNDO to d orbitals: Parameters and results for the second-row elements and for the zinc group. J. Phys. Chem. 100, 616-626 (1996).

[41] Z. Slanina, Equilibrium isomeric mixtures - potential-energy hypersurfaces as the origin of the overall thermodynamics and kinetics, Int. Rev. Phys. Chem. 6, 251-267 (1987).

[42] Z. Slanina and L. Adamowicz, On relative stabilities of dodecahedron-shaped and bowl-shaped structures of C_{20}, Thermochim. Acta 205, 299-306 (1992).

[43] H. Moribe, T. Inoue, H. Kato, A. Taninaka, Y. Ito. T. Okazaki, T. Sugai, R. Bolskar, J. M. Alford and H. Shinohara, Purification and electronic structure of C_{74} fullerene, Paper 1P-1, The 25th Fullerene-Nanotubes Symposium, Awaji, Japan, 2003.

[44] V. I. Kovalenko and A. R. Khamatgalimov, Open-shell fullerene C-74: phenalenyl-radical substructures, Chem. Phys. Lett. 377, 263-268 (2003).

[45] Z. Slanina, L. Adamowicz, K. Kobayashi and S. Nagase, Gibbs energy-based treatment of metallofullerenes: $Ca@C_{72}$, $Ca@C_{74}$, $Ca@C_{82}$, and $La@C_{82}$, Mol. Simul. 31, 71-77 (2005).

Brill Academic Publishers
P.O. Box 9000, 2300 PA Leiden,
The Netherlands

*Lecture Series on Computer
and Computational Sciences*
Volume 5, 2006, pp. 169-174

Fusion and fission of atomic clusters: recent advances

O. I. Obolensky,[1] I. A. Solov'yov, A. V. Solov'yov,[2] W. Greiner

Frankfurt Institute for Advanced Studies,
Johann Wolfgang Goethe-University,
Max-von-Laue str.1, 60438 Frankfurt am Main, Germany

Abstract: We review recent advances made by our group in finding optimized geometries of atomic clusters as well as in description of fission of charged small metal clusters. We base our approach to these problems on analysis of multidimensional potential energy surface. For the fusion process we have developed an effective scheme of adding new atoms to stable cluster isomers which provides good starting points for a global optimization procedure and thus allows one to obtain optimal geometries of larger clusters in an efficient way. We apply this algorithm to finding geometries of metal and noble gas clusters. For the fission process the analysis of the potential energy landscape calculated on the *ab initio* level of theory allowed us to obtain very detailed information on energetics and pathways of the different fission channels for the Na_{10}^{2+} clusters.

Keywords: atomic clusters, atomic cluster fission, atomic cluster fusion, Lennard-Jones clusters, global minimization

1 Introduction

In the following two sections we give an overview of our approach to determination of stable geometries of atomic clusters and to finding the fission pathway minimizing the potential energy barriers needed to be overcome. The approach is based on analysis of the multidimensional potential energy surface. We suggest a scheme of adding new atoms to the optimized geometries of smaller clusters which provides effective sampling over the multidimensional coordinate space resulting in good starting points for optimization procedure. We demonstrate also that analysis of potential energy surface allows one to get very detailed information on energetics of fission and fission pathways.

The physical results obtained within our approach are, briefly, the following.

For Lennard-Jones clusters starting from the initial tetrahedral cluster configuration, by adding new atoms to the system, we were able to find cluster growth paths up to the cluster size of 150 atoms. We demonstrated that in this way all the known global minima structures of the LJ clusters can be found [1, 2].

For metal clusters, the geometries have been optimized for clusters consisting of up to 20 atoms [3, 4, 5]. Many properties of these systems have been calculated.

The impact of cluster structure on the fission process has been elucidated. The calculations show that the geometry of the smaller fragment and the geometry of its immediate neighborhood in the larger fragment (together with the electronic shell effects) play a leading role in defining the fission barrier height [6]. We demonstrated the importance of rearrangement of the cluster structure during fission [6, 7]. The rearrangement may include formation of a neck between the

---

[1] On leave from the A.F. Ioffe Institute, St. Petersburg, Russia. E-mail: o.obolensky@fias.uni-frankfurt.de
[2] On leave from the A.F. Ioffe Institute, St. Petersburg, Russia. E-mail: solovyov@fias.uni-frankfurt.de

two fragments or fissioning via another isomer state of the parent cluster; examples of such processes have been given. Potential energy surface of the Na_{10}^{2+} clusters has been analyzed in detail [6]. For several low lying local minima of the potential energy surface the potential barriers for transitions between the corresponding isomer states are calculated and compared with the corresponding fission barriers. These data suggest that there is a competition between "direct" fission and fission proceeding via intermediate isomer states of the parent cluster [6]. Importance of cluster geometry and, consequently, configurational entropy in thermodynamic aspects (such as the branching ratios between different fission channels) has been elucidated [6]. The experimentally observable changes in the branching ratios between the different channels for fission of the Na_{10}^{2+} clusters have been predicted.

2 Determination of stable geometries of clusters: Cluster Fusion Algorithm

We have developed an efficient scheme of global optimization, called Cluster Fusion Algorithm. The scheme has been designed within the context of determination of the most stable cluster geometries and it is applicable for various types of clusters [1].

We utilized the scheme in search for global minima of the multidimensional potential energy surface of metal and noble gas clusters [1, 2, 3, 4, 5]. With this scheme we were able to determine the most stable cluster geometries for up to 150 atoms for noble gas clusters and for up to 22 atoms for metal (sodium, magnesium) clusters. While the global energy optimization for noble gas clusters is a relatively simple problem and optimization could easily be done for larger clusters, the calculations with metal clusters present a serious challenge and require significant computational resources. The principal difference between these two cases consists in the different nature of the atomic interactions in the clusters. For noble gas clusters the interactions have a pair-wise character and can be very well approximated by the Lennard-Jones type of potential, which has a simple analytical form. Metal clusters cannot be accurately described by a pair-wise potential because of delocalization of valence electrons. For these clusters one has to use *ab initio* quantum mechanical methods (Hartree-Fock-based many-body theory or density functional methods) in order to obtain a good agreement with the experimental data. For both types of calculations our algorithm has proven to be a reliable and effective tool in multidimensional global optimization.

The proposed algorithm belongs to the class of genetic (also called evolutionary) global optimization methods [8, 9]. In applications to clusters the genetic methods are based on the idea that the larger clusters evolve to low energy states by mutation and/or by mating smaller structures with low potential energy. The success of this procedure reflects the fact that in nature clusters in their ground (i.e., the minimum energy) states often emerge in the cluster fusion process. Numerous versions of the genetic strategies has been adapted to global energy optimization in atomic clusters [10, 11, 12, 13]. One of the strategies within the generic approach assumes that the global energy minimum structure for N atoms can be found on the basis of the global energy minimum for $N-1$ atoms. This strategy is implemented, e.g., in the so-called seed growth method [10, 11]. In this method in order to get the most stable cluster of N atoms one atom is added to the most stable cluster of $N-1$ atoms in a stochastic manner, near the boundary of the cluster and then optimization of the structure with a given optimization method is performed.

Our method also uses the strategy of adding one atom to a cluster of size $N-1$. There are, however, two important improvement which allow for a much faster convergence. The first one is the fact that the atom is not added at a random place on the surface of the initial cluster. Rather, we use the deterministic approach and the new atom is added to the certain places of the cluster surface, such as the midpoint of a face. The second important feature of our method is that we add the new atom not only to the ground state isomer of size $N-1$, but also to the other, energetically less favorable, isomers. This insures that we do not miss sizes at which smooth evolution within one family of clusters (say, with the same type of lattice) is interrupted and the global energy minimum of the next cluster size lies within another cluster growth branch.

To illustrate that we show in Figure 1 the global energy minimum geometries for Lennard-Jones (LJ) clusters of sizes 28 through 33. It is seen that the clusters LJ_{30} and LJ_{31} belong to different branches of cluster growth (with icosahedral and decahedral point symmetries).

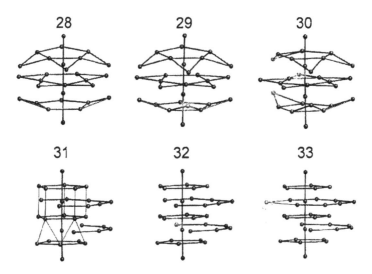

Figure 1: Global energy minimum geometries for Lennard-Jones clusters of sizes 28 through 33. The new atoms added to the cluster are marked by grey circles, while grey rings show the atoms removed.

Another important novel feature of our method is the global optimization technique. Our experience shows that, at least for deterministic addition of one atom to a stable cluster isomer, it is more efficient to perform a three-dimensional optimization of coordinates of the newly added atom rather than applying multidimensional optimization techniques which optimize the coordinates of all atoms in the cluster simultaneously. Therefore, we have employed the following algorithm for optimization of the cluster structure. At each step of the calculation we consider the motion of one atom only, the one, which is the subject to the action of the maximum force. Then we scan the potential energy surface along the direction of the force, keeping the coordinates of all other atoms fixed. At the point in which the kinetic energy of the selected atom is maximum, we set the absolute value of its velocity to zero. This point corresponds to the minimum of the potential valley in which the selected atom moves. When the selected atom is brought to the (local) minimum energy position, the next atom is selected to move and the procedure of the kinetic energy absorption repeats. The calculation stops when all the atoms are at equilibrium.

3   Description of the fission process within potential energy surface approach

We investigate fission of small charged metal clusters, with Na_{10}^{2+} and Na_{18}^{2+} being the examples of such systems. For analysis of the cluster fission process we employ a procedure somewhat different from the usual molecular dynamics simulations techniques. Our approach consists in exploring the multidimensional potential energy surface of the cluster. This allows for a more systematic analysis of various fission scenarios, as compared to the usual methods which try to simulate the evolution of the system with time.

Only very limited subspaces of the multidimensional coordinate space are relevant to the cluster structure optimization or fission problems. Still, the amount of calculations which have to be done is very large and it increases drastically with the growth of the cluster size. Due to the delocalization of electrons and importance of quantum effects in the metal clusters, the use of classical pair-wise potentials is not justified and one has to resort to the quantum treatment of the system. This imposes significant restrictions on the size of the cluster. We have analyzed the potential energy surfaces for metal clusters consisting of up to about 20 atoms with the use of *ab initio* methods of quantum mechanics.

The global minimum on the multidimensional potential energy surface corresponds to the energetically preferred state of the system. Fission takes place for metastable clusters (see [6] and references therein). Therefore, the global minimum corresponds to the system fragmented into two charged parts located infinitely far away from each other. That is, the global minimum is located at the "edge" of the potential energy surface, in the part of the multidimensional coordinate space in which the distance between the two fragments is infinitely large. There are also other local minima at the "edges" of the potential energy surface corresponding to other possible fission channels.

The deepest local minimum on the potential energy surface which is located in the "center" part of the surface, where the two fragments of the parent cluster are close, corresponds to the ground state of the cluster, while other local minima in the "center" part of the surface represent other (meta)stable isomer states.

Therefore, analysis of the potential energy surface allows one not only to determine the ground state of the cluster, but also to find its less energetically favorable isomers. In Figure 2 we present geometries corresponding to several lowest lying local minima in the "center" part of the potential energy surface for Na_{10}^{2+} cluster.

Figure 2: Geometries of the Na_{10}^{2+} cluster corresponding to four lowest lying local minima in the "center" part of the potential energy surface.

The simulation of the fission process in our approach comes to finding a pathway on the system's multidimensional potential energy surface from a minimum in the center part of the surface to a minimum at its edge. The found pathway must minimize the energy barrier for the transition.

In simulation of the fission process we start from the optimized stable geometry of a cluster and choose the atoms the resulting fragments would consist of. The atoms chosen for a smaller fragment are shifted from their optimized locations in the parent cluster to a certain distance.

This corresponds to a shift on the potential energy surface from the local minimum. Then, the energy of the system and its gradient are calculated at that given point. These quantities specify the direction along the surface in which the energy decreases most rapidly and determine the next point of the potential energy surface to be calculated.

If the fragments are removed not far enough from each other then the gradient of the potential energy surface points towards the original local minimum and the system returns to the initial state. Physically speaking, this corresponds to the situation when the cohesive forces in the system prevail over the repulsive ones and the fragments stick together forming the unified cluster again. If the fragments are removed far enough, the minimization procedure on the potential energy surface does not lead to the initial point, but rather it leads away from it. The system can then be trapped in another local minimum which would correspond to changing the isomer state of the cluster. Analyzing the potential energy surface, one can find a potential barrier for such a transition. Alternatively, the minimization procedure leads away from the center part of the potential energy surface towards its edge, i.e. the repulsive forces dominate and the system fragments. The dependence of the total energy of the system on the fragments separation distance forms the potential energy barrier for a given pathway. Hence, finding the fission barrier is equivalent to finding the pathway with the lowest potential energy barrier.

We have observed that often fission barrier can be greatly lowered by drawing the fission pathway via one or more local minima on the potential energy surface. In other words, fission can proceed via formation of intermediate isomers. One can distinguish between two main kinds of the such fission pathways. The pathways of the first kind pass through the local minima located in the "center" part of the potential energy surface, in which the fragments are not spatially separated. In terms of evolution of the cluster geometry in the course of fission, such fission pathways correspond to rearrangement of the cluster structure on the initial stage of the fission process, before the actual separation of the fragments begins. In fact, it is a transition to another isomer state of the parent cluster. The fission pathways of the second kind lead from the local minimum in the center part of the potential energy surface to a minimum at its edge through the local minima located in the "intermediate" part of the surface which corresponds to geometries with the fragments spatially separated, but not removed away each from other. Such metastable states correspond to supermolecules formed by the fragments. As an illustration we plot in Figure 3 two such states for the Na_{10}^{2+} and Na_{18}^{2+} clusters. We note, that the fragments are connected by a "neck" [7, 14, 15, 16]. A similar necking phenomenon is known for nuclear fission [17]. In molecular dynamics simulations necking can be observed as an elongation of the cluster shape during fission [18, 19].

Figure 3: Supermoleculelike geometries of fissioning Na_{10}^{2+} (left) and Na_{18}^{2+} (right) clusters corresponding to local minima in the "intermediate" part of the potential energy surface (see the text).

Acknowledgment

This work is partially supported by the European Commision within the Network of Excellence project EXCELL, by INTAS under the grant 03-51-6170 and by the Russian Foundation for Basic Research under the grant 03-02-18294-a.

References

[1] I.A. Solov'yov, A.V. Solov'yov, W. Greiner, *International Journal of Moderm Physics E* **13** 697-736(2004).

[2] I.A. Solov'yov, A.V. Solov'yov, W. Greiner, A. Koshelev, A. Shutovich *Physical Review Letters* **90** 053401-053404(2003).

[3] I.A. Solov'yov, A.V. Solov'yov and W. Greiner 2002 *Physical Review* A **65** 053203-053222(2002).

[4] A. Lyalin, I.A. Solov'yov, A.V. Solov'yov and W. Greiner *Physical Review* A **67** 063203-063216(2003).

[5] A. Lyalin, A.V. Solov'yov, C. Brechignac and W. Greiner, *Journal of Physics B: Atomic Molecular and Optical Physics* **38** L129-L135(2005).

[6] O. I. Obolensky, A.G. Lyalin, A.V. Solov'yov and W. Greiner, accepted for publication in *Physical Review* B (2005).

[7] A.G. Lyalin, O.I. Obolensky, A.V. Solov'yov, Il.A. Solov'yov and W. Greiner *Journal of Physics B: Atomic Molecular and Optical Physics* **37** L7(2004).

[8] Z. Michalewicz, *Genetic Algorithms + Data Structures = Evolution Programs.* Springer, Berlin, Heidelberg, New York. (3rd Ed.), 1996.

[9] D.E. Goldberg, *Genetic Algorithms in Search, Optimization, and Machine Learning.* Addison-Wesley, Reading, MA, 1989.

[10] J.A Niesse and H.R. Mayne, *Journal of Chemical Physics* **105** 4700(1996).

[11] S.K Gregurick, M.H. Alexander and B. Hartke, *Journal of Chemical Physics* **104** 2684(1996).

[12] D.M Deaven, N. Tit, J.R Morris and K.M. Ho, *Chemical Physics Letters* **256** 195(1996).

[13] D. Romero, C. Barron, S. Gomez, *Computational Physics Communications* **123** 87(1999).

[14] B. Montag and P.G. Reinhard, *Physical Review* B **52** 16365(1995).

[15] C. Bréchignac, Ph. Cahuzac, F. Carlier, M. de Frutos, R. N. Barnett and U. Landman, *Physical Review Letters* **72** 1636(1994).

[16] R. N. Barnett, U. Landman and G. Rajagopal, *Physical Review Letters* **67** 3058(1991).

[17] J. M. Eisenberg and W. Greiner, *Nuclear Theory. vol 1. Collective and Particle Models.* North Holland, Amsterdam, 1985.

[18] P. Blaise, S. A. Blundell, C. Guet and R. R. Zope, *Physical Review Letters* **87** 063401(2001).

[19] Y. Li, E. Blaisten-Barojas and D. A. Papaconstantopoulos, *Physical Review* B **57** 15519(1998).

Brill Academic Publishers
P.O. Box 9000, 2300 PA Leiden,
The Netherlands

Lecture Series on Computer
and Computational Sciences
Volume 5, 2006, pp. 175-186

Structural and Electronic Properties of Gold Clusters

Denitsa Alamanova,[1] Yi Dong,[2] Habib ur Rehman,[3]
Michael Springborg,[4] and Valeri G. Grigoryan[5]

Physical and Theoretical Chemistry,
University of Saarland,
66123 Saarbrücken,
Germany

Abstract: We study the structure and energetics of Au_N clusters by means of parameter-free density-functional calculations ($N \leq 8$), jellium calculations ($N \leq 60$), embedded-atom calculations ($N \leq 150$), and parameterized density-functional calculations ($N \leq 40$) in combination with different methods for determining the structure of the lowest total energy. By comparing the results from the different approaches, effects due to geometric packing and those due to the electronic orbitals can be identified. Different descriptors that highlight the results of the analysis are presented and used.

Keywords: Gold clusters, structure, stability, density-functional calculations, embedded-atom calculations

PACS: 36.40.-c, 36.90.+f, 61.46.+w, 73.22.-f

1 Introduction

Clusters of gold atoms have become the maybe mostly studied class of clusters [1], partly due to the possibility to apply them in electronic devices [2], nanomaterials [3] and catalysis [4]. Despite this popularity only little consensus has been reached concerning the structure of these clusters. Many studies devoted to this issue use combinations of experimental and theoretical methods [5, 6, 7].

From a theoretical point of view, gold clusters offer an additional challenge due to the importance of relativistic effects, most notably the strong spin-orbit couplings. Thus, in parameter-free, electronic-structure calculations, one has to use special, relativistic potentials. With those, the smallest gold clusters are found to be planar [5, 8, 9, 10, 11, 12, 13], whereas their exclusion leads to three-dimensional structures [14, 15].

However, for not-too-small gold clusters, it becomes increasingly difficult to apply parameter-free, electronic-structure methods in the calculation of the properties of the gold clusters, partly because the computational demands scale with the size of the system to at least the third power, and partly because the number of metastable structures grows very rapidly with cluster size. Thus, in parameter-free studies one often has to make significant assumptions on the structure of the system, as for instance is the case in the study of Häberlen *et al.* [16]. One of the greatest disadvantages of the first-principles methods is their incapability of optimizing large number of randomly generated

---

[1] e-mail: deni@springborg.pc.uni-sb.de
[2] e-mail: y.dong@mx.uni-saarland.de
[3] e-mail: haur001@rz.uni-saarland.de
[4] Corresponding author. e-mail: m.springborg@mx.uni-saarland.de
[5] e-mail: vg.grigoryan@mx.uni-saarland.de

initial structures and thereby determining the true global total-energy minimum. One example of this is provided by Au_7 and Au_8 for which the structure was predicted in 2000 by Häkkinen and Landman [10] to be a planar structure with D_{2h} symmetry and a three-dimensional capped tetrahedron, respectively. Three years later, Häkkinen et al. [5] showed that the lowest-total-energy structure of Au_7^- corresponds to a planar structure consisting of a rhombus, capped with an additional atom on three of its sides, and that the ground state of Au_8^- is the same rhombus, with its 4 sides capped. In 2005, the results for Au_8 were confirmed by Walker [12] and Remacle et al. [13], whereas both works found a planar capped hexagon to be the global minimum of neutral Au_7.

Approximate methods may provide a useful alternative to the parameter-free methods. They are computationally less demanding, thus allowing for a detailed search in structure space so that structures for clusters with well above 100 atoms can be predicted in an unbiased way. On the other hand, being approximate it is not obvious how reliable they are. It is the purpose of this work to address this issue. To this end, gold clusters provide an excellent playground, partly because of the large uncertainty concerning their structure in combination with the large amount of studies on these clusters, but also partly because for clusters both geometric packing effects and electronic shell effects may be responsible for the occurrence of certain particularly stable clusters (the so-called magic numbers). The approximate methods often make different approximations on the relative importance of these two effects.

One class of approximate methods is formed by the embedded-atom methods (EAM) that only indirectly includes electronic effects and, therefore, first of all (but not exclusively) put emphasis on packing effects. Both the EAM [17, 18, 19], the Sutton-Chen [14], the Murrell-Mottram [15], and the many-body Gupta potential [20, 21, 22, 23, 24, 25] (that all share the property of including electronic effects only very approximately) have all been applied in unbiased structure optimizations for gold clusters with up to 80 atoms.

One of the, maybe, surprising outcomes of these studies is that the results depend very sensitively on the applied method, i.e., on the (more or less) approximate description of the interatomic interactions and on the method for structure optimization, see, e.g., [26, 27]. One reason may be a subtle interplay between electronic and geometric effects, i.e., that the particularly stable structures of Au_N clusters are dictated partly by the closing of electronic shells and partly by geometric packing effects. Here, the various potentials give different relative importance to the two effects.

The purpose of this contribution is to discuss general methods for calculating the properties of clusters, using gold clusters as the prototype. In parallel we shall also discuss the special properties of the gold clusters, specifically, with special emphasis on the issue above, i.e., whether electronic or packing effects are important in dictating the particularly stable clusters, and, moreover, how the different more or less accurate methods perform in calculating the properties of the clusters.

2 Methods

2.1 Total-energy methods

The smallest gold clusters with up to eight atoms were treated with parameter-free electronic-structure calculations using the GAUSSIAN03 program package [28]. We performed density-functional (DFT) calculations using the generalized-gradient approximation (GGA) of Perdew, Burke, and Ernzerhof [29, 30]. These calculations treat, in principle, all types of interactions, i.e., electronic and geometric effects, at an exact level.

In addition we also performed self-consistent, electronic-structure calculations on spherical clusters where only the 11 ($5d$ and $6s$) valence electrons per Au atom were treated explicitly, whereas all core electrons and the nuclei were smeared out to a uniform jellium background [31, 32]. This model focuses essentially only on electronic effects.

As an alternative we also considered the embedded-atom method (EAM) in the parameterization of Voter and Chen [33, 34, 35]. According to this method, the total energy for a system of N atoms is written as

$$E_{\text{tot}} = \sum_i E_i$$

$$E_i = F_i(\rho_i^h) + \frac{1}{2} \sum_{j(\neq i)} \phi_{ij}(r_{ij})$$

$$\rho_i^h = \sum_{j(\neq i)} \rho_i^a(r_{ij}), \tag{1}$$

i.e., as a sum of atomic components, each being the sum of two terms. The first term is the energy that it costs to bring the atom of interest into the electron density provided by all other atoms, and the second term is a pair-potential term. Both terms are assumed depending only on the distances between the neighbouring atoms, and do therefore not include any directional dependence. Accordingly, the EAM emphasizes geometrical effects, whereas electronic effects are included only very indirectly.

Furthermore, we used the density-functional tight-binding method (DFTB) as developed by Seifert and coworkers [36, 37]. With this method, the binding energy is written as the difference in the orbital energies of the compound minus those of the isolated atoms, i.e., as

$$\sum_i \epsilon_i - \sum_m \sum_i \epsilon_{mi} \tag{2}$$

(with m being an atom index and i an orbital index), augmented with pair potentials,

$$\sum_{m_1 \neq m_2} U_{m_1, m_2}(|\vec{R}_{m_1} - \vec{R}_{m_2}|) \tag{3}$$

(with $\vec{R}_m$ being the position of the mth atom). In calculating the orbital energies we need the Hamilton matrix elements $\langle \chi_{m_1 n_1} | \hat{H} | \chi_{m_2 n_2} \rangle$ and the overlap matrix elements $\langle \chi_{m_1 n_1} | \chi_{m_2 n_2} \rangle$. Here, χ_{mn} is the nth atomic orbital of the mth atom. The Hamilton operator contains the kinetic-energy operator as well as the potential. The latter is approximated as a superposition of the potentials of the isolated atoms,

$$V(\vec{r}) = \sum_m V_m(|\vec{r} - \vec{R}_m|), \tag{4}$$

and subsequently we assume that the matrix element $\langle \chi_{m_1 n_1} | V_m | \chi_{m_2 n_2} \rangle$ vanishes unless at least one of the atoms m_1 and m_2 equals m. Finally, the pair potentials U_{m_1, m_2} are obtained by requiring that the total-energy curves from parameter-free density-functional calculations on the diatomics are accurately reproduced.

2.2 Structure determinations

We used several different methods in determining the structures of the clusters. In the GAUSSIAN03 calculations the clusters were so small that it was possible to determine the structures of the lowest total energy simply through searching in the structure space. In the jellium calculations there is per construction no structure and the system has a spherical symmetry.

In the EAM calculations we optimized the structure using our own *Aufbau/Abbau* method [38, 39, 40]. The method is based on simulating experimental conditions, where clusters grow by adding atom by atom to a core. By repeating this process **very** many times and in parallel also removing atoms from larger clusters, we can identify the structures of the lowest total energy.

Finally, in the DFTB calculations we used two different approaches. In one approach the structures of the EAM calculations were used as input for a local relaxation, i.e., only the nearest local-total-energy minimum was identified. In another set of calculations, we optimized the structures using the so-called genetic algorithms [41, 42, 43]. Here, from a set of structures we generate new ones through cutting and pasting the original ones. Out of the total set of old and new clusters those with the lowest total energies are kept, and this process is repeated until the lowest total energy is unchanged for a large number of generations.

3 Results

The smallest possible cluster is the Au_2 molecule. For this we show in Table 1 the calculated bond length and binding energy from the different methods in comparison with experimental values. Notice that the DFTB method has been parameterized to reproduce results from parameter-free density-functional calculations on precisely the dimer and is, therefore, for the dimer accurate.

Table 1: A comparison between the experimental and the calculated bond length and binding energy of the Au dimer obtained with the parameter-free density-functional calculations and the EAM method.

Au_2	R_e, Å	E_b, eV
DFT	2.55	2.22
EAM	2.40	2.29
EXP	2.47	2.29

Next we show in Fig. 1 the structures of Au_N clusters with $4 \leq N \leq 8$ as obtained with the DFT calculations, the DFTB method, and the EAM method. The results for the trimer correspond to an obtuse triangle in the DFT calculations, and an equilateral triangle for the EAM and the DFTB methods. The figure clearly illustrates the aspects we have discussed above, i.e., the optimized structures of Au clusters result from a subtle interplay between geometric and electronic effects. Thus, in the DFT calculations all clusters are planar, whereas in the EAM calculations they are all three-dimensional (3D). Moreover, it turns out that also relativistic effects are important. Including all relativistic effects (i.e., also spin-orbit couplings) all gold clusters form planar structures at least up to $N = 13$ (see Ref. [5]). If the spin-orbit coupling is neglected, one obtains 3D global minima already at $N = 4$.

The jellium model excludes packing effects and treats exclusively electronic-shell effects. With r_s being the electron-gas parameter of the system of interest (i.e., the radius of a sphere containing one electron) it is well-known [44] that particularly stable clusters (magic numbers) occur for regularly spaced spherical clusters whose radius differ by

$$\Delta R = 0.603 r_s \tag{5}$$

for not too small clusters. For even smaller clusters one finds magic numbers for clusters containing 2, 8, 18, 20, 34, 58, 92, 132, 138, 186, 254, 338, ... electrons (see, e.g., [45]).

In Fig. 2 we show results from the jellium calculations on Au clusters, where it is assumed that each atom contributes with 11 electrons. Thus, the above-mentioned magic numbers are not reached for the gold clusters. Nevertheless, the total energy per atom shows a very regular behaviour that actually can be related to Eq. (5). By comparing the total energy with the orbital energies (also shown) we see that the local minima correspond to structures where the Fermi level makes a jump, i.e., where new electronic shells are being filled.

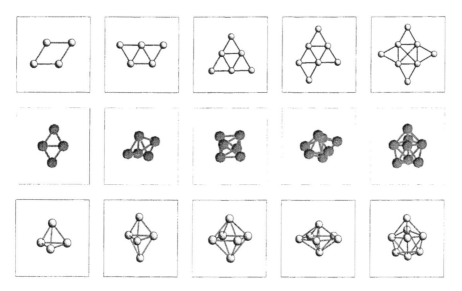

Figure 1: The optimized structures for Au$_N$, $4 \leq N \leq 8$ from (upper row) the DFT calculations, (middle row) the DFTB calculations, and (lower row) the EAM calculations.

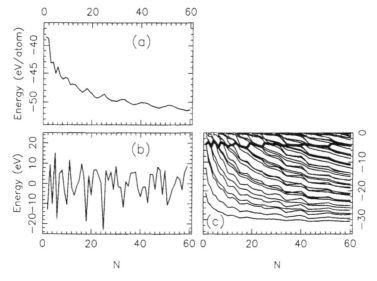

Figure 2: Results from the jellium calculations on Au$_N$ clusters with $1 \leq N \leq 60$. The three panels show (a) total energy per atom, (b) the stability function, and (c) the orbital energies (thin curves) and the Fermi energy (thick curve) as functions of N.

In order to identify the particularly stable clusters we introduce the stability function,

$$\Delta_2 E(N) = E_{\text{tot}}(N+1) + E_{\text{tot}}(N-1) - 2E_{\text{tot}}(N) \qquad (6)$$

where $E_{\text{tot}}(K)$ is the total energy of the Au_K system. $\Delta_2 E(N)$ has local maxima when Au_N is particularly stable, i.e., when $E_{\text{tot}}(N)$ is particularly low compared with $E_{\text{tot}}(N-1)$ and $E_{\text{tot}}(N+1)$. This function possesses a number of maxima, as seen in the figure, i.e., for $N = 3, 8, 11, 16, 21, 22, 26, 28, 30, 36, 37, 38, 47, 48, 50, 58$, and 59.

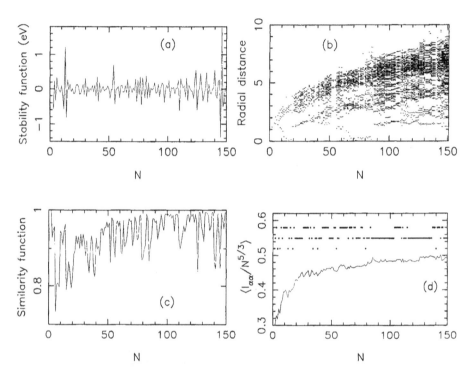

Figure 3: Properties of Au_N clusters from the EAM calculations. The four panels show (a) the stability function, (b) the radial distribution of atoms, (c) the similarity function, and (d) the shape-analysis parameters, respectively. Lengths and energies are given in Å and eV, respectively. In (d) the upper rows show whether the clusters have an overall spherical shape (lowest row), an overall cigar-like shape (middle row), or an overall lens-like shape (upper row).

We shall now compare this purely electronic description of the clusters with those obtained using the other approaches for Au_N. Fig. 3 shows various properties from the EAM calculations on Au_N clusters with N up to 150. Here, we used our *Aufbau/Abbau* method in optimizing the structure. The stability function, Fig. 3(a), has pronounced peaks at $N = 13, 54$, and 146, where the structure corresponds to an icosahedron for the first two and a decahedron for the last (actually, for $N = 55$ we do not find a icosahedron, whereas the structure of $N = 54$ is the 55-atomic icosahedron without the central atom).

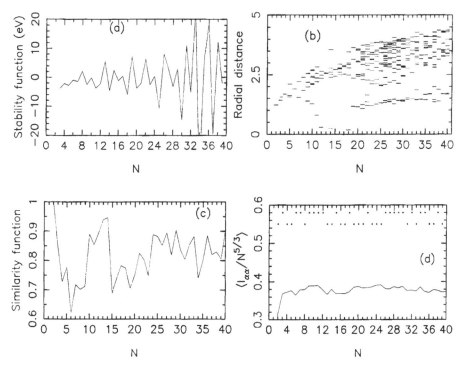

Figure 4: As Fig. 3, but from the DFTB calculations with the structures of the EAM calculations.

Further information on the structure is obtained from the radial distances of the atoms, defined as follows. First, we define the center of the Au$_N$ cluster,

$$\vec{R}_0 = \frac{1}{N} \sum_{i=1}^{N} \vec{R}_i \qquad (7)$$

and, subsequently, we define for each atom its radial distance

$$r_i = |\vec{R}_i - \vec{R}_0|. \qquad (8)$$

In Fig. 3(b) we show the radial distances for all atoms and all cluster sizes. Each small line shows that at least one atom for the given value of N has exactly that radial distance. The figure shows that somewhere around $N = 10$ a second shell of atoms is being built up, with a central atom for $N = 13$. Around $N = 54$, there are only few values of the radial distance, i.e., the clusters have a high symmetry. Around $N = 75$ we see that a third atomic shell is being formed.

We have earlier found [40] that it was useful to monitor the structural development of the isomer with the lowest total energy through the so-called similarity functions. We shall study how clusters grow and, in particular, if the cluster with N atoms can be derived from the one with

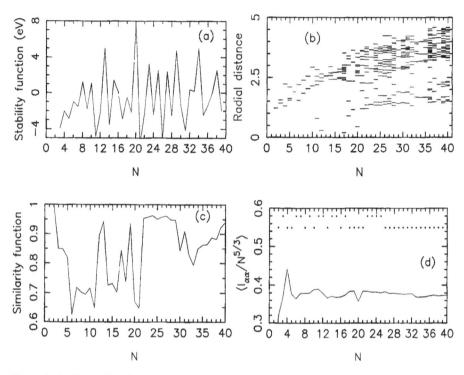

Figure 5: As Fig. 3, but from the DFTB calculations with the genetic-algorithm optimization of the structures.

$N - 1$ atoms simply by adding one extra atom. In order to quantify this relation we consider first the structure with the lowest total energy for the $(N - 1)$-atom cluster. For this we calculate and sort all interatomic distances, d_i, $i = 1, 2, \cdots, \frac{N(N-1)}{2}$. Subsequently we consider each of the N fragments of the N-cluster that can be obtained by removing one of the atoms and keeping the rest at their positions. For each of those we also calculate and sort all interatomic distances d'_i, and calculate, subsequently,

$$q = \left[\frac{2}{N(N-1)} \sum_{i=1}^{N(N-1)/2} (d_i - d'_i)^2 \right]^{1/2}. \tag{9}$$

Among the N different values of q we choose the smallest one, q_{min}, and calculate the similarity function

$$S = \frac{1}{1 + q_{min}/u_l} \tag{10}$$

($u_l = 1$ Å) which approaches 1 if the Au$_N$ cluster is very similar to the Au$_{N-1}$ cluster plus an extra atom. This function is shown in Fig. 3(c). We see that the structural development is very irregular over the whole range of N that we have considered here, with, however, some smaller intervals where S is relatively large, for instance for N slightly above 20.

Finally, we shall consider the overall shape of the clusters. As we showed in our earlier report on Ni clusters [40], it is convenient to study the 3×3 matrix containing the elements

$$I_{st} = \frac{1}{u_t^2} \sum_{n=1}^{N} (R_{n,s} - R_{0,s})(R_{n,t} - R_{0,t}) \tag{11}$$

with s and t being x, y, and z. The three eigenvalues of this matrix, $I_{\alpha\alpha}$, can be used in separating the clusters into being overall spherical (all eigenvalues are identical), more cigar-like shaped (one eigenvalue is large, the other two are small), or more lens-shaped (two large and one small eigenvalue). The average of the three eigenvalues, $\langle I_{\alpha\alpha} \rangle$, is a measure of the overall extension of the cluster. For a homogeneous sphere with N atoms, the eigenvalues scale like $N^{5/3}$. Hence, we show in Fig. 3(d) quantities related to $I_{\alpha\alpha}$ but scaled by $N^{-5/3}$. In this figure we also mark the overall shape of the clusters through the upper points with the lowest row meaning spherical, the middle row meaning cigar-shaped, and the upper row meaning lens-shaped clusters. Some clusters with an overall spherical shape can be recognized, that, simultaneously, are clusters of particularly high stability according to Fig. 3(a).

By comparing with the results of the jellium calculations, we see that the EAM method predicts a completely different set of particularly stable clusters. Moreover, compared with the results of the parameter-free density-functional calculations, the EAM method tends to produce more compact clusters.

We shall now turn to the results obtained with the DFTB method. In Fig. 4 we show results similar to those of Fig. 3, but obtained by letting the clusters of the EAM calculations relax locally using the DFTB method, whereas we in Fig. 5 show the results for the DFTB calculations where the structure was optimized with the genetic algorithms.

The structural information from all three sets of calculations is very similar. The radial distances show in all cases that a second atomic shell is being constructed starting from slightly above 10 atoms. First above $N = 40$ a third atomic shell is formed [see Fig. 3(c)]. Moreover, the similarity function shows that clusters in a narrow window just above $N = 10$ as well as in a wider window above $N = 20$ resemble each other, independently of the theoretical approach. There are, however, some differences in the overall shape, as seen in the shape-analysis parameters. In the EAM calculations several roughly spherical clusters with $N \leq 40$ are found, whereas the symmetry is broken when including electronic effects with the DFTB method, so that in these calculations no cluster is found to have an overall spherical structure. Moreover, the structures of the DFTB calculations are overall slightly more compact than those of the EAM calculations.

On the other hand, the stability function of Fig. 4(a) shows a much more irregular behaviour than the one of Fig. 3(a), although the structures are very similar. This emphasizes that electronic effects indeed are important. By comparing with Fig. 5(a) we see that through further relaxations the stability function becomes less irregular, although its variation (over a range of roughly 12 eV) is significantly larger than the range of the stability function in Fig. 3(a) (roughly 2 eV). It is interesting to observe that in the jellium calculations (where there is per construction no structural relaxation) the stability function spans a range of roughly 35 eV, which is comparable to the range we see in Fig. 4(a). This means that electronic effects are very important for the stability of the clusters, but also that through structural relaxations the role of the electronic effects can be somewhat reduced.

Finally, we see in Fig. 1 that the DFTB calculations lead to essentially the same (type of) structures as the EAM calculations, with $N = 4$ being the only significant exception. Here, the DFTB calculations predict a planar structure (as is the case for the relativistic DFT calculations), whereas for larger values of N, non-planar structures result in all our calculations except for the relativistic DFT calculations.

4 Conclusions

In this work we have discussed the interplay of electronic and packing effects in clusters. We have used Au_N clusters as a prototype in order to illustrate the effects of different types of approximations on the description of the interatomic interactions. We have, moreover, demonstrated how carefully chosen descriptors can be constructed that clearly grasp the essential outcomes of the calculations. Moreover, we hope also to have demonstrated the complexities related to unbiased, accurate calculations of the properties of not-too-small clusters.

Our results indicate the existence of a tendency for simple potentials that do not directly include effects due to electronic orbitals (i.e., due to directed chemical bonds) to prefer closed packed structures. Including the electronic orbitals the structures may become less symmetric, and when increasing the accuracy of the treatment of the electronic orbitals and, simultaneously, the structure, the geometric arrangement of the atoms becomes less and less closed packed. Moreover, the electronic effects lead to a much stronger variation in stability as a function of size.

We have in this presentation focused on Au_N clusters. These clusters are among the most studied ones and are simultaneously very difficult to treat theoretically (as discussed in the introduction), which was the motivation for the present work. Nevertheless, we believe that most of our conclusions are valid also for other types of metal clusters, thus emphasizing the importance to perform different types of calculations with different types of (approximate) descriptions of the interatomic interactions before making finite conclusions about the properties of the clusters of a specific element.

Acknowledgment

We gratefully acknowledge *Fonds der Chemischen Industrie* for very generous support. This work was supported by the SFB 277 of the University of Saarland and by the German Research Council (DFG) through project Sp439/14-1.

References

[1] P. Pyykkö, Angew. Chem. Int. Ed. **43**, 4412 (2004).

[2] M. Dorogi, J. Gomez, R. Osifichin, R. P. Andres, and R. Reifenberger, Phys. Rev. B **52**, 9071 (1995).

[3] R. L. Whetten, M. N. Shafigullin, J. T. Khoury, T. G. Schaaff, I. Vezmar, M. M. Alvarez, and A. Wilkinson, Acc. Chem. Res. **32**, 397 (1999).

[4] A. Sanchez, S. Abbet, W. D. Schneider, H. Häkkinen, R. N. Barnett, and U. Landman, J. Phys. Chem. A **103**, 9573 (1999).

[5] H. Häkkinen, B. Yoon, U. Landman, X. Li, H.-J. Zhai, and L.-S. Wang, J. Phys. Chem. A **107**, 6168 (2003).

[6] S. Gilb, P. Weis, F. Furche, R. Ahlrichs, and M. M. Kappes, J. Chem. Phys **116**, 4094 (2002).

[7] M. Neumaier, F. Weigend, and O. Hampe, J. Chem. Phys. **122**, 104702 (2005).

[8] G. Bravo-Pérez, I. L. Garzón, and O. Novaro, J. Mol. Str. (Theochem) **493**, 225 (1999).

[9] H. Grönbeck and W. Andreoni, Chem. Phys. **262**, 1 (2000).

[10] H. Häkkinen and U. Landman, Phys. Rev. B **62**, 2287 (2000).

[11] J. Wang, G. Wang, and J. Zhao, Phys. Rev. B **66**, 035418 (2002).

[12] A. V. Walker, J. Chem. Phys. **122**, 094310 (2005).

[13] F. Remacle and E. S. Kryachko. J. Chem. Phys. **122**, 044304 (2005).

[14] J. P. K. Doye and D. J. Wales, New J. Chem. 733 (1998).

[15] N. T. Wilson and R. L. Johnston, Eur. Phys. J. D **12**, 161 (2000).

[16] O. D. Häberlen, S. C. Chung. M. Stener, and N. Rösch, J. Chem. Phys. **106**, 5189 (1997).

[17] C. L. Cleveland, U. Landman, T. G. Schaaff, M. N. Shafigullin, P. W. Stephens, and R. L. Whetten, Phys. Rev. Lett. **79**, 1873 (1997).

[18] R. N. Barnett, C. L. Cleveland, H. Häkkinen, W. D. Luedtke, C. Yannouleas, and U. Landman, Eur. Phys. J. D **9**, 95 (1999).

[19] C. L. Cleveland, U. Landman, M. N. Shafigullin, P. W. Stephens, and R. L. Whetten, Z. Phys. D **40**, 503 (1997).

[20] I. L. Garzón and A. Posada-Amarillas, Phys. Rev. B **54**, 11796 (1996).

[21] I. L. Garzón, K. Michaelian, M. R. Beltrán, A. Posada-Amarillas, P. Ordejón, E. Artacho, D. Sánchez-Portal, and J. M. Soler, Phys. Rev. Lett. **81**, 1600 (1998).

[22] I. L. Garzón, K. Michaelian, M. R. Beltrán, A. Posada-Amarillas, P. Ordejón, E. Artacho, D. Sánchez-Portal, and J. M. Soler, Eur. Phys. J. D **9**, 211 (1999).

[23] K. Michaelian, N. Rendón, and I. L. Garzón, Phys. Rev. B **60**, 2000 (1999).

[24] T. X. Li. S. Y. Yin, Y. L. Ji, B. L. Wang, G. H. Wang, and J. J. Zhao, Phys. Lett. A **267**, 403 (2000).

[25] S. Darby, T. V. Mortimer-Jones, R. L. Johnston, and C. Roberts, J. Chem. Phys. **116**, 1536 (2002).

[26] F. Baletto and R. Ferrando, Rev. Mod. Phys. **77**, 371 (2005).

[27] V. G. Grigoryan, D. Alamanova, and M. Springborg, Eur. Phys. J. D (in press).

[28] M. J. Frisch, G. W. Trucks, H. B. Schlegel, G. E. Scuseria, M. A. Robb, J. R. Cheeseman, J. A. Montgomery Jr., T. Vreven, K. N. Kudin, J. C. Burant, J. M. Millam, S. S. Iyengar, j. Tomasi, V. Barone, B. Mennucci, M. Cossi, G. Scalmani, N. Rega, G. A. Petersson, H. Nakatsuji. M. Hada, M. Ehara, K. Toyota, R. Fukuda, J. Hasegawa. M. Ishida, T. Nakajima, Y. Honda, O. Kitao, H. Nakai, M. Klene, X. Li, J. E. Knox, H. P. Hratchian, J. B. Cross, C. Adamo, J. Jaramillo, R. Gomberts, R. E. Strattmann, O. Yazyev, A. J. Austin, R. Cammi, C. Pomelli, J. W. Ochterski, P. Y. Ayala, K. Morokuma, G. A. Voth, P. Salvador, J. J. Dannenberg, V. G. Zakrzewski, S. Dapprich, A. D. Daniels, M. C. Strain, O. Farkas, D. K. Malick. A. D.

Rabuck, K. Raghavachari, J. B. Foresman, J. V. Ortiz, Q. Cui, A. G. Baboul, S. Clifford, J. Cioslowski, B. B. Stefanov, G. Liu, A. Liashenko, P. Piskorz, I. Komaromi, R. L. Martin, D. J. Fox, T. Keith, M. A. Al-Laham, C. Y. Peng, A. Nanayakkara, M. Challacombe, P. M. W. Gill, B. Johnson, W. Chen, M. W. Wong, C. Gonzalez, and J. A. Pople, GAUSSIAN03, *revision C.02*, Gaussian Inc., Wallingford, CT, 2004.

[29] J. P. Perdew, K. Burke, and M. Ernzerhof, Phys. Rev. Lett. 77, 3865 (1996).

[30] J. P. Perdew, K. Burke, and M. Ernzerhof, Phys. Rev. Lett. 78, 1396 (1997).

[31] W. A. de Heer, Rev. Mod. Phys. **65**, 611 (1993).

[32] M. Brack, Rev. Mod. Phys. **65**, 677 (1993).

[33] A. F. Voter and S. P. Chen, in *Characterization of Defects in Materials*, edited by R. W. Siegal, J. R. Weertman, and R. Sinclair, MRS Symposia Proceedings No. 82 (Materials Research Society, Pittsburgh, 1987), p. 175.

[34] A. Voter, Los Alamos Unclassified Technical Report No LA-UR 93-3901 (1993).

[35] A. F. Voter, in *Intermetallic Compounds*, edited by J. H. Westbrook and R. L. Fleischer (John Wiley and Sons, Ltd, 1995), Vol. 1, p. 77.

[36] G. Seifert and R. Schmidt, New J. Chem. **16**, 1145 (1992).

[37] G. Seifert, D. Porezag, and Th. Frauenheim, Int. J. Quant. Chem **58**, 185 (1996).

[38] V. G. Grigoryan and M. Springborg, Phys. Chem. Chem. Phys. **3**, 5125 (2001).

[39] V. G. Grigoryan and M. Springborg, Chem. Phys. Lett. **375**, 219 (2003).

[40] V. G. Grigoryan and M. Springborg, Phys. Rev. B **70**, 205415 (2004).

[41] J.-O. Joswig, M. Springborg, and G. Seifert, Phys. Chem. Chem. Phys. **3**, 5130 (2001).

[42] J.-O. Joswig and M. Springborg, Phys. Rev. B **68**, 085408 (2003).

[43] Y. Dong and M. Springborg, in *Proceedings of 3rd International Conference "Computational Modeling and Simulation of Materials"*, Ed. P. Vincenzini *et al.*, Techna Group Publishers, p. 167 (2004).

[44] R. Balian and C. Bloch, Ann. Phys. New York **69**, 76 (1972).

[45] M. Springborg, J. Phys. Cond. Matt. **11**, 1 (1999).

Brill Academic Publishers
P.O. Box 9000, 2300 PA Leiden
The Netherlands

*Lecture Series on Computer
and Computational Sciences*
Volume 5, 2006, pp. 187-192

Cluster Origin of the Solubility of Single-Wall Carbon Nanotubes

F. Torrens[1a] and Gloria Castellano[b]

[a]Institut Universitari de Ciència Molecular,
Universitat de València,
Edifici d'Instituts de Paterna, PO Box 22085, E-46071 València, Spain
[b]Departamento de Ciencias Experimentales,
Facultad de Ciencias Experimentales,
Universidad Católica de Valencia *San Vicente Mártir*,
Guillem de Castro-106, E-46003 València, Spain

Abstract: The possibility of the existence of single-wall carbon nanotubes (SWNT) in organic solvents, in the form of clusters containing a number of SWNTs, is discussed. A theory is developed based on a *bundlet* model for clusters, which enables describing the distribution function of clusters by size. Comparison of the calculated values of solubility with experimental data would permit obtaining energetic parameters characterizing the interaction of an SWNT with its surrounding in a solid phase or solution. Fullerenes and SWNTs are unique objects, whose behaviour in many physical situations is characterized by remarkable peculiarities. Peculiarities in solutions show up in that fullerenes and SWNTs represent the only soluble forms of carbon, what is primary related to the originality in the molecular structure of fullerenes and SWNTs. The fullerene molecule is a virtually uniform closed spherical or spheroidal surface, having no sharp ridges or dents. Similarly, an SWNT is a smooth cylindrical unit. Both structures give rise to the relatively weak interaction between the neighbouring molecules in a crystal, and promote effective interaction of the molecules with those of a solvent. Another peculiarity in solutions is related to their tendency to form clusters, consisting of a number of fullerene molecules or SWNTs. The energy of interaction of a fullerene molecule or SWNT with solvent molecules is proportional to the surface of the former molecule, and roughly independent of the relative orientation of solvent molecules. A unified treatment is proposed in the framework of the bundlet model of a cluster, in accordance with which the free energy of an SWNT involved in a cluster consists of two components: a volume one proportional to the number of molecules n in a cluster and a surface one proportional to $n^{1/2}$.

Keywords: Solubity of carbon nanotubes, *Bundlet* model for clusters, Droplet model for clusters, Nanotube, Fullerene, Nanohorn

PACS: 36.40.Ei; 36.40.Ei; 61.46.+w; 81.07.De

In earlier publications, periodic tables of single-wall carbon nanotubes (SWNT) were discussed [1,2]. A program based on the AQUAFAC model was applied to calculate the solubility of SWNTs [3]. A comparative study of SWNT solvents and co-solvents provided a classification of solvents [4-8]. The aim of the present report is to present the *bundlet* model for clusters of SWNTs, performing a comparative study of the solubilities of fullerenes (droplet model) and SWNTs (bundlet model).

1. Computational Method

A new mechanism of solubility, which may explain the solubility of SWNTs of different sorts, is based on the possibility of formation in solution of clusters consisting of a number of SWNTs. The aggregation phenomenon changes the thermodynamic parameters of SWNTs in solutions, which displays, naturally, the phase equilibrium and changes the magnitude of solubility. The thermodynamic approach to the description of the phenomenon of solubility of SWNTs, taking account cluster formation, is based on the *bundlet* model of clusters, which is valid under conditions when the characteristic number of SWNTs in the cluster is $n \gg 1$. The problem of determining the temperature dependence of solubility of SWNTs is formulated in terms of the possibility of forming clusters consisting of several parallel SWNTs. In accordance with the general principles of thermodynamics, in a saturated solution of SWNTs, the magnitudes of the chemical potential per SWNT for dissolved

---

[1] Corresponding author. E-mail: francisco.torrens@uv.es

substance and for a crystal, which is in equilibrium with solution, are equal. This equality is valid not only for isolated SWNTs in a solution, but also for clusters consisting of several SWNTs. According to the bundlet model of clusters, the free energy of a cluster in a solution is made up of two parts: the volume part proportional to the number of SWNTs n in the cluster, and the surface part proportional to $n^{1/2}$ [9–11]. The problem of growing a bundle of parallel cylinders in the space can be reduced to that of growing a packet of circles on a plane. The model corresponds to the assumption that clusters consisting of $n \gg 1$ particles have a cylindrical bundlet shape, and permits the Gibbs energy G_n for a cluster of size n to be represented by the sum

$$G_n = G_1 n - G_2 n^{1/2} \tag{1}$$

where the parameters G_1 and G_2 are responsible for the contribution to the Gibbs energy of the molecules placed inside the volume and on the surface of a cluster, correspondingly. The chemical potential μ_n of a cluster of size n in a solution is expressed via the equation

$$\mu_n = G_n + T \ln C_n \tag{2}$$

where T is the temperature. Having regard to relation (1), this results in

$$\mu_n = G_1 n - G_2 n^{1/2} + T \ln C_n \tag{3}$$

where the parameters G_1 and G_2 are expressed in temperature units. In a saturated solution of SWNTs, the cluster-size distribution function is determined via the equilibrium condition linking the clusters of a specified size with a solid phase, which corresponds to the equality between the magnitudes of the chemical potential (per molecule), for molecules incorporated into clusters of any size and into crystal. This results in relation (4) for the cluster-size distribution function in a saturated solution:

$$f(n) = g_n \exp\left[\left(-An + Bn^{1/2}\right)/T\right] \tag{4}$$

where the parameter A is the equilibrium difference between the energies of interaction of an SWNT with its surroundings in the solid phase and in the cluster volume; B is the similar difference for SWNTs located on the cluster surface; g_n is the statistical weight of a cluster of size n, which can depend, generally speaking, on both temperature and cluster size n. However, we will further neglect these dependences in comparison with the much stronger exponential dependence in relation (4). Form (4) for the cluster-size distribution function is based on the structural features of SWNTs. In essence, an SWNT is a homogeneous surface structure that, unlike planar or elongated molecules, interacts with its surroundings almost irrespectively of the orientation about its axis. The large number of similar elements of the SWNT surface makes possible to represent the interaction energy of this molecule with the solvent molecules, having essentially smaller size, as the product of a specific surface interaction energy by surface area of the molecule. The feature of the SWNT structure may be further used in the description of the interaction between clusters, made up of SWNTs, and the solvent. This is purely surface interaction and, because the interaction energy of SWNTs with each other, both in a cluster and in a solid, is low in comparison with the binding energy of C atoms in an SWNT, one can assume that the specific surface energy of interaction of SWNTs with one another and with solvent molecules is not sensitive to the relative orientation of parallel SWNTs in a cluster. Broadly speaking, the parameters A and B may have any sign. However, the normalization condition for the distribution function (4), having the obvious form

$$\sum_{n=1}^{\infty} f(n)n = C \tag{5}$$

causes the requirement $A > 0$. Here C is the solubility expressed in relative units. In view of the condition $n \gg 1$, the normalization relation (5) may be replaced by the integral

$$C = \overline{g}_n \int_{n=1}^{\infty} n \exp\left[\left(-An + Bn^{1/2}\right)/T\right] dn = C_0 \int_{n=1}^{\infty} n \exp\left[\left(-An + Bn^{1/2}\right)/T\right] dn \tag{6}$$

Here $\bar{g}_n$ is the statistical weight of a cluster, averaged over the range of values of n that makes the major contribution to integral (6). This parameter includes the entropy factor, governs the absolute value of solubility and may depend on the type of solvent. C_0 is the SWNT molar fraction. In first approximation, parameters A, B and C_0 have been taken equal to those fitted for fullerene C_{60} in hexane, toluene and CS_2: $A = 320K$, $B = 970K$, $C_0 = 5 \cdot 10^{-8}$ for $T > 260K$. In order to improve the model, a correction has been introduced to take into account the effect of the different packings in C_{60} and SWNTs

$$A' = \left(\eta_{cyl}/\eta_{sph}\right)A \quad \text{and} \quad B' = \left(\eta_{cyl}/\eta_{sph}\right)B \quad (7)$$

where $\eta_{cyl} = \pi/2(3)^{1/2}$ is the density of close packing of cylinders (which is equal to that of circles on a plane), and $\eta_{sph} = \pi/3(2)^{1/2}$ is that of spheres.

2. Calculation Results and Discussion

The equilibrium difference between the Gibbs energies of interaction of an SWNT with its surroundings, in the solid phase and in the cluster volume or on the cluster surface (Figure 1), shows that, on going from C_{60} (droplet model) to SWNT (*bundlet* model) the minimum is less marked (55% of droplet), which causes a lesser number of units in SWNT ($n_{minimum} \approx 2$) than in C_{60} clusters (≈ 8). Moreover, the abscissa is also shorter in SWNT (≈ 9) than in C_{60} clusters (≈ 28). In turn, when the packing correction (relation 7) is included the C_{60}–SWNT shortening decreases (68% of droplet), while keeping $n_{minimum} \approx 2$ and $n_{abscissa} \approx 9$. The temperature dependence of the solubility of SWNT (Figure 2) shows that solubility decreases with temperature, because solubility is due to cluster formation. The reduction is less marked for SWNT, in agreement with the lesser number of units in SWNT clusters (Figure 1). In particular at $T = 260K$ on going from C_{60} (droplet model) to SWNT (bundlet model), the solubility drops to 1.6% of droplet (Figure 2). In turn, when the packing correction is included (relation 7) the shortening decreases (2.6% of droplet).

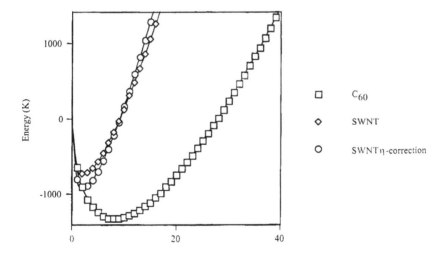

Number of molecules in cluster

Figure 1: Energy of interaction of an SWNT with its surroundings in the cluster volume or surface.

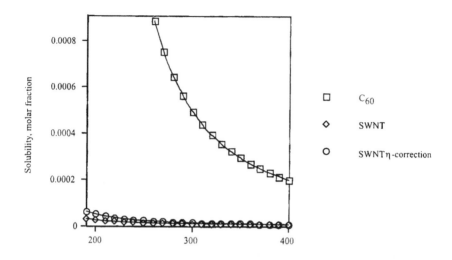

Temperature (K)

Figure 2: Temperature dependence of solubility of C_{60} (droplet) and SWNT (*bundlet–η-correction*).

The cluster distribution function by size in a solution of SWNT in CS_2, calculated for saturation concentration at solvent temperature $T = 298.15K$ (Figure 3), shows that on going from C_{60} (droplet model) to SWNT (bundlet model), the maximum cluster size decreases from $n = 8$ to 2 and the

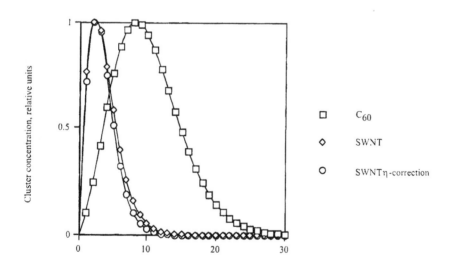

Number of molecules in cluster

Figure 3: Cluster distribution by size saturated in CS_2 at $T = 298.15K$ of C_{60} (droplet) and SWNT.

distribution is rather narrowed, in agreement with the lesser number of units in SWNT clusters (Figures 1–2). On the other hand when the packing-density correction (relation 7) is included, the distribution is somewhat narrowed while keeping $n_{\text{maximum}} = 2$ (Figure 3).

The following conclusions can be made from this study.

1. For a cluster nature of the SWNT solubility to be completely established, direct experimental exploration is necessary. As a possible scheme for such experiments, the measurements of infrared absorption spectra of an SWNT solution, involving concentrations at various temperatures and a constant optical path length, can be conceived. The existence of such a dependency will indicate the presence of SWNT clusters in solution. Another way is based on applying Raoult's law, according to which the saturation vapour pressure of a solvent above a solution differs from that above a pure solvent, by a value being proportional to the concentration of solute particles. The measurement of the flow of the solvent vapour, being determined by the difference of the pressures, will enable obtaining the dependence of the solute particle concentration on the concentration of the solute. Provided this dependence is nonlinear, it will form a basis to draw a quantitative conclusion concerning the existence of SWNT clusters in solution.

2. Along with solubility, cluster formation also must affect the transport properties of SWNTs in solution, particularly diffusion. It can be shown that a characteristic size of clusters decreases as the SWNT concentration drops below the saturation value. Since the mobility of a cluster increases with its decreasing size, it leads to the dependence of an effective diffusion coefficient on concentration. This can serve as a basis for the method of diffusion separation of higher SWNTs, being usually of a tiny concentration in solution.

3. Fullerenes–SWNTs are unique objects of chemical physics whose behaviour, in many physical situations, is characterized by remarkable peculiarities. Fullerenes–SWNTs represent the only soluble forms of carbon, what is primary related to the originality in the molecular structure of fullerenes–SWNTs. The fullerene molecule (SWNT) is a virtually uniform closed spherical or spheroidal (cylindrical) surface, having no sharp ridges or dents. Both structures give rise to the relatively weak interaction between the neighbouring molecules in a crystal, and promote effective interaction of the molecules with those of a solvent.

4. Another interesting peculiarity of the behaviour of fullerenes–SWNTs in solutions is related to their tendency to form clusters consisting of a number of fullerene molecules–SWNTs. The energy of interaction of a fullerene molecule–SWNT with solvent molecules is proportional to the surface of the former molecule, and roughly independent of the relative orientation of solvent molecules.

5. The performed analysis of experiments concerning the behaviour of fullerenes–SWNTs in solutions shows that, over a wide range of conditions, fullerenes in solutions exist in the form of aggregates containing from ten up to tens of thousands of particles. However, the size of clusters of SWNTs is smaller. This peculiarity makes fullerenes–SWNTs in solutions interesting objects from the viewpoint of the investigation of the properties of *cluster* substances.

6. Aggregation of fullerenes–SWNTs is reflected in various physical and chemical properties of fullerene–SWNT solutions. Thus, this phenomenon causes the extraordinary (decreasing) temperature dependence of solubility.

7. All these phenomena have a unified explanation in the framework of the droplet–*bundlet* models of clusters, in accordance with which the free energy of a fullerene molecule (SWNT) involved in a cluster consists of two components: a volume one, which is proportional to the number of molecules n in a cluster, and a surface one, which is proportional to $n^{2/3}$ ($n^{1/2}$).

8. Experimental SWNT properties depend on the sample, since some samples: (a) contain fullerenes, (b) consist of different diameters (metallic–semimetallic or semiconductor SWNTs), (c) show polydispersity between short and large SWNTs; (d) solubility of SWNTs differ for different diameters; (e) SWNTs thinner than (5,5) are scarce. The trend of SWNTs to form clusters in solutions must be taken into consideration when further developing the technology of enrichment, separation and purification of SWNTs.

9. It has not escaped our notice a droplet model for clusters of conical single-wall carbon nanohorns, following modified relations (1')–(7')

$$G_n = G_1 n - G_2 n^{2/3} \tag{1'}$$

$$\mu_n = G_1 n - G_2 n^{2/3} + T \ln C_n \tag{3'}$$

$$f(n) = g_n \exp\left[\left(-An + Bn^{2/3}\right)/T\right] \tag{4'}$$

$$C = \bar{g}_n \int_{n=1}^{\infty} n \exp\left[\left(-An + Bn^{2/3}\right)/T\right] dn = C_0 \int_{n=1}^{\infty} n \exp\left[\left(-An + Bn^{2/3}\right)/T\right] dn \tag{6'}$$

$$A' = \left(\eta_{con}/\eta_{sph}\right)A \quad \text{and} \quad B' = \left(\eta_{con}/\eta_{sph}\right)B \tag{7'}$$

where η_{con} is the density of close packing for cones ($\eta_{sph} < \eta_{con} < \eta_{cyl}$), e.g., for cones with a solid angle of one stereoradian, $\eta_{con} = (1-1/\pi)^{1/2}$.

Acknowledgments

The authors thank support from the Spanish MEC DGI (Project No. CTQ2004-07768-C02-01/BQU) and Generalitat Valenciana (DGEUI INF01-051 and INFRA03-047, and OCYT GRUPOS03-173).

References

[1] F. Torrens, Periodic table of carbon nanotubes based on the chiral vector, _Internet Electron. J. Mol. Des._ 3 514-527(2004).

[2] F. Torrens, Periodic properties of carbon nanotubes based on the chiral vector, _Internet Electron. J. Mol. Des._ 4 59-81(2005).

[3] F. Torrens, Calculations on organic-solvent dispersions of single-wall carbon nanotubes, _Int. J. Quantum Chem._, in press.

[4] F. Torrens, Calculations on cyclopyranoses as co-solvents of single-wall carbon nanotubes, _Mol. Simul._ 31 107-114(2005).

[5] F. Torrens, Calculations on solvents and co-solvents of single-wall carbon nanotubes: Cyclopyranoses, _J. Mol. Struct. (Theochem)_ 757 183-191 (2005).

[6] F. Torrens, Calculations on solvents and co-solvents of single-wall carbon nanotubes: Cyclopyranoses, _Nanotechnology_ 16 S181-S189(2005).

[7] F. Torrens, Calculations on solvents and co-solvents on single-wall carbon nanotubes: Cyclopyranoses, _Probl. Nonlin. Anal. Eng. Syst._ 11(2) 1-16(2005).

[8] F. Torrens, Calculations on fullerenes, single-wall carbon nanotubes, solvents and co-solvents, _Molecules_, submitted for publication.

[9] V.N. Bezmel'nitsyn, A.V. Eletskii and E.V. Stepanov, Cluster origin of fullerene solubility, _J. Phys. Chem._ 98 6665-6667(1994).

[10] V.N. Bezmel'nitsyn, A.V. Eletskii and E.V. Stepanov, _Zh. Fiz. Khim._ 69 735-735(1995).

[11] V.N. Bezmel'nitsyn, A.V. Eletskii and M.V. Okun', Fullerenes in solutions, _Physics–Uspekhi_ 41 1091-1114(1998).

Brill Academic Publishers
P.O. Box 9000. 2300 PA Leiden
The Netherlands

*Lecture Series on Computer
and Computational Sciences*
Volume 5, 2006. pp. 193-198

The story of the Si_6 magic cluster

Aristides D. Zdetsis

Department of Physics,
University of Patras,
GR-26500 Patras, Greece

Abstract: The Si_6 cluster is considered as one of the best studied and well established theoretically and experimentally. Due to dynamic on top of static Jahn-Teller distortions its structure is not rigid and its energy hyper-surface is extremely flat. As a result high level correlation, beyond single-reference perturbation theory is necessary for the description of the electronic and geometric characteristics of this cluster. Failure to recognize this can lead to misunderstandings and discrepancies. The present work examines the geometric and electronic structure of Si_6 using various theoretical techniques. This work can serve as a simple example of a case where a seemingly good agreement between theoretical and experimental results can be fortuitous or misleading.

Keywords: Atomic clusters, silicon clusters, structural properties, Jahn-Teller effect

PACS: 36.40-c, 61.46+w, 73.22.-f

1. Introduction

The field of atomic clusters, which constitutes a link between molecules and crystals, is of interdisciplinary nature involving Physics, Chemistry and Materials science. This field is very important and active over the last 30 years due to its fundamental scientific and technological importance as a consequence of novel properties found neither in molecules nor in infinite solids. In addition, atomic clusters serve as model systems in atomistic calculations in solid state theory and in particular in nanocrystals. Nanocrystals, which preserve most of the symmetry properties of the corresponding infinite crystals, can be readily produced by different technological techniques now days. Among the various types of atomic clusters (and nanocrystals) the semiconductor clusters have a special technological importance especially for micro and nano-electronics. As a result, the literature for small silicon clusters is extremely rich and the number of publications ranges to several hundredths or even thousandths [1-7]. Nevertheless here too, controversial results and interpretations do exist despite the widespread believe that most of the major problems are well understood and resolved, especially for the small clusters [1, 7]. Surprisingly enough even Si_6, which is considered as one of the best understood and extensively studied small clusters, is full of puzzles and paradoxes about its molecular, electronic and optical structure [1, 7]. Thus, even today several questions and puzzles still remain open, especially for bonding and structural properties, for which comparison between experimental and theoretical results is only indirect. This is especially true for large and moderate size clusters. For small clusters, such as Si_6, any ambiguities or discrepancies are unexpected and very surprising. And yet, as will be illustrated bellow, despite a seemingly good agreement of theoretical and experimental results, Si_6 is not a "platonic" molecular system of well defined (high) symmetry. Therefore each one of the three structures of figure 1, visualized by the usual ball-and-stick diagrams, is not correct (if considered independent of each other). The claimed real structure of Si_6 could be one of them, none of them or all of them!

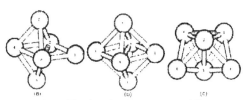

Fig. 1: The three lowest structures of Si_6.

2. The magic story of Si_6

As mentioned before, the Si_6 cluster, which is a magic cluster with increased stability, is considered one of the best and fully understood clusters [1, 3-7]. Its structural and electronic properties have been studied theoretically (among others) by K. Ragavachari [3, 5-6], who is one of the pioneers of the small cluster theoretical research. Ragavachari's final calculations [6], based in higher level methods (MP2 geometry optimization compared to his initial calculations with HF), suggested the structure of fig. 1(b) as the ground state, instead of structure 1(a). Ragavachari's final suggestion was confirmed by experimental Raman measurements. The confirmation was accomplished through the comparison and identification of the calculated and measured Raman-active vibration modes [6]. Thus, contrary to most of the other small Si clusters, Si_6 is considered as fully and well understood. Due to its "magic" property, Si_6 is very popular and has been studied extensively both theoretically and experimentally. The popularity of this cluster is related to its small size, which makes the use of highest levels theoretical techniques possible, and its relative stability which facilitates its experimental characterization. Furthermore the characteristics of Si_6 have been used extensively to model and parameterize much larger systems through empirical and semi-empirical calculations. However, this is not the end of the story. More recent theoretical results [1, 7], with much higher level theoretical techniques for both energy gradients (geometry optimization, vibration frequencies) and energies, suggest different equilibrium structure(s) for Si_6 than the one proposed (and "verified") by Raghavachari and co-workers [6]. The irony of the story is that the new structure is similar to the structure Raghavachari has suggested earlier [3, 5] by lower level methods. Not to mention also that Raghavachari himself have pioneered the development and implementation of some of the high-level techniques in popular computer packages such as the one used in the present calculations. Thus, the story of Si_6 has "suspense" and "drama"! Yet it can serve at the same time as a best and worse case example of "agreement" between (higher level) theory and experiment.

3. Results and discussion

The initial structure proposed by Raghavachari on the basis of HF geometry optimization is the first structure on the left in figure 1; structure 1(a) [5]. This structure is an edge-capped trigonal bipyramid of C2V symmetry. Following this structure there is a very close lying (in energy) bicapped tetrahedron, fig. 1(c), which can be also viewed as a face-capped trigonal bipyramid of near C2V symmetry. This last structure, initially of C2V symmetry was unstable to distortions and was finally stabilized by further geometry optimization into the CS (near C2V) symmetric structure of figure 1(c). The distorted octahedron of D4h symmetry in figure 1(b) was unstable at the HF level of theory, so it was rejected as a local minimum of the energy "hyper-surface". When the geometry optimization is repeated at the MP2 level of theory, both of the low-lying structures, 1(a) and 1(b), collapse into the same distorted octahedron structure of figure 1(b). This lead Raghavachari to suggest that the real structure of Si6 was the D4h structure. On the experimental side, the measured Raman spectrum [6], seems to provide indirect support to the MP2 predictions, since the MP2 calculated spectrum for the D4h structure, after a 5% scaling, appears to be in quite good agreement with experiment. Everything looks pretty natural up to here. Not quite!

In spite of this ideal agreement of (higher than before) theory and experiment, more recent results obtained with higher order perturbation as well as DFT/B3LYP theories by the present author [1, 7] do not agree with the MP2 predictions. Instead, they agree with the general predictions of the HF gradients which favour the structure in figure 1(a), but also the structure in fig. 1(c). The D4h structure is not a local minimum for higher order perturbation theory as well as QCISD(T) and B3LYP [1,7]. This discrepancy is rather surprising since Si6 is widely considered as a well-established system, almost a textbook case. Apparently, the perturbation expansion is not well converging and the energy hyper-surface is very flat. As a result of this flatness, the MP2 gradients fail to converge to the right structure. This can be understood from the results of figure 2, which shows a selected energy hyper-surface scan, and table 1 which includes the energies of all three structures in various levels of theory (starting from top to bottom with MP2 and ending with the results of the QCISD(T) method).

Table 1: The energies of the structures of fig. 1, in atomic units.

Method	Structures (at the B3LYP geometry)			
	C_S	C_{2v}	D_{4h}	D_{4h} / MP2
HF	-1733.360551	-1733.360679	-1733.354206	-1733.354710
MP2	-1733.931275	-1733.929716	-1733.932939	-1733.933733
MP3	-1733.917838	-1733.917543	-1733.916229	-1733.916229
MP4SDTQ	-1734.001835	-1734.000550	-1734.001572	-1734.001579
CCSD	-1733.932769	-1733.932240	-1733.931700	-1733.930998
CCSD(T)	-1733.982118	-1733.981508	-1733.9801816	-1733.980490
State	$^1A^{'}$	$^1A_1$	$^1A_{1g}$	$^1A_{1g}$

Thus the paradoxical answer to the question "Which structure of the three is the true structure of Si6?" is either "all of them" or "neither one of them". To see why, let as have a closer look at table 1. These calculations have been performed with a high quality basis set (so the technical approximations are at a relatively high level). As we can see, although the C2v is the lowest possible structure, the energy differences between the three structures are marginal. The structures are practically and truly isoenergetic. This is verified by the energy-surface scan in fig. 2. Similar diagrams (involving different angles) exist also for the distortion of the D4h to the Cs structure. In both cases the energy differences are smaller or comparable with the energy-accuracy of the calculations. The differences become even smaller when the accuracy of the calculation (depending on the level of correlation and the quality of the basis set) increases (compare the b3lyp results in fig. 2 for the two basis sets).

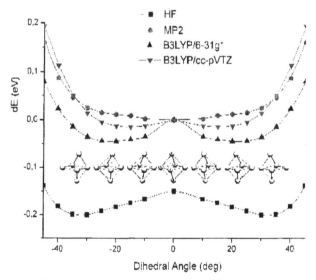

Figure 2: Variation of the relative (to the D_{4h} structure) energy (in eV) with distortion of the dihedral angle from zero to +/- 45° for various models. The HF curve has been shifted vertically for clarity.

What is even more important is that these differences are much smaller than the zero point energy of the nuclear vibrations or even smaller than the energies of the low frequency "soft" modes. This is highly suggestive that the three structures could be continuously transforming between themselves at no energy cost through the soft vibrations. Are there any soft modes? Yes indeed. First of all, as we can see in table 2, at all levels of theory except MP2, the D4h symmetric structure shows soft modes with imaginary frequencies. This indicates that this structure is not a global or local minimum but a saddle-point and that a lower symmetry structure can be more stable. Indeed, distorting the D4h structure according to the displacement patterns of the imaginary frequency mode, shown in figure 3, we obtain under geometry optimization at higher levels of perturbation theory (e.g. MP3, MP4, etc) or B3LYP the edge-capped trigonal bipyramid of figure 1 (a).

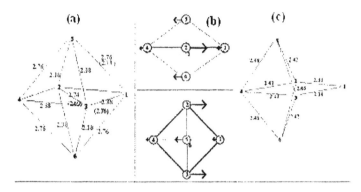

Figure 3: Transformation of the D_{4h} distorted tetrahedron the structure (a), according to the displacements patterns of the first E_u mode (b), into the edge-capped trigonal bipyramid , (c) . The bond lengths in (a) and (c) are in Å and correspond to the B3LYP optimized geometry. The MP2 bond lengths are given in parenthesis. The displacement vectors in (b) are given in the plane defined by the atoms 1,4,5,6, (top), and in the plane of the atoms 1,2, 4 and 5, (bottom) The Calculated Raman spectrum is shown in figure 4.

Table 2: Vibrations of D_{4h} structure at various levels of theoretical treatment along with some "corresponding" B3LYP of the C_{2v} and C_s structures. Frequencies are given in cm⁻¹. The symbol i indicates imaginary frequencies. Experimental measurements are from ref. 45.

D_{4h}	D_{4h}					C_{2v}	C_s
Exp	Sym.	MP2	MP3	MP4	B3LYP	B3LYP	B3LYP
-------	E_u	52	81i	75i	79i	-------	-------
-------	B_{2u}	197	117	149	117	-------	-------
252	B_{2g}	220	252	225	234	276	276
300	A_{1g}	314	331	319	312	295	295
-------	A_{2u}	358	344	347	315	-------	-------
386	B_{1g}	396	418	404	386	361	360
404	E_g	447	424	421	395	395	370
458	A_{1g}	481	480	476	442		439
-----	E_u	482	483	480	443	436 460	448 451

On the other hand soft modes (with no imaginary frequencies) have been also found in the other two structures. Thus, we have arrived to the same conclusion through a different route.

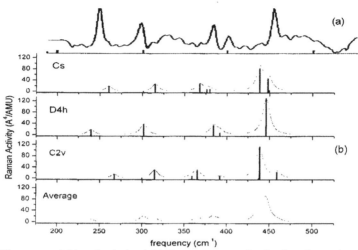

Figure 4: The measured (a) and calculated (b) Raman spectrum for the three lowest isoenergetic structures of the Si6 cluster.

The three structures could transform dynamically into each other through the coupling with soft (or unstable) vibration modes. We could recognize this effect as a dynamical Jahn-Teller effect, in analogy to the more familiar (static) Jahn-Teller effect, which is responsible for the (static) distortion of the high-symmetry ideal octahedron into the D4h structure. The resulting structural plasticity of Si6 is very unusual for such "well-defined" system. There is an intriguing possibility that this structural non-rigidity of Si6 could be related to its magic property. In this case the enhanced stability of the magic clusters would be a dynamic rather than a static property. This possibility is considered by the present author as highly probable [1, 7]. Now everything seems to fit together nicely in principle, except for one thing. What about the experimental evidence (Raman frequencies) in favour of the D_{4h} structure? Let us have a closer look at table 2. The last two columns of table 2 show some selective frequency results for these structures, for modes compatible with D_{4h} Raman active modes and with large intensities. As we can see, these frequencies are comparable in magnitude to the experimental results and to the values predicted by MP3, MP4, B3LYP (and MP2) for the corresponding D_{4h} structure. However, both of these structures have a larger number of active modes (with much smaller intensities) than the ones shown in table 4. Therefore, one possibility is that the experiment cannot detect all active Raman modes below some threshold value, or that it could not resolve frequencies which are "nearby". Both of these statements are true. However, independent of these experimental limitations, there is a stronger, additional scientific reason for a misleading interpretation of the experimental results. Since all three isomers coexist and transform into each other, according to the present results, the experimental values in reality reflect time-averages over the three structures. This last possibility is certainly more convincing after a closer look in the plots of figure 4, which shows the calculated Raman spectrum of all three structures, together with the average of this spectrum and the experimentally measured Raman spectrum. This work is still in progress. More convincing arguments and results will be published soon.

4. Concluding remarks

It has been illustrated here that Si₆ is not an ordinary cluster, as the ones we are familiar so far (or maybe we are not familiar enough with the other magic clusters). It is very tempting to suggest that the structural plasticity of this magic cluster is inherently connected to the "magic" property. The present author has many reasons to believe and strongly suggest this intriguing possibility. Future work towards this direction will clarify this proposition. Finally, from the "epistemological" point of view, let me conclude with the profound statement that "results (theoretical or experimental) are not always what they claim (or appear) to be, unless proven otherwise". This certainly applies to the results presented in this work.

References

[1] A. D. Zdetsis, to appear in *Reviews on Advanced Materials Science* (*RAMS*) (January 2006)
[2] R. E. Honig, *J. Chem. Phys.* **22**, 1610 (1954)
[3] K. Raghavachari and V. Logovinsky. *Phys. Rev. Lett.* **55**, 2853 (1985)
[4] M. F. Jarrold, *Science* **252**, 1085 (1991)
[5] K. Raghavachari, *J. Chem. Phys.* **84**, 5672 (1986)
[6] E. C. Honea, A. Ogura, C. A. Murray, K. Raghavachari, W. O. Sprenger, M. F. Jarrold and W. L. Brown, *Nature* **366**, 42 (1993)
[7] A. D. Zdetsis, *Phys. Rev. A* **64**, 023202 (2000); A.D. Zdetsis to be published

Brill Academic Publishers
P.O. Box 9000, 2300 PA Leiden
The Netherlands

Lecture Series on Computer
and Computational Sciences
Volume 5, 2006, pp. 199-203

Structures and Stability of a Small Silicon Cluster: High-Level *Ab initio* Calculations of Si$_6$

Yi Gao, Chad Killblane, and X.C. Zeng[1]

Department of Chemistry,
University of Nebraska-Lincoln,
Lincoln, Nebraska, 68588, USA

Abstract: The lowest-energy structure of Si$_6$ has been controversial. In this paper, we studied relative stability of this cluster by using the B3LYP, PBE1PBE, MP2, MP4, CCSD, CCSD(T), and QCISD(T) calculations with large basis sets (cc-pVTZ and cc-pVQZ). Our results indicate that the octahedral structure (D$_{4h}$) is the lowest-energy structure among three isomer candidates studied previously. Our results are also supported by a previous experimental measurement.

Keywords: Si$_6$, silicon cluster, CCSD(T), QCISD, T$_1$ value

1. Introduction

Small-sized silicon clusters have been the subjects of extensive research.[1-31] Their structural properties have been explored via both spectroscopic and ab initio methods. However, there are still discrepancies between the observed spectroscopic data and calculations for some of these clusters. Among small-sized clusters, Si$_6$ is an exceptionally difficult case.[5,11,18,20,28,30] This paper will focus on the relative stability of three Si$_6$ isomers in an attempt to resolve the lowest-energy Si$_6$ structure.

Spectroscopic measurements performed by Honea *et al* have shown the Si$_6$ cluster appears to be a distorted octahedron with D$_{4h}$ (**a**) symmetry.[11] Further molecular calculations at the MP2/6-31G* level provide indirect support for this observation.[11] However, two other isomers were also identified with different levels of theory. The first is a bicapped tetrahedron (**b**) with C$_s$ symmetry, and the second is a capped trigonal bipyramidal structure (**c**) with C$_{2v}$ symmetry. These structures were the subject of a later study by Zdetsis using the MP2, MP3, MP4(SDTQ), CCSD and CCSD(T) methods with the 6-31G* and D95* basis sets.[28] Zdetsis found that at MP2 level **a** was lower in energy than two other structures. However, **b** becomes the most stable with MP3, MP4(SDTQ), CCSD and CCSD(T) methods. Thus, the lowest-energy Si$_6$ geometry was still controversial. This work attempts to address the discrepancy between the observed structure and those determined by ab initio theory.

2. Computational Details

All calculations in this work were performed by the Gaussian 98 program.[32] The three structures provided by Honea *et al*[11], and investigated by Zdetsis,[28] as shown in Figure 1, served as the starting point for the calculations. Initial optimizations of all three structures were performed at the density-functional theory (DFT) B3LYP level with the 6-31G* basis sets. After completion of the initial optimizations the three structures were then re-optimized at the MP2/cc-pVTZ level, B3LYP/cc-pVTZ and PBE1PBE/cc-pVTZ levels. Upon completion of the final geometry optimizations frequency calculations were performed respectively at the MP2/cc-pVTZ, B3LYP/cc-pVTZ and PBE1PBE/cc-pVTZ levels. Finally, it was necessary to carry out a high-level MP4(SDTQ)/cc-pVTZ, QCISD(T)/cc-pVTZ, CCSD(T)/cc-pVTZ, and CCSD(T)/cc-pVQZ single-point energy calculations to determine the true ground state.

---

[1] Corresponding author. E-mail: xczeng@phase2.unl.edu.

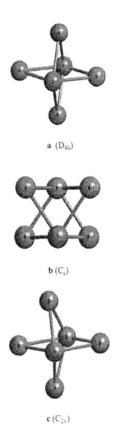

a (D_{4h})

b (C_s)

c (C_{2v})

Figure 1. The optimized three Si_6 cluster structures with B3LYP/6-31G* level.

3. Results and Discussion

Optimized structure and harmonic vibrational frequencies are collected in Table 1 and Table 2. During the optimization with the cc-pVTZ basis sets, we found that the isomer **b** can be discounted immediately because it readily collapses to either isomer **a** or **c** depending on the level of theory used. In particular, the MP2/cc-pVTZ optimizations indicated that structure **a** was the global minimum, and both **b** and **c** transformed into **a**. The B3LYP/cc-pVTZ and PBE1PBE/cc-pVTZ optimizations however showed **c** was slightly lower in energy than **a**, whereas **b** collapsed to **c**. Therefore it became only necessary to differentiate between the two isomer **a** and **c**.

Table 1. Calculated bond lengths at MP2/cc-pVTZ and B3LYP/cc-pVTZ optimized structures for **a**(D_{4h}) and **c**(C_{2v}).

Bond	MP2/cc-pVTZ	B3LYP/cc-pVTZ	
	a (D_{4h})	a (D_{4h})	c (C_{2v})
	Length (Å)	Length (Å)	Length (Å)
Si_1-Si_2	2.7189	2.7418	2.7069
Si_1-Si_3	2.3797	2.3848	2.4305
Si_1-Si_4	2.3797	2.3848	2.4107
Si_1-Si_5	2.3797	2.3848	2.4108
Si_1-Si_6	2.3797	2.3848	2.3465

Si$_2$-Si$_3$	2.3797	2.3848	2.4305
Si$_2$-Si$_4$	2.3797	2.3848	2.4108
Si$_2$-Si$_5$	2.3797	2.3848	2.4108
Si$_2$-Si$_6$	2.3797	2.3848	2.3465
Si$_3$-Si$_4$	2.7621	2.7597	2.5195
Si$_3$-Si$_5$	NA	NA	2.5192
Si$_3$-Si$_6$	2.7621	2.7597	NA
Si$_4$-Si$_5$	2.7621	2.7597	NA
Si$_4$-Si$_6$	2.7621	2.7597	NA
Si5-Si$_6$	2.7621	2.7597	NA

Table 2. Harmonic vibrational frequencies, IR intensity and their group symmetry of **a** and **c**.

MP2/cc-pVTZ			B3LYP/cc-pVTZ					
a (D$_{4h}$)			**a** (D$_{4h}$)			**c** (C$_{2v}$)		
Frq	Int.	Sym.	Frq	Int.	Sym.	Frq	Int.	Sym.
63.4156	0.4857	E$_u$	-61.7147	0.5477	E$_u$	33.7403	0.4114	B$_2$
197.8217	0.0000	B$_{2u}$	125.1064	0.0000	B$_{2u}$	86.0415	0.0008	A$_1$
233.6820	0.0000	B$_{2g}$	239.6996	0.0000	B$_{2g}$	124.0547	0.0032	B$_1$
293.5034	0.0000	A$_{1g}$	301.6021	0.0000	A$_{1g}$	266.6989	0.3952	B$_2$
346.1896	0.5250	A$_{2u}$	315.1694	1.0374	A$_{2u}$	299.5636	1.1936	B$_1$
383.8440	0.0000	B$_{1g}$	384.3082	0.0000	B$_{1g}$	314.4814	0.0007	A$_1$
437.2451	0.0000	E$_g$	391.6555	0.0000	E$_g$	358.9359	0.0000	A$_2$
466.2478	0.0000	A$_{1g}$	446.0317	0.0000	A$_{1g}$	365.2908	0.3313	A$_1$
473.8690	20.1026	E$_u$	446.3670	23.0887	E$_u$	391.6604	0.4057	B$_1$
						437.6343	22.1648	B$_2$
						438.5532	1.8246	A$_1$
						458.5390	18.8626	A$_1$

To account for the zero-point energy contribution, it is necessary to perform frequency calculations on the optimized structures. Structure **a** and **c** were both analyzed at the B3LYP/cc-pVTZ and PBE1PBE/cc-pVTZ level, and structure **a** was also analyzed at the MP2/cc-pVTZ level. The results of the DFT calculations were as follows. Isomer **a** showed two imaginary frequencies, whereas isomer **c** did not. This would seem to suggest that isomer **c** is in fact the global minimum, and that isomer **a** is a transition state. However, the MP2 calculation had good convergence, and did not show any imaginary frequencies for the structure **a**. These results are consistent with those reported by Zdetsis.[28]

Table 3. Absolute Energies in atomic units. Boldface denotes lower-energy isomer.

Ab Initio Methods	**a** (D$_{4h}$)	**c** (C$_{2v}$)
MP2/cc-pVTZ// MP2/cc-pVTZ	**-1734.265056**	--
B3LYP/cc-pVTZ// B3LYP/cc-pVTZ	-1737.06414481	**-1737.06491747**
MP4(SDQ)/cc-pVTZ// B3LYP/cc-pVTZ	**-1734.2522485**	-1734.2519487
CCSD/cc-pVTZ// B3LYP/cc-pVTZ	-1734.244962	**-1734.245179**
CCSD(T)/cc-pVTZ// B3LYP/cc-pVTZ	**-1734.3159117**	-1734.3155139
QCISD(T)/cc-pVTZ// B3LYP /cc-pVTZ	**-1734.3168322**	-1734.3164987
MP2/cc-pVQZ// B3LYP/cc-pVTZ	**-1734.3254685**	-1734.32308
MP4(SDQ)/cc-pVQZ// B3LYP/cc-pVTZ	**-1734.2993909**	-1734.2992222
CCSD/cc-pVQZ// B3LYP/cc-pVTZ	-1734.2935256	**-1734.2938367**
CCSD(T)/cc-pVQZ// B3LYP/cc-pVTZ	**-1734.3704209**	-1734.3700912
PBE1PBE/cc-pVTZ// PBE1PBE/cc-pVTZ	-1736.2784158	**-1736.2785017**
MP4(SDQ)/cc-pVTZ// PBE1PBE/cc-pVTZ	**-1734.2522521**	-1734.2519488
MP4(SDTQ)/cc-pVTZ// PBE1PBE /cc-pVTZ	**-1734.3487473**	-1734.3468893

Finally we performed a high level single-point energy calculation of both **a** and **c**, based on the B3LYP and PBE1PBE optimized structures. The absolute energies of **a** and **c** were evaluated at the MP2, MP4(SDQ), MP4(SDTQ), CCSD, CCSD(T), and QCISD(T) methods with large cc-pVTZ and cc-pVQZ basis sets. The results are collected in Table 3. It is shown that, with both basis sets, **a** is lower in energy than **c** based on the MP2, MP4(SDQ), MP4(SDTQ), CCSD(T) and QCISD(T) methods, but is a little higher in energy with the CCSD method. Considering that MP4(SDTQ), CCSD(T) and QCISD(T) methods are more precise methods than the CCSD method, D_{4h} (**a**) structure should be more stable than C_{2v} (**c**) structure. On the other hand, Lee and Taylor have suggested the norm of the T_1 amplitudes obtained from the CCSD method as a diagnostic to evaluate the reliability of the single-reference calculations.[33] They concluded that a T_1 value of 0.02 or larger would correspond to multi-reference character. In our calculations, the T_1 values for **a** and **c** are 0.0184 and 0.0198, respectively, which indicate that our single-reference calculations are reliable.

Upon examination of all available evidences it seems reasonable to conclude that Si_6 is in fact the distorted octahedron first reported by Honea *et al.*[11] Discrepancies in earlier computational work are now resolved by use of the larger cc-pVTZ and cc-pVQZ basis sets. Furthermore, the agreement between the vibrational data, and MP2 calculations is a strong indicator of true minima. Finally, the consistency among most high-level calculations [e.g, MP4, CCSD(T) and QCISD(T)] based on the DFT optimized structures also support the conclusion that the distorted octahedron structure D_{4h} is more stable than C_{2v} structure.

In summary, we show that the distorted octahedron structure D_{4h} of Si_6 is most likely the global minimum. The results of high-level ab initio calculation support this conclusion, while the calculated spectra fit the D_{4h} group. Thus, the discrepancy between experimental and theoretical data can be put to rest.

Acknowledgements

This work was supported by grants from US NSF (CHE, DMII, MRSEC), DOE (DE-FG02-04ER46164) and the Nebraska Research Initiative, and by the Research Computing Facility at University of Nebraska-Lincoln.

References

[1] L.A. Bloomfield, R. R. Freeman, and W. L. Brown, *Phys. Rev. Lett.* **54** 2246-2249 (1985).

[2] K. Raghavachari and V. Logovinsky, *Phys. Rev. Lett.* **55** 2853-2856 (1985).

[3] G. Pacchioni and J. Koutecky, *J. Chem. Phys.* **84** 3301-3310 (1986).

[5] K.Raghavachari, *J. Chem. Phys.* **84** 5672-5686(1986).

[6] K. Raghavachari and C. M. Rohlfing, *J. Chem. Phys.* **89** 2219-2234 (1988).

[7] P. Ballone, W. Andreoni, R. Car and M. Parrinello, *Phys. Rev. Lett.* **60** 271-274 (1988).

[8] C. M. Rohlfing and K. Raghavachari, *Chem. Phys. Lett.* **167** 559-565 (1990).

[9] M. F. Jarrold and E. C. Honea, *J. Phys. Chem.* **95** 9181-9185 (1991).

[10] M. F. Jarrold and J. E. Bower, *J. Chem. Phys.* **96** 9180-9190 (1992).

[11] E. C. Honea, A. Ogura, C. A. Murray, K. Raghavachari, W. O. Sprenger, M. F. Jarrold and W. L. Brown, *Nature* **366** 42-44 (1993).

[12] I. H. Lee, K. J. Chang, and Y. H. Lee, *J. Phys.: Condens. Matter* **6** 741-750 (1994).

[13] D.J. Wales, *Phys. Rev. A* **49** 2195-2198 (1994).

[14] J. M. Hunter, J. L. Fye, M. F. Jarrold, and J. E. Bower, *Phys. Rev. Lett.* **73** 2063-2066 (1994).

[15] S. Li, R. J. Van Zee, W. Weltner Jr. and K. Raghavachari, *Chem. Phys. Lett.* **243** 275-280 (1995).

[16] J. C. Grossman and L. Mitas, *Phys. Rev. Lett.* **74** 1323-1326 (1995).

[17] T. Frauenheim, F. Weich, T. Kohler, S. Uhlmann, D. Porezag, and G. Seifert, *Phys. Rev. B* **52** 11492-11501(1995).

[18] N. Binggeli and J. R. Chelikowsky, *Phys. Rev. Lett.* **75** 493-496 (1995).

[19] S. Wei, B.N. Barnett, and U. Landman, *Phys. Rev. B* **55** 7935-7944 (1997).

[20] I. Vasiliev, S. Ogut, and J. R. Chelikowsky, *Phys. Rev. Lett.* **78** 4805-4808 (1997).

[21] B. Liu, Z. Y. Lu, B. Pan, C.-Z. Wang, K.-M. Ho, A.A. Shvartsburg, and M.F. Jarrold, *J. Chem. Phys.* **109** 9401-9409 (1998).

[22] K. Ho, A. A. Shvartsburg, B. Pan, Z. Yilu, C. Wang, J. G. Wacker, J. L. Fye and M. F. Jarrold, *Nature* **392** 582-585 (1998).

[23] Y. Luo, J. Zhao, and G. H. Wang, *Phys. Rev. B* **60** 10703-10706 (1999).

[24] B. X. Li, P. L. Cao, and M. Jiang, *Phys. Stat. Sol.(b)* **218** 399-409 (2000).

[25] B. X. Li and P. L. Cao, *Phys. Rev. A.* **62** 023201(2000).

[26] I. Rata, A.A. Shvartsburg, M. Horoi, T. Frauenheim, K.W.M. Siu and K.A. Jackson, *Phys. Rev. Lett.* **85** 546-549 (2000).

[27] A. A. Shvartsburg, R. R. Hudgins, P. Dugourd and M. F. Jarrold, *Chem. Soc. Rev.* **30** 26-35 (2001).

[28] A. D. Zdetsis, *Phys. Rev. A.* **64** 023202 (2001).

[29] X. Zhu and X.C. Zeng, *J. Chem. Phys.* **118** 3558-3570 (2003).

[30] G. Maroulis, D. Begué and C. Pouchan, *J. Chem. Phys.* **119** 794-797 (2003).

[31] A. Tekin and B. Hartke, *Phys. Chem. Chem. Phys.* **6** 503-509 (2004).

[32] M. J. Frish, G. W. Trucks, H. B. Schlegel *et al.*, GAUSSIAN 98, Revision A.9, Gaussian, Inc., Pittsburgh, PA, 1998.

[33] T. J. Lee, A. P. Rendell and P. R. Taylor, *J. Phys. Chem.* **94** 5463-5468 (1990).